Ruch and the Upper Applegate Valley

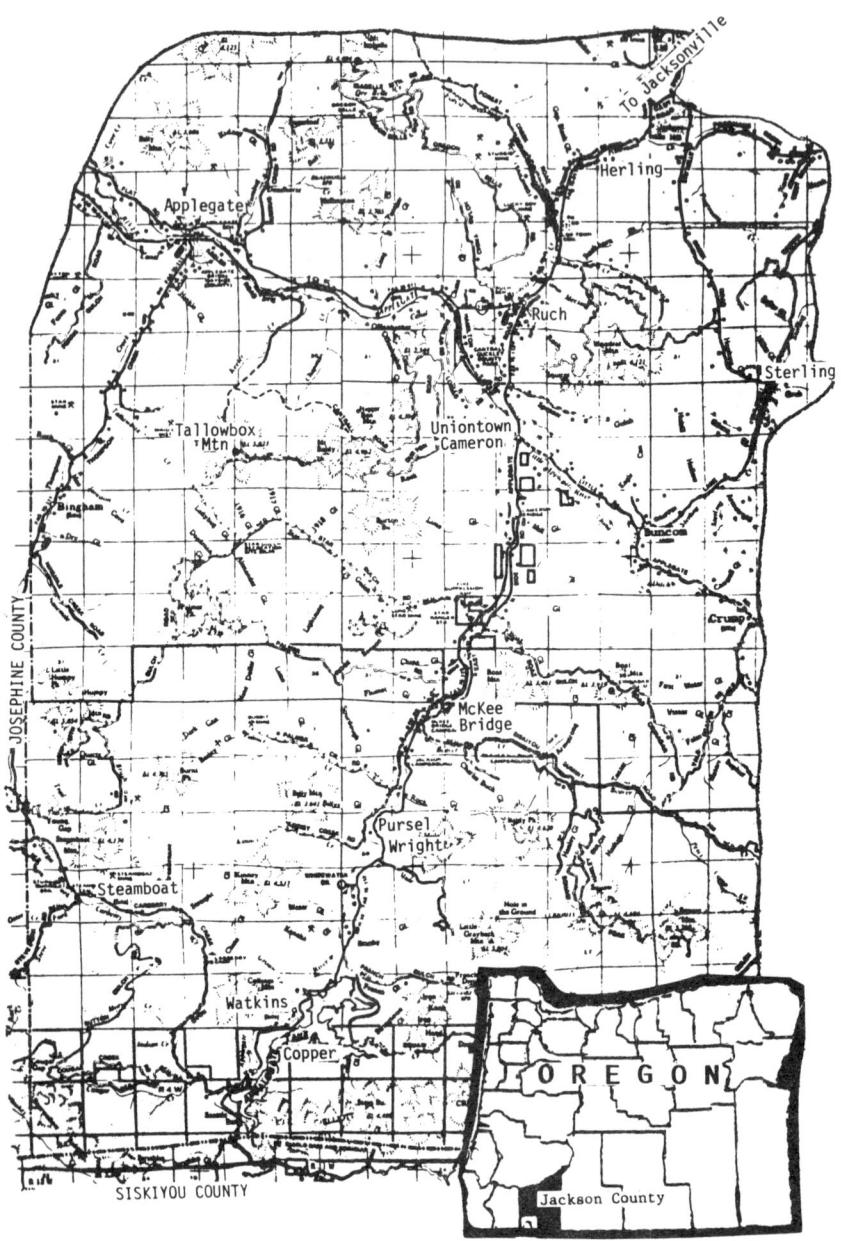

RUCH

(ROOSH)

And the Upper Applegate Valley

An Oregon Documentary

JOHN and MARGUERITE BLACK

WEBB RESEARCH GROUP

Published by: WEBB RESEARCH GROUP
Direct all inquiries to the distributor:
> PACIFIC NORTHWEST BOOKS COMPANY
> SAN 200-5263
> P.O. BOX 314 Medford, Oregon 97501

LIBRARY OF CONGRESS
Cataloging in Publications Data

Black, John, 1911-
Ruch and the upper Applegate Valley.

Bibliography: p.
Includes Index.
1. Jackson County (Or.)—History, Local. 2. Jackson County (Or.)—Description and travel. 3. Applegate Valley Region (Or.)—History. 4. Applegate Valley Region (Or.)—Description and travel. I. Black, Marguerite. II. Title.

F88s.J14B55 1989 979.5'27 89-16617
ISBN 0-936738-39-1

TABLE OF CONTENTS

Ruch, Oregon along Highway 238 in southwest Jackson County as viewed in aerial photograph by Bert Webber on October 30, 1989.

PREFACE
THE ROUTE FOR A TOUR OF
THE UPPER APPLEGATE VALLEY

This tour forms a geographical loop with Ruch (pronounced: *Roosh*) along the way and as destination, a distance of about sixty miles. The historic sites described are situated along this loop.

The Route:

Start at the summit of Jacksonville Hill, just west of City of Jacksonville. Proceed southwesterly along Highway 238 to Ruch. Turn on to Upper Applegate Road at Hamilton Road and turn right and go two miles to the intersection of Hamilton Road and Highway 238. Proceed toward Ruch.

Return to Upper Applegate Road, go about two miles, turn left on Little Applegate Road, continue to the intersection of Sterling Creek Road (Buncom). Turn up Sterling Creek Road about two miles, and return to Little Applegate, continue up Little Applegate to Yale Creek, return to Upper Applegate Road.

Turn left on Upper Applegate and continue 15 miles to Applegate Lake and Carberry Road. Continue on Carberry to Steamboat Ranch, on over the divide down Thompson Creek to Applegate and the intersection of Highway 238.

* * *

This project has been partially funded by the 1976 Applegate Valley Bicentennial Committee. Members included Phil and Freddie Holt, George and Harriet Watson and Maude Ziegler. They had faith that a book would be forthcoming. Here it is.

We owe sincere thanks to Evelyn Byrne Williams for her contribution of the drawing of McKee Bridge for the book cover and the use of many photographs from her collection. Fred and Ethel Pursel West whose recall of life and times in the thirties have been most helpful.

Carol Smith Webb shared her family genealogy records and edited the section on the life of her grandparents and great grandparents.

7

Lewis Buckley and Gerald Pearce gave us information on their families for which we thank them.

The work of Ruby Lacy and Lida Childers in extracting and publishing Jackson County, Oregon, census and marriage records was especially valuable to us. We extend our appreciation to them.

Rich Thelin, at the Jackson County Historical Society Archives, made us very excited when he produced from the files the original coroner's inquest documents on the deaths of Fredolin and Anna Ruch.

Librarians Carol Harbison and Karalee Newberg at the library of the Jacksonville Museum of Southern Oregon History always responded promptly to appeals for information. For their efforts we are most grateful.

To Linda Morehouse Genaw, one of my former students, I am indebted for biographical materials, advice and encouragement. The staff of the Reference Department of the Jackson County Library System gave assistance which we appreciate.

We thank Barbara Hegne for information on the Louis C. Garey family and a copy of an early township map of the Ruch area.

A sincere thank you to Leonard Lukens, postal historian, for the loan of rare postmarks from discontinued post offices in the Applegate Valley.

We are indebted to Bert and Margie Webber, authors, for their great assistance with editing and practical encouragement throughout the writing of this work.

Local history has been our hobby for over 20 years. We personally knew many of the residents of the area since the 1920s. Over the years we saw them grow old and die, their way of life gone forever. Their farms and ranches have new owners and there are many changes. A strong desire to preserve and document the history of the Valley from the time of the early settlers to the 1980s, has motivated this book.

It has been a team effort. John Black's lifetime knowledge of the people and the area, his ability to locate sites by legal description and his expertise in researching court house records have been invaluable. He mastered a word processor and then gave countless hours of typing to produce the manuscript. Marguerite's writing came from years of teaching experience and a natural desire to share fascinating stories. Together we studied maps, went on field trips and took photographs to supplement our collection of pictures taken many years ago. We became very familiar with indexes and volumes of deed records in the Jackson County Clerk and Recorder's office. Kathy Beckett, the County Clerk, and her staff permitted us to come and go freely.

Every effort has been made to avoid errors in this book but a few may appear. Some omissions have occurred when documentation was not available. For any errors or omissions we are totally responsible.

John and Marguerite Black
Forest Creek Road
Jacksonville, Oregon
October 1989

Chapter 1

APPLEGATE VALLEY BEGINNINGS

The headwaters of the Applegate River are in the Siskiyou Mountains in California. The river flows in a northwesterly direction through Oregon's Jackson and Josephine Counties to the confluence with the Rogue River about three miles west of Grants Pass.

The river was named by Lindsay Applegate in 1849 when he was traveling south to the gold fields of California with a party of adventurers. As they crossed the divide overlooking the valley of the Rogue, near present day Grants Pass, they saw, in the distance, the waters of an unknown river. Some of the group thought it was a curve of the Rogue but Lindsay was convinced it was a different stream. The party found this was true, and did some prospecting along it before continuing south. They began calling it Applegate's Creek. Subsequently the official name became Applegate River.

GOLD FEVER SETTLEMENTS
YREKA

When gold was discovered in California in 1848, travel on the north-south California-Oregon trail increased dramatically. The pack trail was soon improved so that wagons could travel it. Certain sections were built by settlers who charged a toll for use of the road.

As miners and prospectors explored the creeks and rivers in northern California and southern Oregon in 1851, 1852 and 1853 gold was discovered in several areas. Settlements quickly sprang from the wilderness.

In March 1851, Abraham Thompson and a party of prospectors found gold while camped on a large grassy flat between two creeks, near present day Yreka, California.

They noticed there were flakes of gold clinging to the roots of bunch grass pulled up by grazing pack animals. Thompson and others remained in the area prospecting and recovering some of the gold. Other miners flocked to the site and set up camps. This area soon became known as Thompson's Dry Diggings. A main

10

town was established south of Dry Diggings and was called Shasta Butte City.

In the spring of 1852, the California legislature created Siskiyou County and named the town Wyreka. This became Yreka by common usage.

JACKSONVILLE

Two packers, James Cluggage and James Pool, camped overnight in Bear Creek Valley in early 1851, and discovered free gold in the gravel of a small creek flowing from a gulch in the hills. News of this strike traveled fast and in weeks there were hundreds of miners in camp. This camp became the town of Jacksonville.

Since it was the largest settlement, when Jackson County was organized in 1852, Jacksonville became the seat of county government.

SAILOR'S DIGGINGS—WALDO

In 1851 a big gold strike was made on the Illinois River in what is now Josephine County. Attracted to this strike were sailors from ships standing in to the newly established settlement of Crescent City. So many sailors jumped ship to go to the gold mines, that the main camp on the Illinois River was called Sailor's Diggings. This camp also took on the name Waldo. When the Territorial Legislature created Josephine County (1856), it provided that Sailor's Diggings would be the provisional county seat until the first election. There is no mention of "Waldo" as such, but many believe the two names were very probably for the same place. The name Waldo survived probably because the post office established for the settlement bore that name. The post office finally closed in 1928. In 1989 there is no trace of this once prosperous town. Of the other two major gold camps, Yreka and Jacksonville, each today are thriving cities.

PACK TRAILS AND EARLY ROADS

Not all of the emigrants into the area were miners. There were also farmers, traders and store keepers who recognized the tremendous market potential for food and supplies for the population of the mining camps, as well as settlers who were taking up land. Pack trains were in use before 1850. An article in the *Sacramento Transcript*, January 22, 1850, states that long trains of mules heavily laden with food and other supplies leave

Draft horses and freight wagon used in Jacksonville Jubilee parade early 1930s, depicts typical scene from 1880s. (Photo courtesy O. L. Wheeler)

Sacramento every day for the northern mines. These pack trains were reorganized at Yreka after off-loading goods for the merchants there. The trains then continued over the mountains into Jacksonville. The trek from California saw the train going from 25 feet elevation at Sacramento to 2,635 at Yreka then over the Siskiyous between 4,500 and 5,000 feet altitude then dropping down to 1,569 at Jacksonville. The leg of the trip between Yreka and Jacksonville was about 60 miles and could only be traversed in good weather.

Another source of supplies was established, to the north, on the Umpqua River. Levi Scott founded the settlement of Scottsburg in 1851. Boats came up the Umpqua from the coast where the cargoes were transferred to pack trains for the trip south to Jacksonville.

In 1853 still another route was established when a way was found to unload ships at Crescent City. Supplies were then reloaded on pack trains of mules for the 120 mile journey to Jacksonville.

Inland from Crescent City, the tail followed Elk Valley over a divide into Smith River Valley, then over Cold Spring Mountain and the summit of the Siskiyous into Oregon. Continuing northward, the trail crossed the Illinois River passing through Waldo and newly settled Kerbyville. Across one more divide, the trail came to the Applegate River. Here it crossed the river on a ferry near the present Fish Hatchery Bridge. The route followed on the north side of the river upstream about 28 miles toward Jacksonville.

In the meantime, in Jacksonville, the newly appointed Jackson County Board of Commissioners held their first formal session in March 1853. The first commissioners were: James Cluggage, Nathaniel Dean and Abel George. C. E. Alexander was clerk. These men were appointed by the Territorial Legislature.

The commissioners issued a statement with regard to public roads. It was the opinion of the Board that it was absolutely necessary for the public good and the citizens of Jackson County that public roads should be laid out and located through the entire Valley.

A list was made of every existing trail and road which passed through Jackson County. Each one was declared to be a Public Road. Most of these trails eventually became the basis of the present State and County road systems in the county.

A petition to view and mark out a wagon road from Jacksonville to Crescent City was presented to the Board of Commissioners in the May 1854 session by M. Russell, Cyrus Lomas, J. W. Farnsworth and others.

This road was to be from Jacksonville to Applegate Creek Valley, touching Spencer's ranch and on down the Creek to the most practicable place to cross the mountains into the Deer Creek Valley. From there the road would enter the Illinois Valley and the most practical route to Crescent City, California. (Vol. 1, p. 31 *Commissioner's Journals*) Appointed to view and then mark out this road were W. W. Fowler, G. B. Davidson and Daniel Newcomb. They were to complete this project and report to the next session.

The Board of Commissioners at this session were Martin Angel, T. Dunn and B. B. Griffin. The route was viewed and marked past Rich Gulch, from the end of Oregon Street in Jacksonville, up the ridge to the divide, down Poormans Creek to Logtown. According to the early road records, this has always been a wagon road to the settlement of Logtown. This route is now State Highway 238 from Grants Pass, through Murphy, Provolt, Applegate, Ruch and Jacksonville terminating in Medford.

CRESCENT CITY TO JACKSONVILLE WAGON ROAD

Pressure for a wagon road from Crescent City to Jacksonville grew rapidly during this time. A company called the "Crescent City Plank Road Company" was organized at Crescent City in 1856 and the route was surveyed. In 1857, contracts were let and construction started. The route did not follow the old pack trail all the way. A better grade was selected in the Smith River Valley, over the Oregon border and into the Illinois River Valley. The settlements along the road were Waldo, Fort Briggs, Kerbyville, Fort Hayes and Wilderville. From there a new road was built on the south side of the Applegate River to the mouth of Thompson Creek. A bridge was constructed in 1858 just in time for the road to be opened for travel. The section from George Long's claim to the Josephine County line was designated as a Road District in September 1856. This meant that the road was open and would be kept in repair by the settlers who lived in the district.

The first stage coach to travel the newly opened road arrived in Crescent City from Jacksonville on May 19, 1858. The stage bound for Jacksonville left Crescent City the same day. Within weeks freight wagons began to roll and pack trains became history on this route.

The use of the road was not free. Tolls were charged. The right to pass was $5.00 for a two-horse team; $8.00 for a four-horse team and $10.00 for a six-horse team. Early toll roads served their purpose of improving travel and transportation as farms and villages were being established.

UPPER APPLEGATE ROADS

Trails to the Upper Applegate country were in use by the miners, packers and settlers as early as 1853. A gold strike on Sterling Creek led to a busy mining camp there in 1854.

A road from Jackass Gulch (Forest Creek) up Applegate Creek through Buncom to Sterling and over the divide to Wait's Mill (Phoenix) via Griffin Creek was viewed in 1856. This road branched off the Jacksonville-Crescent City road at present day Ruch.

From Little Applegate River crossing, a road up Big Applegate was formally viewed and opened in June 1876. It crossed the river at John Wright's ford and crossed again near the mouth of Palmer Creek ending at Nicholas Wright's place. The next year a road was viewed and surveyed from Nicholas Wright's to Mark Watkins' and the mouth of Squaw Creek. From there up Carberry Creek to Steamboat remained only a pack trail until the early 1900s.

DONATION LAND CLAIMS

Even before roads were established, many settlers were coming into the Rogue and Applegate Valleys to take up Donation Land Claims. In 1850, Congress passed the Donation Land Claim Law for the purpose of encouraging settlement of the Oregon Territory. It offered a half section of land (320 acres), to any one who would occupy and cultivate the land for four consecutive years. If a man were married by December 1, 1851, his wife could also claim 320 acres. Thus, a man and wife could own a square mile of virgin Oregon land, much of which was covered with heavy timber. Martin and Anna Angel had their 640-acre claim near the present city of Central Point. Burril Griffin had 640 acres along the creek now bearing his name, south of Jacksonville.

The law was amended to the effect that settlers arriving in Oregon between December 1, 1851 and December 1, 1853 had to be 21 years old and could only claim 160 acres. If there was a wife she could also claim 160 acres.

Another amendment was passed in February 1853, which reduced the occupancy time to two years and required the payment of $1.25 per acre. The Donation Land Claim law expired in 1855, its purpose accomplished. By that time most of the best land in the Bear Creek and Applegate Valleys had been located and claimed.

There were six Donation Land Claims in Upper Applegate Valley. These were for James Bishop, Xavier LaClair, Willard Spencer, Henry H. Brown, Gideon B. Davidson and George Long. Their histories will be discussed in a succeeding chapter.

Since the land survey of Oregon did not reach Jackson County until 1853, the early Donation Land Claims were laid out by compass plus a system of metes and bounds. The boundaries were described by local geographical features and neighboring claims. When the surveys began, there had to be some adjustment in these boundaries, but all were honored. To the present time the legal descriptions contain the name and number of the original locator. Many of these claims were sold or traded several times before the patents were issued. Some had been claimed for speculation, but eventually nearly all became productive farms.

For those who were too late to file on a Donation Land Claim, there was the Act of 1820 which provided for the sale of public domain lands, and the Homestead Act of 1862.

Many settlers took up homesteads on marginal lands which lay along narrow creek valleys and hillsides. Most of these eventually failed. □

Typical homestead in Upper Applegate Valley is the John and Marguerite Black place on Forest Creek. The property includes grain fields and timber. Hidden in shadow of trees at right is original rail fence. (Author collection)

Chapter 2

TOURING THE AREA
HISTORIC SITES: JACKSONVILLE
TO RUCH

In 1959, Oregon's Centennial year, there was a group of historically-minded citizens in Jacksonville called the Siskiyou Pioneer Sites Foundation. Their centennial project was to erect historical markers made of heavy wood cut in the shape of the State of Oregon. These are about 16 inches by 24 inches in size. The names and dates are painted.

There are four markers still in existence in 1989. One is at the Herling-Bauten place, one at Logtown Cemetery and one at Uniontown. The other is on a curve of Highway 238 a few yards up the hill from the 30 mile marker on Jacksonville Hill. This sign is mounted on a post a few feet from the edge of the pavement on the north side of the highway. Although weathered and faded, the block lettering is still readable in 1989:

**MARTIN ANGEL
AMBUSHED AND KILLED IN 1850
BURIED ON SPOT**

Martin Angel, his wife and three small children came to Jackson County in 1852 and took up a 640-acre Donation Land Claim near the present city of Central Point. By 1855 he had land cleared and was raising hay and grain which he sold to the Army at nearby Fort Lane.

Martin Angel was active in the local Indian affairs and had a reputation for dealing harshly with Indians.

He was a member of the board of Manzanita School District No. 6 and was appointed to the board of County Commissioners in 1854. He was elected President of the Board in July 1855 to serve a one year term. He never made it.

In the fall of 1855, a small band of Applegate Indians (Dakubetede), 12 or 13 in number, moved into two deserted mining cabins in the Star Gulch area of Upper Applegate. They went into winter quarters in the cabins, piling up soil around the walls for protection. Some scouts exploring the area discovered

Martin Angel was ambushed, killed by Indians at this spot on January 2, 1856. (Author photograph, 1989)

them and reported it. Word was sent to the military officers at Fort Lane. They set out for the Applegate on the last day of December 1855. The troops included 25 regular soldiers and a company of volunteers from Jacksonville. James Buckley from the Applegate area was with them.

Among the volunteers was Martin Angel and a man named Walker. These two were riding about 250 yards ahead of the main company. When they were about two-and-one-half-miles from Jacksonville on the Crescent City road, gunfire erupted from the brush where Indians were lying in wait for them.

Martin Angel, hit in the head and neck, died instantly. Another shot killed his horse. Walker escaped with only a bullet grazing his beard. The Indians rapidly stripped the dead man and his horse and disappeared into the brush and trees before the rest of the troops came to the scene of the ambush. Apparently these troops heard the shots then took time to load their rifles to be ready if their were a large band of Indians.

This was on January 2, 1856.

In an interview with Lewis Buckley in 1976, he stated that the story of the Martin Angel ambush had been handed down in his family as follows: his grandfather, James Buckley, was riding in advance of the main company with Martin Angel and Mr. Walker. James Buckley was not carrying a gun and he escaped without injury. The Indians were after Martin Angel's gun. Other sources claim that the Indians shot Martin Angel in revenge.

Angel was buried in the "old" Jacksonville Cemetery which was located on the slope near the present day Touvelle House. In 1865 his grave was moved to the "new" Cemetery on the hill.

The story appeared in the *Table Rock Sentinel*, published in Jacksonville, on Saturday, January 5, 1856. It generated intense excitement and anger among the citizens. The war against the Indians had been further inflamed by the killing of Martin Angel.

OLD STAGE STOP: HERLING

About a mile east of Logtown on the Jacksonville-Crescent City road, a settler named Louis Herling took up a homestead before 1860. It was two 80-acre parcels mostly hillside land on both sides of Poormans Creek.

Louis Herling was born in Prussia and came to America when he was a young man. He was a gunsmith. His wife Catherine was born in Hesse. They had three children, each born in a different state: Louis Jr. born 1852 in New Jersey, Emma born 1855 in Wisconsin and Edward born in California.

A large house was built on the homestead, with a well dug in the front yard. Travelers began stopping there to water and rest their teams. Stages stopped there, too.

Land was cleared on the hillside. An irrigation ditch to bring water from Poormans Creek was constructed. In a few years there were alfalfa fields as well as an apple orchard.

Soon Louis Herling was in business serving the traveling public. He was granted a liquor license in July 1866 for the fee of $15.00. The license was renewed every year until June 1870 when the fee was $30.00. His name does not appear in subsequent records. By 1870 his son Louis Jr., 17, was working as a blacksmith apprentice. Their daughter Emma was 14. The little boy Edward was not listed on the census. It is presumed that he had died.

In the Jacksonville City records it was found that Louis Herling owned two lots in Jacksonville known as the "Hog Pit." This is where strayed hogs were penned until their owners retrieved them. On June 3, 1875 Louis Herling sold the "Hog Pit" lots 1 and 2 to the City of Jacksonville for $400.00. Location of the lots is behind the Brunner building, which in 1989 houses the Jacksonville Public Library.

A patent to the 160-acre homestead was granted to Louis Herling in 1871 (Vol. 7, p. 344 Deed Records).

On May 28, 1971, daughter Emma Herling married Thilo Gassman in her father's house. Witnesses were Joseph Wetterer and Max Muller. He was 35 and she just turned 15. The marriage was performed by Justice of the Peace James R. Wade. Thilo Gassman was from Prussia. He came to Jacksonville before 1870 and had a butcher shop.

Information about the Herling house drops from sight until 1880. Nevertheless there seems no reason to believe the public did not continue to stop there. Business was carried on even though no liquor license is on record for the 1870s.

For the Herlings, the 1880 census lists only Louis, age 54, and his wife Mary, age 61. His occupation was farmer.

HERLING: HENRY A. BAUTEN

In 1882 the name Henry A. Bauten appeared in the records. It seems that Louis Herling had died and the place was up for sale. The Herling place was sold at public auction on October 28, 1882. Bauten won the bid at $950.00. Emma Gassman was administratrix of the estate of Louis Herling. She made out the deed to Henry A. Bauten on November 7, 1882.

Bauten came to the United States from Germany in 1880, age 37. He was a farmer. He moved into the Herling house and was soon open for business. He applied for and was granted a liquor license on March 1, 1883. The fee was $50.00 for six months. His license was annually renewed until April 1886, when the fee was $100.00. The book of records ended in 1888 thus no further liquor licenses were available. It is known by many old timers that Henry Bauten continued to sell liquor for many years. Drinks were to be had from the customer's own bottle as late as 1910. The term "gallon house" meant that liquor could only be sold by the gallon under county license.

The year 1888 was eventful for Henry Bauten. On June 25, 1888 he married Mary Pulzer in the house of Max Muller in Jacksonville. The minister was F. S. Noel. Witnesses were John Pulzer and Patrick Ivory. Henry was 45 and Mary was 19.

Since it was three miles over the hill to the nearest post office in Jacksonville, Bauten applied for a post office. He named it

Herling. The opening date was July 26, 1888 with himself as postmaster.

A daughter named Wilhelmina was born in 1892. Her nickname was "Minnie." In 1892 Henry Bauten deeded the homestead of 160 acres to his wife. Included was a parcel of 120 acres which he had purchased in recent years. The deed was signed May 21, 1892. (Vol. 25 p. 123 Deed Records)

Minnie Bauten grew up on her parents' farm. She attended Forest Creek School in 1898 and later continued her education in Jacksonville. She became an accomplished pianist.

Henry Bauten died in 1912 and was buried in Ashland. Minnie married Gordon Stout, who lived near the Bautens. Gordon and Minnie farmed the place for many years.

A bachelor, Pryor Eaton, lived in a small box-type cabin on patented mining about one half mile from the Bautens. When he died he willed his property to Minnie Stout. The small cabin still stands in 1989, on the west side of Highway 238 about 300 yards from milepost 30. It dates from before the turn of the century. It is a typical miner's cabin.

Pryor Eaton house near milepost 30 on Highway 238. This typical miner's cabin was built in late 1800s and is still standing in 1989. (Photo made April 10, 1987 by author)

Stories about the good times that took place at the Herling-Bauten house are corroborated by a newspaper article discovered in a scrapbook in the Southern Oregon Historical Society Library collection. The compiler of the scrapbook was Corrine Linn, daughter of David Linn, carpenter and builder of Jacksonville.

One headline and article was: "Southern Oregon Landmark in Hands of Wreckers—Hurling Place Center of Gay Life 50 to 75 Years Ago." (Jacksonville, October 26, 1921 Medford *Mail Tribune*).

Old stagecoach stop at Herling about 1900. Man on left is Henry A. Bauten, girl with doll is his daughter, Mary. Wife, Minnie Bauten on right. Men in center unidentified. (Photo from Southern Oregon Historical Society)

Only a short time and one more Southern Oregon landmark, a reminder of Jacksonville in back years, will be gone. Hurling's place, at least all that remains of it, is in the hands of the wrecking crew.

Hurling's was for many years the gathering place for pioneer social life of Jacksonville vicinity. No ball or dinners were ever gayer than those given there and early residents still tell stories of the masquerades and holiday balls and suppers. Just how long ago the road house was built is doubtful. One woman remembers going to her first dance in 1869 when she was a girl of 7. She believes it was built in the early 1860's about fifty or sixty years ago. The history of Hurling is linked with the history of Jacksonville. During the 1860s through the 1880s its popularity grew.

Those were the days when the gold mines were paying and money was plentiful. The Southern Oregon boom had attracted many who had been in the California rush a few years earlier. Prospectors, traders and gamblers as well as settlers were drawn here. As many as 500 Chinese lived in Jacksonville's Chinatown then. But when the mines failed, Hurling's place was left alone and was soon forgotten.

Where once camped miners and outlaws, cattle now graze in the historic place. The rocky road over which untold wealth had been hauled has been made into a paved highway for busy farmers and hurrying tourists.

There is no place for hospitality; it's the end of a way of life.

Hurling's place is but a memory.

FOREST CREEK—POORMANS CREEK

Forest Creek rises on the slopes of Mt. Isabelle and flows about three miles in a southeasterly direction to the confluence with the east fork, then flows two miles to another tributary, Poormans Creek. This creek rises along the ridge south of Jacksonville and flows southwesterly to confluence with Forest Creek. Today's Highway 238 follows Poormans Creek. Forest Creek with its tributaries is about eight-and-one-half miles in length and empties into the Applegate River near the present Cantrall-Buckley Park. Until about 1910, Forest Creek was called Jackass Creek and was so marked on early maps.

Miners first worked on upper Jackass Creek in the early 1850s. Some mining was done by Chinese who bought claims from white men. Later when the easiest gold was mined out, miners turned to farming in the summer and mining in the winter.

One of the first miners to purchase government land on Upper

Jackass was Daniel Hopkins before 1872. He established a sawmill and had the land cleared by logging, which became farm fields. Other early day settlers were Levi Sebring, S. S. Baird, Jacob Smith, James Armpriest, Ed Manville, Frank Logg, John Horn and Harry Wulf.

A county road was surveyed in 1871 to the upper mines. It was laid along the hillsides to be above the mining operations in the creek. In 1898 the farmers petitioned for a change in the road to go around and above their farm fields.

The school district was organized on Sept. 10, 1878 and called Forest Creek District No. 43. It was partitioned off Logtown District No. 3. The school house was located at the confluence of the east fork and the main creek by the road.

ALBERT W. STURGIS, MINER-FARMER

Albert W. Sturgis was a farmer who turned to mining and made a success of it. He was a shrewd trader and a hard worker. In the 43 years he lived in the Ruch area, he owned parts of three Donation Land Claims and several miles of mining claims along Forest Creek.

He came to Applegate Valley in 1861 when he was 25 years of age. That year he married Mary E. Talley on Dec. 2, 1861. Their first child, named Winter, was born in 1863.

Sturgis purchased the Henry H. Brown Donation Land Claim in 1864 for the sum of $1,000.00. This claim was located about a half mile down stream from Uniontown, on the Applegate River. Two more children were born to them while they lived on this place, Albert Jr. In 1865, and Fred T. in 1874.

They suffered the loss of Albert Jr. in 1875 at the age of 10. He was buried in the Jacksonville Cemetery.

Sometime in the next two years Mary Sturgis left her husband and sought a divorce. She brought suit against him for possession of the property. She won and Albert Sturgis was forced into bankruptcy to comply with the court order which awarded her the 160-acre D.L.C., also three lots in Sec. 4 totaling 70 acres. (Vol. 8 p. 96 Deed Records, May 28, 1878).

After losing the property, Albert Sturgis remained in the area, working to acquire more land. On July 21, 1885, he married Pauline Coffman, daughter of early settlers William Issac and Anna Coffman. The ceremony was performed by E. D. Foudry, Minister, at the home of her parents.

They had one daughter named Pauline, who was born in May

1886. Her nickname was "Sadie" and she was known by it all her life.

During the years after his marriage to Pauline, Albert Sturgis located and purchased mining claims. In 1892 he purchased the 160-acre John McKee homestead from Austin Albright, and 17.5 acres of mining ground adjacent to it along Forest Creek.

He organized the Sturgis Mining Company with headquarters about two miles up Forest Creek Road. Here he built a large frame house, shop, barn, bunkhouse and store building.

The house had running water, which was unusual in those days. Up a gulch across the road was a well with a pump powered by a little steam engine. Water was pumped into a tank from which it was piped to the house. There was a small store in a separate building where supplies were sold to the miners who worked for him. A few gnarled fruit trees remain where an orchard was once planted.

Water for the mining operation was delivered by about a mile of ditch built around the hillsides from Forest Creek. The Sturgis Mining Company prospered for about 10 years. By this time, he owned approximately 640 acres of deeded land on Forest Creek plus the 160-acre McKee homestead at Logtown.

Sturgis decided to sell his properties and discontinue mining in 1903. The buyer was S. A. Vance. The deal included all placer claims, patented or otherwise, water rights, water ditches, rights of way and easements and all deeded land he owned in the upper Forest Creek mining area. The price was $35,000.00.

S. A. Vance was from Los Angeles, California. He and his wife Marie, with their small son Albert S., moved to Forest Creek to operate the mining property. He had a small office built on the rear of the dwelling house. They lived there less than two years because Vance became seriously ill in the fall of 1905 and they returned to Los Angeles for medical treatment. He died on October 25, 1905.

His wife, Marie Vance, was appointed administratrix of the estate and guardian of their son. Mrs. Vance's brother, C. H. Anderson, became involved in her affairs. He established a corporation called the Vance-Anderson Mining Company with stock for sale to investors. In order to hold the claims, Mrs. Vance leased the mining ground to Lewis Stone and others for several years. She received little if any royalty.

Litigation of a dispute with Fred J. Blakely and others of the Sterling Mining Company took time and money.

By 1910 David Hyatt, guardian of Albert in Oregon, petitioned the court for an order to sell all of the Forest Creek mining property for the benefit of the boy. An order was granted for it to be sold to the highest bidder. On August 22, 1911, the records show that the highest bidder was the Vance-Anderson Mining Company. They bid $10,000. The court further ordered that this sum of money be invested back into stock of the Vance-Anderson Mining Company. Albert S. Vance received 100 shares of stock. Apparently these transactions were all on paper. No money changed hands. David L. Hyatt filed his final guardianship report.

On May 17, 1912, his case was closed. The deed complying with the court order is recorded in Vol. 91, p. 429 dated November 6, 1911, Jackson County Deed Records.

The mining claim on which the house was located was never patented. It remains a mining claim in 1989.

In 1902 Albert Sturgis purchased the west half of the Willard Spencer D.L.C. which was located near the confluence of Forest Creek and Applegate River. A new bungalow-type house was built about 1912. The old house nearby was rented to men with families who worked on the ranch. The buildings were about an eighth-of-a-mile from the highway on a knoll overlooking the river.

Daughter "Sadie" Pauline Sturgis married John J. Ossenbrugge on December 17, 1910. They had two daughters.

After Sturgis' death in 1913, his widow, Pauline, continued to manage the ranch. She died in 1937 and was buried beside him in Jacksonville Cemetery. Sadie inherited the property and managed it for many years. It was still in the Ossenbrugge estate in the early 1980s when it was purchased by a family from California.

LOGTOWN—FRANK LOGG

By the time the Jacksonville-Crescent City road was opened for wagon traffic in 1858, a bustling mining camp was established on both sides of it near the confluence of Poormans and Jackass Creek (Forest Creek).

The camp expanded into a settlement with several saloons, a store, a hotel with a livery stable and a blacksmith shop. There were miners' cabins, barns and corrals. It became a major stopping place for the travelers on the Jacksonville-Crescent City Road.

Frank Logg was a prominent miner in the settlement. He owned mining claims and other land. He was one of the organizers of what became the "Lower Jackass Mining District." An agreement setting forth rules and regulations for the miners was signed on March 17, 1860. The settlement was called "Logtown" by most people.

Another name was found on written records and legal papers as early as 1861. This was Forestville. The voting precinct was listed as Forest Precinct when it was established in 1868. This name did not survive. The area has always been called Logtown long after the settlement declined and was abandoned. Logtown was never awarded a post office.

Frank Logg's wife was named Magdalena. She died in childbirth on May 13, 1871. She was 38. She was buried in Jacksonville Cemetery. Frank never remarried. He lived out his life with a partner, John McDonnel (called Mac). Logg had deeded land on the east fork of Forest Creek, just above the school house.

Old timers tell a story about Frank and Mac. One day Frank fired off a rickety old gun. A piece of the gun flew back and hit him in the forehead. He fell as if shot. Mac ran in panic to the neighbors to report that Frank was killed. When they arrived at the cabin, Frank was found alive except for a lump on his head.

It is also told about Frank and Mac how they worked faithfully mining all winter. After the gold clean-up in the spring, they would take off for San Francisco and proceed to "live it up." In the fall, they would return, broke but happy, and go to work again. This was typical of several bachelor miners in the area.

DANIEL J. S. PEARCE

An early settler on Poormans Creek near the intersection of Highway 238 and Forest Creek Road was Daniel Jones Sweeny Pearce. He was born in Mansfield, Ohio, February 19, 1835. He traveled across the plains to the California gold fields in 1856. The next year he was in Jacksonville and mined on Jackson Creek during the height of the boom.

He was attracted to the gold strike in the Boise Basin (Idaho) in 1862. Two years later, he was at a strike on McLellan Creek in Montana. When this strike failed, he joined a group of miners who whipsawed lumber and built boats to carry them down the Yellowstone and Missouri Rivers to St. Joseph. Not only was this a rough and dangerous water route, but there was constant threat of Indian attacks.

In Memphis, Missouri, he married Sarah Alice Watts on February 26, 1866. He was 31, she was 15. They farmed in Kansas for several years. Six children were born to them. These were:

Floyd (1867), Merrell (1870), Ada (1873), Leona (1874), Louella (1876), and Grace (1879). Daniel J. S. Pearce brought his family to Jackson County in 1880 where he took up a homestead on Sterling Creek. Here he was active in mining and some farming. The two oldest boys did the work of grown men on the homestead. A patent to this property was granted on Dec. 14, 1891. Five more children were born during this decade: Enan (Evan) (1881), Daniel (1884), Paul (1887), Cordelia (1890), and George (1893). This made 11 children. Seven of them grew to adulthood.

During the early 1890s, Pearce purchased a group of patented mining claims on Poormans Creek and built a house for his family on one of them. His children attended Forest Creek School, married and established families of their own. Some descendants still live in the area.

Daniel Jones Sweeny Pearce died on November 26, 1923, age 88 years, and was buried in the Logtown Cemetery. His wife Sarah outlived him by three years. She died April 6, 1926, and is also buried in Logtown Cemetery. For a period it was called Laurel Grove Cemetery.

LOGTOWN—HINKLE FAMILY

Among the earliest settlers at Logtown (1855) were the Hinkles. There was Edwin Hinkle and his wife Mary (b. 1815). They had two daughters, Ferba (Phoebe), born 1845, and Mary, born 1855.

The family group included four brothers. William, the oldest, was born in 1830, George was born in 1835; Riley and Calvin were twins, born in 1838. They came from Tennessee and all were illiterate. Records are not clear as to the relationship of Edwin Hinkle to the brothers. They worked together establishing a farm and a homestead claim taken up about 1855, adjoining Frank Logg's claim.

They soon had land cleared and were raising hay and grain to sell to packers and teamsters on the Jacksonville-Crescent City trail. Edwin and Mary Hinkle operated a combined hotel and store. Records show that Edwin Hinkle had a liquor license and a stock of groceries and supplies purchased from P. J. Ryan of Jacksonville. He was a partner with William H. Tinsley in operating a pack train to Crescent City in 1856.

This family group suffered a setback when Edwin Hinkle died in April or early May 1856. There is no record of the exact date of his death or where he was buried.

The estate was filed for probate on May 24, 1858. These records reveal fascinating information about the operation of this early pioneer business.

The estate was appraised by William H. Tinsley, Riley Hinkle and William Hinkle. The land claim with improvements was valued at $1,000.00.

The inventory of household goods, farm equipment and livestock revealed:

Table and Tin ware .... $	15.00
Cooking utensils Churn and wooden bucket	21.00
1 Camp Kettle and Wash tub	5.00
1 Feather bed and Equipages	30.00
4 Oregon beds and Equipages	40.00
2 Rifle guns	20.00
1 Shot gun $4. 1 Box chairs and table	10.00
1 Looking glass and Shaving tools	2.00
1 X cut saw $6. 1 handsaw & 3 augers $4.	10.00
1 Iron wedge $2.50, 2 Axes 2.50, 1 Froe 2.50	7.50
1 Hatchet, 5 maul rings, Hammer and chisel, 3 hoes	5.50
1 Pair Candle molds and balances 2 doll, 2 log chains	7.00
	$ 173.00

An inventory of farm equipment and livestock itemized:	
1 Ox wagon $100. 2 Turning plows $30 .... $	130.00
1 Horse cart $15, two pair harness, saddle & bridle $15	30.00
1 Mule $30. 1 bay mare $40. 2 sows & pigs $20	90.00
1 Sow & 5 shoats $25, 3 doz. fowl $6 doz $18	43.00
9 Cows & Calves $_0$ $45 a piece 2 cows $_0$ $90	495.00
5 Heifers yearlings $100, 1 yoke Oxen $100	200.00
1 Bull $25, 1 Scythe & Cradle $8	33.00
	$1021.00
	$2294.00

The appraisal was signed on May 26, 1858 by:

W. H. Tinsley
Wm. Hinkle
Riley Hinkle

When the bills were all presented for settlement it was found that the estate had debts of less than $100.00.

For the next three years Mary Hinkle and her teenage daughter Ferba (Phoebe) continued to operate the hotel and store. Riley,

William and George tended the farm, raised and harvested the crops in summer and worked on their mining claim in winter.

Tragedy overtook them on the night of June 18, 1861, when Mary Hinkle's house caught fire. All three women were burned to death. Samuel Bowen, a neighbor, gave the following testimony before the coroner's jury the next day, June 19:

> About midnight on the night of Tuesday, June 18, 1861, I heard the alarm of fire [and] ascertained that the residence of Widow Hinkle was in flames. I got up and went out. There were men there trying to put the fire out and get the family. The flames kept the men out of the building. When I got there, the building was falling in. Mrs. Hinkle and her two daughters [who] lived there, perished in the flames.

The coroner's jury gave the decision that Mrs. Mary Hinkle, Miss F. Hinkle and Miss Mary Hinkle came to their deaths by fire in the accidental burning of their residence on the night of the 18th of June 1861. The following jurors signed their names: John McKee, Thomas Farris, H. Sabine, Henry Gregg, George Long and Samuel Bowen.

The fire burned with such intensity that the destruction was complete. Examination of the ashes revealed nothing in the way of evidence of how it happened, but parts of charred skeletons were located.

Almost immediately, a rumor began circulating through the camp that Mary Hinkle and her daughters were murdered by a robber who was after a cache of gold, then set the house on fire to cover up the robbery.

On Aug. 31, 1861, the *Oregon Sentinel* carried this story headlined "Murder Will Out" to the effect that a party of miners assisted a man with a band of loose horses, which turned out to be stolen. By threatening to hang him they extracted a confession from him that, with the help of two men, Springer and Bullock, they had not only stolen the horses in the Rogue River Valley, but also had set fire to Mrs. Hinkle's house, after murdering her and her daughters. This story is the sole evidence available that Mary Hinkle and her daughters were murdered.

There is no record of where Mary Hinkle and her daughters were buried. In Logtown Cemetery there are a number of very old graves with no markers that are listed on the cemetery maps as unknown. It is on record that Burpee and Linn provided the caskets and dug the graves, but the record does not give the location were the remains were buried.

On an early map made by Elva Smith, who kept a record of burials, there is the grave of a Hinkle baby who died in the 1850s. A bill for $8.00 to Edwin Hinkle from J. S. Burpee for making a coffin and digging a grave was found in his probate records.

It is known that the Reverend James Dunlap, a minister who lived in the camp, conducted the funeral for the Hinkles in June of 1861. The next year Rev. Dunlap died and is one of the first recorded graves in Logtown Cemetery.

After Mary Hinkle's death, George Hinkle was appointed administrator of her estate. The appraisers were John McKee, Robert Casteal and J. T. Williams. Their report was dated August 7, 1861. The land and improvements were appraised at $600. A long list of cattle, horses, turkeys, chickens, and farm equipment totaled $1370.00. There was a doctor bill to Thompson and Greer for Mary Hinkle from Dec. 1, 1858, to Dec. 12, 1858, in the sum of $45.00. This had to be for Mary or the girls, because Edwin Hinkle died in April or May 1858. A bill for a coffin to J. S. Burpee, $40.00 was dated June 20, 1861, and $8.00 for digging a grave to D. Linn, Jacksonville. Other medical bills Aug. 4 to Sept. 5, 1860, showed 4 visits and medicine, $15.00 each. Some money had been paid on this but balance due was $16.50.

George Hinkle submitted a bill to the estate for work performed on the place from July of 1860 to January 1861 at $50.00 per month. The court awarded him $279.00. George Hinkle signed his name to this paper because someone had taught him to write it thus he no longer had to sign with a mark.

Among the papers was a note in which Mary Hinkle borrowed $100.00 from Peter Inyard. It was headed "Forestville, Ore. May 29, 1861" and signed with her mark. It was witnessed by R. H. Casteal. She had purchased various goods from P. J. Ryan on Sept. 17, 1861, including: bed cord, smoothing iron and stand, combs, calico, fine linen, saleratus, nails, 100 lb. crushed sugar and 10 lbs. fine sugar.

By Sept. 1861, all the bills were filed and the court ordered the property sold to settle the estate.

The highest bidder for the land claims was Hugh Donnelly who got it for $300.00. The deal was closed Dec. 6, 1861. The final settlement of the Mary Hinkle estate was dated Dec. 6, 1862.

Although the Hinkle family lived in Logtown only a short time (1856-1861), their story is important as documentary evidence of life at Logtown in its early days.

Riley, Calvin and William remained in Jackson County during the 1870s and 1880s. Calvin married and had a family. William made his home with them. George Hinkle was married and moved to Washington Territory where he had several children. William Hinkle died in 1892, Calvin Hinkle died in 1896. His wife Matilda lived till 1921. Riley Hinkle died in 1897. They are buried in Jacksonville Cemetery and all have permanent stone markers.

Hugh Donnelly was a miner and a neighbor. He worked claims along both creeks and while it was legal to do so, he took up claims then sold them to the Chinese. All transactions had to be signed with his mark. He was a shrewd trader.

LOGTOWN—McKEE FAMILY

Another well known settler at Logtown was John McKee. He and his wife Maryum (Bowen) and two small children, Maxmilly and Adelbert had come across the plains in 1852-53 in a wagon train which included his wife's parents, John and Roxyann Bowen. The Bowen's adult son Samuel was also with them. The group arrived in August 1853, and by October John McKee had filed on a Donation Land Claim on the foothills of a mountain east of present day Medford, later named Roxy Ann Butte.

As John McKee started to prove up on his claim he became discouraged by the difficulty of farming the unfamiliar sticky clay soil. Maryum had brought with her from Missouri a slip of a yellow rose bush, which she planted in the yard of their cabin. It took root and lived.

John McKee soon became interested in the mining boom in progress over the hill west of Jacksonville at the mining camp of Logtown. By 1855 he had located a mining claim on Poormans Creek just above the crossing of the Jacksonville-Crescent City road. In 1862 he purchased 40 acres of the Hinkle claim from Hugh Donnelly and built a house for his family.

McKee had experience as a blacksmith. He set up a shop to do work for the miners and a few settlers who were starting to farm in the area. He sharpened tools and plows, shod horses, mules and oxen. He invented and improved a miner's pick which he called a "strap-eye pick." It was much in demand as word of its usefulness spread through the camps.

As soon as the family was moved into the new house at Logtown, Maryum transplanted her yellow rose from the Roxy Ann Butte property to her new yard. Remnants of this yellow rose still bloom at the site in 1989. Slips taken from it over the years are growing in gardens all over the Applegate Valley. In 1989 a historical marker stands near the original rose bush.

County records show that John McKee served as a member of the Forest Precinct election board in 1858, indicating that they were living at Logtown at this time. The house that John McKee built was a large log structure with a big room where dances were held. There was space for two squares or quadrilles, and many a "ball" was held there. They were also enthusiastic card players. In summer, ball games, races and other contests were held. People came for miles to participate in these activities.

The big house gradually filled with children. A daughter, Martha Jane, was born in 1855, and was followed by a new baby about every two years, until 1878, when John B., the last one, was born. There was a total of fourteen, but not all of them lived to adulthood. Those who grew up, married and had families were: Adelbert (1852), Maximilly (1850), William H. T. (1857), Sarah Elizabeth (1859), George S. (1861), Amos Milton (1864), Emma Eva (1867), Silas H. (1870), Rachel Teresa (Tressie) (1872), Mary, (1876), and John B. (1878).

As in most large families in those days, the older children were soon helping with the younger ones. Girls did endless household tasks. Boys worked on the farm with their father. Maryum was often called on to help when illness struck the neighbors. She was famous as a midwife.

John McKee also continued to prove up on his Donation Land Claim on the slopes of Roxy Ann Butte. He was granted the patent to it on July 26, 1867. There were 320 acres, the north half in John's name, and the south half in Maryum's name. The patent was signed by President Andrew Johnson and was recorded in the Jackson County deed records on February 18, 1873. A few months later, April 1873, John McKee sold the Donation Land Claim to George W. Stephenson for $600 in gold coin. (Vol. 6, p. 160, Deed Records). Eventually this property became part of today's Hillcrest Orchards.

Sometime in the 1860s, John McKee let the Hinkle claim revert to the government, and filed on a 160-acre homestead adjacent to it. He completed proving up on it, and was granted a patent on December 13, 1878. (Vol. 10, p. 174, Deed Records). The graveyard where early Logtown miners and settlers were buried was just inside the south boundary of John McKee's homestead.

Another land deal took place in 1888 which brought about a change in the lives of John and Maryum McKee. It appears that

John knew a man named William Sutherland who owned 280 acres of timber and farm land on Big Butte Creek, off present day Cobleigh Road. Sutherland owed a large sum of money and he could not pay it thus the property was sold at sheriff's sale. John McKee bid at $415.00. As the highest bidder, he became the owner of a ranch on Big Butte Creek in the Rogue Valley. The deed was recorded June 16, 1888. (Vol. 16, p. 83, 84, 85, Deed Records). Sometime in the next two years, John and Maryum McKee moved to the ranch on Big Butte Creek.

On September 20, 1892, John McKee sold his 160-acre homestead at Logtown to Austin Allbright for $600.00. This included the house, barns, sheds, farm land and some mining ground. It also included the graveyard, which by this time contained several rows of graves of miners and early settlers, some of them McKees. However, John McKee's deed to Austin Allbright did not mention any land set aside, or reserved for a cemetery. Legal ownership of this graveyard was passed along to each purchaser of the property until 1929.

On the Big Butte Creek ranch, John McKee had the help of two of his children to operate it. Amos McKee and his wife, Lottie, with their two sons, Ernest and Floyd. This family lived in a small cabin near the main house. A daughter, Pearl, was born there on December 20, 1894. Mary (McKee) and her husband, John Higginbotham came to live there and help after Amos moved his family back to the Applegate Valley about 1897.

Amos worked at a mine on Palmer Creek for several years. Another daughter, Clara Hester, was born there on November 2, 1905.

Mary and John Higginbotham gradually took complete charge of the Butte Creek Ranch, as John and Maryum were becoming elderly and were in failing health. Amos and Lottie McKee took the couple into their home and cared for them. Maryum died on October 28, 1908. She was buried in Logtown Cemetery.

John McKee lived for three more lonely years with the John Higginbothams. He deeded 160 acres of the ranch to Mary in 1910. He died on February 6, 1911, and was buried beside his wife and other kin in Logtown Cemetery.

John left many descendants. They are scattered far and wide. As of this writing (1989), one granddaughter, Pearl McKee Byrne, age 94, lives in the Upper Applegate Valley. Her daughter, Evelyn, with her husband, Clarence Williams, lives nearby. Two other granddaughters, Clara Smith and Dorothy Hackert, live in Jacksonville, as does Luella Dunnington Parker.

Long before the John McKee family moved away, the easiest gold was mined out on Poormans Creek and Forest Creek. Logtown diminished to a few cabins and outbuildings by the turn of the century. The mining claims were patented and became private property. The last building remaining from the old Logtown settlement was a large pole barn. The barn burned to the ground about 1923. The fire was said to have been caused by young boys smoking inside it.

However, mining was not entirely finished. Years later, there was to be a revival of mining with modern equipment which paid very well.

LOGTOWN CEMETERY

In pioneer days a graveyard in a rural area was merely an acre or so of land where the dead were buried by their families and neighbors. A coroner often had to render a decision as to the cause of death when it was under unusual circumstances. The coffin was often homemade, but sometimes a fancy coffin was purchased from a cabinet maker such as David Linn in Jacksonville. A grave was usually dug by some of the family or friends. At ceremony time, the coffin was hauled from the family home by family members or relatives. Close friends often served as pall bearers. Funerals were considered important and these services were a final tribute to the deceased and usually presided over by a minister. Funerals were highly religious in character. Many families erected marble or granite monuments, but some markers were just a slab of wood with a name etched or painted on it. Due to the actions of the elements, these wooden markers soon disintegrated, those graves were then left unmarked. In later years, mortuaries installed small metal markers, but unfortunately, these did not last long, either.

The old cemetery was located about 400 feet up the hill on the east side of the Jacksonville-Crescent City road.

In 1929, a group of local people rebuilt the wire fence with new cedar posts donated by Mark Winningham.

No written records of burials in Logtown Cemetery were kept in the early days, but Elva Smith, who grew up near Logtown and knew everybody, kept track of names and dates on hand drawn maps as best she could. She kept the maps up-to-date during the twenties and thirties. Issac Coffman, long time sexton of the Jacksonville Cemetery, often assisted with burials in Logtown in the 1930s.

Building the rustic gate at Logtown Cemetery in 1939. On top, Byron Winningham (left) and Lloyd Whitney. Woman standing at left is Pearl Whitney. Man at far right is Walter Armpriest. (Author collection) Lower: After the logs in the gate became unstable in later years, they were replaced with a "lifetime" arch built of scrap rail. (Author photo in 1987)

As more old timers passed away and burials were made during the thirties, Elva Smith and a few other interested families decided to organize a cemetery association. It seemed the time had come to obtain legal title to the land and carry out various improvement projects to preserve the pioneer graveyard. It was and still is the only active cemetery between Jacksonville and Missouri Flat, Josephine County.

Logtown Cemetery Association was formally organized at a meeting held at the cemetery on May 14, 1939. Those who attended were:

Elva and Ed Smith, Ruch
Pearl and Harry Whitney, Jacksonville
Bill and Gertrude Winningham, Medford
L. Frank and Anna M. Lozier, Medford
Emma Snith, Ruch
E. Igo (and wife), Medford
Minus Pence (and wife), Jacksonville
Leonard McKee, Jacksonville
John and Marguerite Black, Forest Creek

Anna Lozier was chairman *pro-tem* and conducted the meeting. The following were elected as a board of trustees: Gertrude Winningham, Pearl Whitney, Anna Lozier, Leonard McKee and John Black. Gertrude Winningham was elected chairman, and Marguerite Black was elected secretary-treasurer.

It was voted to change the name of the cemetery from "Laurel Grove" back to Logtown, and the organization to be officially called Logtown Cemetery Association. It was agreed that all persons who have relatives buried there are considered members with a right to attend annual meetings and vote.

In subsequent meetings, application for incorporation was filed, and plans to obtain legal title to the south half of the cemetery were made. At this time the owners were Walter W. and Edith Bell, who lived in California.

Harry Skyrman, a Medford attorney, handled the legal matters. The certificate of Articles of Incorporation was received dated May 23, 1939.

Paul E. and Mildred Pearce donated to the Cemetery Association the part located in Sec. 14 Twp. 38 S. R. 3 W. Walter W. and Edith Bell donated the part located in Sec. 23 Twp. 38 S. R. 3 W. W.M. The deeds were signed on October 17, 1940.

During 1939, plans were carried out to build a large rustic

archway of cedar logs at the highway entrance. A carved wooden sign was donated by local Civilian Conservation Corps artists and mounted over the archway.

The next project was employing a professional surveyor to make a legal survey and prepare a map. W. W. Walker of Ashland completed this work in 1944. Existing graves were drawn on the blocks wherever they fell. New graves were put in according to block and lot. Later, the aisles and blocks in the cemetery were marked with concrete markers and steel pins.

By 1949, the big cedar archway became unsafe and was replaced with railroad iron and a wire gate. A well was drilled in 1950 and a hand pump installed. Plans for a well house never materialized partly on account of maintenance concerns.

All of these improvement projects were on a "pay as you go" basis. Donations of time and money came generously from members and the community. Work days were well attended and the projects were completed.

In 1958, a group of members planted a row of slips from Maryum McKee's yellow rose bush across the front of the cemetery, on the north side of the gate. These took root and grew very well.

Later on, the Applegate Valley Garden Club set out more slips on the south side of the gate. Garden Club members cultivate and fertilize the roses every year and have them watered two or three times during the hot summers. The results are spectacular. In spring, the roses bloom profusely, and last for several weeks. Few passersby are aware that this rose garden is the end result of the late Maryum McKee's earlier transplant of a single yellow rose from her garden in Missouri, and long trek over the Oregon trail in 1853 to this area.

The Oregon State Centennial marker installed by the gate in 1958 has been refinished once, and mounted on a new post. The marker is number 24, and reads: "CEMETERY, Logtown Rose Planted Here in 1863 and 1958."

Another historical marker was installed in 1976, by the Applegate Bicentennial Committee, and the Southern Oregon Historical Society. This was part of a project to place historical markers at the most important sites in the Applegate Valley. The committee succeeded in placing markers at Sterling Cemetery, McKee Bridge, and Ruch. The markers consist of an anodized aluminum plaque mounted on a pedestal built of river rocks and concrete. The text of the marker:

Logtown

Logtown, a mining community located on both sides of the road one-quarter mile north of here, is believed to have been named for Francis Logg, miner and homesteader. In the 1860s and 70s there was a livery stable, store, meat market, hotel, church, three saloons, and two Chinese stores. When miners left for other gold fields, buildings were abandoned. The last house burned about 1910. An old-fashioned yellow rose survived for over one hundred years on the site of the homestead of John and Maryann McKee. First recorded burial in Logtown Cemetery was 1862.

The officers and members of Logtown Cemetery Association observed the fiftieth anniversary of the organization at the annual meeting on May 21, 1989. It appears that the goals of the original organizers have been attained. Accurate records have been kept and the cemetery grounds are well preserved.

Many years ago, a man named Fred Law, whose family were early settlers near Ruch, wrote a poem about the Logtown Rose.

The Logtown Rose
By Fred M. Law

To the young and the old and one who knows
Let me tell you the story of the Logtown Rose.
It's the emblem of beauty that does display
The old pioneer of an early day.

It was back in the year of '63
When to Forest Creek came John McKee,
And then his friends all gathered round,
Cut logs for his home in old Logtown.

When his home was built, it was snug and warm,
It protected his children through winter's storm.
And Mirium spun yarn to make socks and hose.
Once in spare time, planted a yellow rose.

It was a tiny slip she placed in the ground;
Then its roots spread out, and slips gathered 'round,
As the years come and as the years go,
Its friends would die, while the rose would grow.

It was a beautiful flower of yellowish hue,
For over 50 years, it weathered through.
To live as it did, you would never suppose,
But it really did, the Logtown Rose.

Wooden marker for the Logtown Rose was hand-carved by Myrtle Krouse in the 1970s.

Now the nails that they used have turned to rust,
And the logs that once stood have turned to dust,
But remaining there as winter winds blows,
On this historic spot, stands the Logtown Rose.

Protect it, friends, as you pass by,
Give it a drink, don't let it die,
On the earth so dry from the sun so hot,
Please let the rose live on this sacred spot.

It's a friend of the family of John McKee,
And also a friend to that old oak tree,
Though too far away from the shade it gives
Through the summer heat, so it may live.

So take care of it, friends, and do it soon
And in a very short time for you it'll bloom.
You see, my friends, it cannot cry;
It can only bloom and say good-bye.

Its breath is sweet; its heart is gold,
Now this is the story, as I've been told.
So long may it grow in sweet repose,
And bloom for you all, the Logtown Rose.

JAMES BISHOP

A half mile to the south of Logtown Cemetery is the James Bishop Donation Land Claim. James Bishop came to Oregon from Vermont, arriving in Jackson County in November 1852. His wife's name was Anne (Anna). They had ten children, six boys and four girls. They settled on this claim in November 1853, and set about clearing the land to put in a crop.

A creek about three miles long flows through the claim and empties into Forest Creek. It was named for the Bishop family.

They had only been on the claim two years when James Bishop was killed by Indians during the uprising of 1855. No details were available as to where or how it happened. Anna Bishop and her children inherited the claim. In September 1859, the heirs were listed: James Bishop, Jr., Henry, Charles, Oskar, Emeline, Mary Ellen, Elizabeth, William, Harriette, Martin and the widow, Anna. It was reported that the claim had been surveyed by David P. Thompson, and was ready for division among the heirs.

At this time, Anna and her family were living in Josephine County. On November 15, 1867, Anna Bishop recorded a deed for the sale of the land to Theodoric Cameron of Uniontown. (Vol. 4, p. 618 Deed Records.)

Among the subsequent owners of the Bishop D.L.C. was W. H. Bostwick who purchased it from Theodoric Cameron in 1888. Bostwick and his wife Eva had ten children, among the older ones was William T., who was born in 1868. Others were Walter, Gertrude, Bert, Hattie, Lena, Irvin and Vance. W. H. Bostwick lived on the Bishop place about twelve years. A photo of the family beside the house was taken about 1900. It shows Walter Bostwick, Jim Buckley, Ed Bostwick, Bert Bostwick, mother and father Bostwick (W. H. and Eva) and three children, Lena, Irvin and Vance. William T. Bostwick was married to Rhoda Dunlap in 1888. She died in childbirth the next year. She and the infant are buried together in Logtown Cemetery.

In 1890 William Bostwick married Augusta Schneider. Their children include Josie, Earl, Henry, Everett and Harold. They lived on upper Forest Creek where he carried on mining and farming. The children attended Forest Creek School. In 1904 Bostwick sold the north half of the Bishop D.L.C. to Albert W. Sturgis. He had it farmed by various tenants until 1908 when he sold this half to Robert F. Holzgang who moved there with a large family. Some of them were Anna, Elizabeth, Frank, Joseph, Mary, Martha, John, George, Godfrey, Margaret and Victor.

House on Bishop Donation Land Claim occupied after 1888 by the Bostwick family for about twelve years. Pictured are: Walter Bostwick, Jim Buckley, Ed, and Bert Bostwick. W. H. and Eva Bostwick (father and mother) and children Lena, Irvin and Vance. Old dog at gate is "Carlo." (Harry Bostwick collection)

In 1920 Robert Holzgang purchased the south half of the Bishop D.L.C. from the estate of William Ray, and lived there until he was killed in an accident with a buzz saw. The family remained a few years before moving to Medford. The place was sold to R. B. Carr about 1928. Other owners included Martin and Chester McDonough, who sold to Applegate Valley Investment Co. The house was replaced with a mobile home. The old barns and other outbuildings across the road were taken down.

In 1989, the ranch is farmed by Billy Joe Hunter, his wife Joanne, and his sons Timothy and Daniel. They operate a feed yard for cattle on a year-around basis. They produce the feed by renting and farming other ranches besides their own.

There was some mining done in the upper valley of Bishop Creek in the early days. It is now subdivided into a rural residential community. □

Chapter 3

RUCH

The first permanent settler at the intersection of the road to Upper Applegate and the Jacksonville-Crescent City road was James McDonough. He came to the United States from Ireland at an early age and made his way to Jackson County in the 1870s. The 1880 census lists him as a farm laborer living in the household of James Buckley. McDonough took a 160-acre homestead adjoining Buckley to the north. The Jacksonville-Crescent City road lay across the south end of the property. The house and outbuildings were on the hillside across Forest Creek. A long lane gave access to the homesite. The house and some of the buildings are still standing in 1989.

James McDonough married Lillie Smith on Dec. 7, 1886, at the home of her parents, Elijah and Margaret Smith, early settlers who lived west of Ruch. Four children were born to them: Ivan, Dec. 12, 1887; Bertha, 1891; Chester, August 5, 1893; and William Martin, 1899. All of them, except Bertha, lived out there lives on the home place.

About two and one half miles south of the McDonough homestead, on the road to Upper Applegate, was the settlement of Uniontown. The Cameron family had established a store and post office in the early 1860s. Uniontown flourished during the same years as Herling and Logtown.

By the time Casper Ruch came into the area, in the 1890s, Herling, Logtown, and Uniontown were declining. Uniontown post office closed in 1891, and the postmaster, Theodoric Cameron, moved to Jacksonville. Herling post office closed in 1895.

Casper (Cap) Ruch recognized the opportunities of a site at the intersection of Uniontown road and the Jacksonville-Crescent City Road as a location for his blacksmith shop. In 1895, he purchased from James and Lillie McDonough "a parcel of land, containing 10 acres, more or less, lying between Applegate and Uniontown roads." The deed was signed on May 18, 1895. (Vol. 40, p. 493, Deed Records).

In 1896, Cap Ruch paid $40.00 taxes on his land, and $150.00

Cap Ruch's store was constructed in 1898 and with the Post Office in it, became the community focal point. Undated early picture shows Cap Ruch at left on porch, hands on hips wearing vest and hat. Then, that's Ed Smith leaning on post with shoulder; Matt Ray, front row third from left with white shirt; Bob Ray, front row, 5th, arms folded wearing suspenders. Two children at right are Martin and Chester McDonough, brothers. Elijah Smith, bearded man leaning against 3rd post from left of picture, right side of the post; Dave Buckley, next to Elijah Smith, head tilted without hat. Dave Roten, to right of 2nd post, back row, black hat. Dog, "Tybo." (Photo courtesy of Don Wendt)

on his improvements. He built a blacksmith shop and a cabin below the road.

The story of Casper (Cap) Ruch goes back to the 1860s, when his parents, Fredolin (Fritz) Ruch and his wife, Anna, came to the United States from Switzerland. They made their way to Oregon and were in Jackson County by 1870. At that time, Fritz was 46 years of age. His occupation was miner. His wife, Anna, was 38. They had these children: Fritz Jr., age 10; Katherine, 9; Elizabeth, 6; Casper (Cap), 5; and Henry, age 1. By 1875 they had another child, William.

At this time they were living on a mining claim about four miles up Humbug Creek. The mining claim was owned by John Johnson, and it is believed that Ruch and Johnson were mining together.

In the spring of 1875, Fredolin Ruch purchased an undivided half interest in Johnson's claim:

> ...mining ground and claims on the left branch of Humbug Creek, Jackson County, from a point where the creek forks thence a distance of 800 yards...includes ditches, water rights, blacksmith shop and tools, sluices, picks, mining tools, house, stable and outhouses.

The price was $1,600.00 in gold coin. The deed was signed April 30, 1875, and was recorded in the court house in Jacksonville the next day, May 1, 1875. (Vol. 7, p. 70, Deeds Records). Spelling of name in Deed Records: Fredolin Ruhe.

On the following day, Sunday, May 2, in the morning, Fredolin Ruch committed suicide. In the coroner's inquest held at the Ruch residence, these people testified: Anna Ruch, wife; Fredolin Ruch, Jr., eldest son; Dr. J. A. Callender, a physician from Jacksonville; John Newcomb, John Bolt, Riley Hinkle, and Thomas Basye, neighbors. The coroner was H. T. Inlow and the jury was H. V. Helms, William Pernoll, John Pearson, Peter Burkhalter, John Christopher, and Orlando Rose.

After hearing the evidence and examining the body of the deceased, they announced that Fredolin Ruch had come to his death by committing suicide. He had taken strychnine.

Anna Ruch testified that her husband had been having some "spells." The neighbors said he had not been acting "right," lately. Fredolin Jr. told that when he came home about 3:00 o'clock on May 1, his father shook his hand and said he would not live much longer. The next morning they tried to restrain him, but he slipped from their grasp and went to where he had hidden a bottle of strychnine. He returned to the house and told them he had taken some of the strychnine and would die soon. Anna and Fredolin Jr. did what they could to save him. A messenger was sent to Kubli and Bolt store for help, but when Mr. Bolt and others arrived, Ruch was breathing his last. He was age 54 years, 5 months. He was buried in Jacksonville Cemetery.

The widow Anna Ruch was distraught with the loss of her husband and apparently could not contain her grief.

Administrator for the estate was John Bolt. But before he could really get started on his duties, further tragedy struck the Ruch family.

On the night of May 14, 1875, while her children were sleeping, Anna Ruch pinned a folded handkerchief over her eyes and drowned herself, and four-year-old William, in the mining reservoir. Again, a coroner's inquest was held. The jury was John O'Brien, John Christopher, Thomas Basye, William Basye, Henry York and William Pernoll.

Fredolin Ruch Jr. (Fritz) testified that in the morning when he could not find his Mother and William, he sent his brother Cap to get Mr. Johnson "quick." Then he went down to John Bolt's house to tell him that his Mother and William were gone. When he and Mr. Bolt returned, Johnson and Cap told him that Mother and William were in the reservoir. They were dead.

Mr. Johnson said he had walked by the reservoir on the way back to his house and saw the bodies in the water. Asked about the size of the reservoir, he stated it was 50 yards wide by 60 yards long and 5 to 6 feet deep.

Rial Benedict, John Stockberger and John Bolt removed the bodies to the house. Miss Sarah M. Gall and Mrs. M. J. Benedict dressed and prepared the bodies for burial. The jury rendered the verdict that Anna Ruch came to her death by voluntarily drowning and that William came to his death by his mother drowning him. She and William were buried beside her husband in Jacksonville Cemetery.

Guardianship papers were filed on May 25, 1875, with Kaspar Kubli as guardian for the girls. Katherine was age 13, and Elizabeth 11. Peter Britt was guardian for the boys, Casper age 10, and Henry 6. Fredolin Jr. (Fritz), age 15, found a home with Thomas Bayse, a farmer. Henry grew up in the home of Jacob Kubli. There is no record of where Casper lived during the 1880s. He received a grade school education and he learned blacksmithing.

Soon after he built his blacksmith shop at the busy intersection of Uniontown and Jacksonville-Crescent City Road, his business began to grow. He put up some shelves to sell tobacco, candy, a few nails and other supplies.

Since the community was without a post office, Cap Ruch applied for one. The applicant for a post office was usually given the privilege of naming it. Cap offered his own name and it was accepted. Ruch post office was open for business on May 4, 1897. Some time during the next year he constructed a store building, with a porch overlooking the intersection of Uniontown and

Cap Ruch remodeled his store which included all-new front porch, false front and siding. The building burned and was a total loss in the 1960s. Men in the photo left to right: Vance Bostwick, Aris Throlkmorton, Cap Ruch, _____ Johnson, Harve Cameron.

Jacksonville-Crescent City roads.

He put in supplies for the country trade. Across the road he built a smoke house where he smoked hams and bacon to sell in the store. Attending the store and post office kept him so busy that he gave up blacksmithing.

About 1912, Cap contracted with carpenters to build a modern frame bungalow on the hill behind his store. Many people wondered about a bachelor having such a fine house. They found out when Cap Ruch married Anna Boylan, who was teaching at the nearby school. They were married on June 11, 1913, by Father Joseph O'Neil.

Casper Ruch's house was behind his store. Although the house has seen considerable remodeling, it is still occupied in 1989. (Author photo)

Among other buildings Cap built was a large hall (1900), where dances, programs, elections and other meetings were held. Dances at Ruch hall were very popular in the early days.

Robert L. Hughes, a local bachelor, purchased the hall in the 1940s. According to a newspaper article dated Aug. 31, 1960, he had it taken down and used the lumber to build a cabin for himself on the site.

Some time before World War I, Cap Ruch remodeled the store building, making it larger. As times changed, Cap and Anna Ruch expanded their business by installing a gas pump and other facilities. In the 1920s they faced competition for the first time in their lives.

SUNNYSIDE SERVICE STATION

After World War I, Jackson County embarked on a widespread road improvement project. This was financed partly by the Federal Government, by the State of Oregon, and by the County. Certain rural roads were designated as "market roads." These were improved and paved to facilitate transporting farm products to market centers.

48

Some of the "good old boys" gather with Cap Ruch and "Tybo" at left. Others are (unidentified) Chinese, Glen Downing, Dick Lousigmont, Lester Throckmorton, Bob Ray, Vance Bostwick. Most men wore mid-calf, heavy leather boots due to the roughness of outdoor work. (Harry Bostwick collection)

In 1921, work was begun on the Jackson County section of the Jacksonville-Crescent City Road from Provolt to Jacksonville. Near the Ruch store, the road construction crews made a fill on the property of James McDonough. In exchange for this easement, the McDonough family received title to a strip of land along the north side. The road improvement project included plans for paving the highway from Ruch through Jacksonville to Medford.

When the paving was started at Ruch, people in the area objected to extending the paving over and down the Jacksonville Hill. The grade on the north side was a series of short steep curves, and paving this was considered foolhardy. They filed a petition to this effect. The protesters prevailed. The paved section ended just beyond the Bauten place and remained that way for over 10 years. Another sidelight about this stretch of pavement was that the county road officials prohibited solid tire logging trucks from using it. Loggers drove their trucks on a separate road along the paved section from Forest Creek road to the Bauten place.

Sunnyside Service Station. Most early service stations got their start with the coming of automobiles but in recent years and with change in owners many of the buildings now serve different purposes. With gas pumps removed, this is, in 1989, a restaurant and pizza parlor on the side of Highway 238. (Author photo)

Valley Country Store on Upper Applegate Road in 1989. (Author photo)

James McDonough died in 1923. Ivan and Bertha were both married and moved away. This left Chester and Martin to make a living on the farm and take care of their mother. As traffic increased on the highway, they saw an opportunity to start a business of their own. About 1928, they put up a small building on the edge of the highway fill and put in a service station. They installed two gas pumps, sold tires, tubes and other supplies. A lube and oil change pit was built over the edge of the bank. They put rest rooms on a lower level. They called their enterprise Sunnyside Service Station and soon had all the business they could handle.

Two years later they built an addition onto the service station room and put in a stock of groceries.

When the power line was built through the Applegate Valley in 1930, they wired for electricity and installed refrigeration. They were the first store in the area to sell ice cream cones and soda pop. This was a big treat for rural people, especially the children.

Cap Ruch was stricken with cancer and died on June 10, 1930. Anna continued to run the store, alone, for about fifteen years. The post office was discontinued on July 15, 1939, and after that business steadily declined. Anna closed the store and retired. She died on April 1, 1945. Her only survivor was her sister, Margaret Bigelow, wife of Frank Bigelow, of Medford. Anna did not have a will, so the court appointed Margaret Bigelow as administrator of the estate. Margaret died within the year, and her son, Earl Bigelow, was appointed administrator. The estate was appraised at $14,000, much of it was properties that Cap Ruch had purchased over the years. Before he died, he subdivided a few parcels. Earl Bigelow filed his final account on December 29, 1947 and inherited the entire estate.

The store building was leased for a grocery store and lunch counter for a few years. In the early 1960s the old building burned to the ground as a result of a flue fire.

The house Cap Ruch built for his bride is still standing and in fairly good condition. All that remains of the original Ruch store is a slab of concrete, where the gas pump stood.

In 1976 a permanent historical marker of anodized aluminum, mounted on a river rock pedestal, was installed by the Applegate Bi-Centennial Committee and the Southern Oregon Historical Society. The text of the marker is:

Casper Ruch started Ruch settlement at the crossroads site between Crescent City and Jacksonville in 1896. On ten acres purchased from J. M. McDonough, he built home, blacksmith shop, warehouse, dance hall, store and smoke house, curing meat he sold. A school district known as Logtown No. 3, organized in 1863, later became Drake School, then Ruch School in 1897. Land was donated by James B. Buckley from his 350 acre land grant. Ruch post office existed from 1897 to 1939 with "Cap" Ruch and his wife, Anna, as postmasters.

After Ruch store was closed for good, business at Sunnyside remained steady during the ensuing years. Chester McDonough married the former Valera Winningham Merritt, who had a daughter, Eugena. They built a modern house on the hill overlooking the store and highway.

Martin McDonough served as a Private in the U.S. Army during World War II. Chester and his wife, Valera, operated the store. After Martin returned, he married a woman with children by a former marriage, and they moved to Medford.

The store was offered for sale or lease, but this did not succeed.

Martin McDonough's home in Ruch as it appears in 1989. (Author photo)

Martin and his wife had a house built below the store and they moved back to Ruch. They continued to operate the store until 1972 when they found a buyer. Loren Hardy and Joel Brown of Jacksonville purchased it. Under the new management, the store was remodeled to include a coffee shop, a new line of meats and groceries, a new beverage case, and delicatessen items. They started a series of humorous advertisements featuring their location in "Downtown Ruch," which became a local joke.

Valera McDonough died in 1974, Martin died in 1975, and Chester died in 1976. They are all buried in Logtown Cemetery.

As the center of a large rural residential community in 1989 Ruch has a variety of businesses. There is a supermarket, beauty shop, cafe, public library, video shop and a real estate office. Mary Jacks, who built several of the buildings, operates a logging and construction business on the site of the former Hunter-Best sawmill. Sunnyside Service Station has become a tavern. A separate building has gas pumps and limited service.

Developments on Upper Applegate road, a few hundred yards from Highway 238 intersection, include another store, a church and a mobile home park. A subdivision called Sunshine Village, extends along the road and on the hillside to the east.

The store was established in 1958 by Robert L. and Alma Christean. They called it Christean's Service. The property included a laundromat, the mobile home park, a garage and shop building. The store carried basic groceries and had gas pumps. A lunch counter became very popular with loggers, hunters and local residents. Christean's sold the property to Anthony Ryan and family in August 1968. They named it Ryan's Outpost. The store has been leased to other operators twice. In 1989 it is the Valley Country Store.

RUCH COMMUNITY BIBLE CHURCH

Across the road from the store is the non-denominational Ruch Community Bible Church. This church was organized in 1956 by Reverend Earl Best and Reverend Lester Stevens. Others involved were Glen and Grace Hunter, Glen and Nellie Best and Rex Davis. They rented the Ruch store building for a few months, then purchased an adjoining acreage from the Buckley family and started construction of the church. The lumber came from the local Hunter-Best sawmill. Much of the work was done by volunteers. Rev. Earl Best served as minister until 1963. Reverend

The Upper Applegate area has a strong church-oriented population. The three major churches are Ruch Community Church (top), Applegate Community Church (lower) and Applegate Christian Fellowship (right). (Author photographs)

Earl Mortlock was there 10 months. Reverend Lester Stevens was pastor 17 years. In 1989 the pastor is Rev. Ron McKay. The church operates a kindergarten and child care center for the community.

APPLEGATE CHRISTIAN FELLOWSHIP

On the north side of Highway 238 at Ruch is another church, the Applegate Christian Fellowship. The main building, with two wings, is located in the center of a well-landscaped acreage which includes a parking lot for hundreds of cars.

In 1989 the pastor is Reverend Jon Courson. In 1976 he came from San Jose, California, and organized a small non-denominational congregation in his own home. As the membership grew they moved to Upper Applegate Grange hall until 1980. During the summer, services were held at Cantrall-Buckley Park. Meetings were also held at Ruch School gym and in a rented section of the Sunshine Plaza building for several years. As membership increased, the group outgrew all these facilities. About 1986, land was acquired adjoining McDonough's property and a building program was initiated. The church complex in 1989 accommodates a membership of over 2,000. Many of them come from Medford, Ashland, Central Point and other Rogue Valley areas. Others come from Josephine County. Plans for a kindergarten and a Christian elementary school are under consideration for the future, according to one of the church planners.

The two pioneer trails through Ruch are right where they always have been but they have become busy highways carrying unending traffic to all parts of the area and beyond. □

Chapter 4

UNIONTOWN

About two and one half miles south of Ruch on Upper Applegate Road was the settlement of Uniontown. Here was the home of the Cameron brothers: Theodoric (Tod), Zachary (Zack), Robert (Bob), and William (Billy). They were the children of James R. and Emeline (Kendall) Cameron. The family had lived on a farm in Van Buren County, Iowa. Theodoric and his brother Robert came across the plains in 1852 driving their own ox team and wagon. They arrived in southern Oregon August 1852 and joined the mining activity on Sterling Creek. During 1853, Tod took up several mining claims and had other folks help operate them. Next, he filed on a Donation Land Claim on Little Butte Creek, in the Rogue River Valley. He settled on this claim on May 10, 1854. It is part of the present city of Eagle Point. The land was cleared for farming and Tod Cameron leased it to Peter Simon. Simon raised truck garden produce to sell to the miners who had congregated at Jacksonville and to other early settlers. (Vol. 2, p. 182, Sept. 6, 1858, Deed Records). Eventually, he sold the claim and the patent was granted on June 26, 1895, to Elizabeth Simon.

Returning to the Sterling mining camp, Tod Cameron opened a bakery, which he operated successfully for several years. About 1860, he purchased 40 acres of land from the Government. It was located along the Big Applegate River one half mile downstream from the confluence with Little Applegate River. (Vol. 91, p. 115, Deed Records). Here he built a cabin and put in a stock of supplies to sell to miners and settlers. His brothers soon joined him. In 1858, Robert returned to Iowa, where he married Esther Le Fever. They made the journey across the plains in 1863. William also arrived in 1863. Soon after he arrived, William Cameron filed on a homestead adjoining Tod's acreage on the north. (Vol. 7, p. 287, Deed Records). Robert and Esther Cameron purchased the G. B. Davidson Donation Land Claim, which was located upstream on Little Applegate River about one fourth mile. (Vol. 6, p. 196, Deed Records).

They built their houses on a strip of land between the road and the river. Barns and corrals were on the hill across the road. By

1864 they were settled and in business. They called the settlement "Uniontown" because of strong sympathies for the northern government during the civil war.

In 1869 the parents, James and Emeline Cameron, with Zachary, arrived to join the family group. A house was built for the parents where they lived out their lives among their sons and families.

A saloon separate from the store was built, also a blacksmith shop and storage sheds. A negro blacksmith worked for them. He was called Nigger Ben. Ben was a skilled blacksmith and he had the respect of the community. A prominent 4,394-foot elevation peak in the Siskiyou Mountains, on the west side of the Applegate River, was named Nigger Ben Mountain. Ben's last name was apparently never used and has been lost. In 1964 when racial integration was being popularized, the United States Bureau of Geographic Names in *Decision List 6402*, changed the name to Negro Ben Mountain. As Lewis McArthur points out in *Oregon Geographic Names*, there has never been any evidence the original name was derogatory. McArthur declared, "If every name that might now or in the future offend some ethnic group must be altered to suit the changing times, the authorities might just as well resort to simple numerical designation."

In the saloon, Val Comstock was the keeper and helped in the store when he was needed. He was also a teamster and hauled freight from Crescent City for the store. Comstock owned and operated several mining claims.

As the eldest, Tod Cameron was the head of the clan. He was a shrewd businessman interested in politics and government. He enjoyed a busy social life attending dances and parties all over the area. He remained single until 1892. In addition to the store, he owned farm lands, mining claims, and a saw mill. He made the plans, his brothers did the work, and they all prospered. As soon as his mining claims failed to make a profit, he sold them. He purchased the saw mill with a partner, U. S. Hayden of Jacksonville, in 1866.

This water-powered saw mill had been established by Justus Wells, of Ashland, in the early 1850s. It was located about a mile upstream on Big Applegate River from the confluence of Little Applegate River. There was enough of a settlement around it that it was called Wellsville. During the Indian troubles of 1854-55, the settlement was attacked and burned. Several people were reported killed and they were buried on a bluff above the mill site. For many years there was a fence around these graves but today there is no sign of them. After the Indians were removed to the reservation, the mill was rebuilt and continued to operate. Tod Cameron paid $4,500.00 for it. The deal included "blacksmith tools, 4 yoke of cattle, yokes and chains belonging thereto; one logging wagon, together with all significant appurtenances thereto." (Vol. 4, p. 409, August 20, 1866). William and Robert operated the mill and sold lumber to miners and settlers for miles around. They drove team and wagon and delivered lumber to the mining camps when it was needed.

As the store prospered during the 1870s, Tod Cameron recognized the need for a post office. On April 21, 1879, Uniontown post office was established. Tod Cameron was postmaster.

William attended to the store and post office as Tod carried on other activities. In 1876, he became a member of Warren Lodge No. 10 A.F. & A.M. in Jacksonville, and served in various offices. When Adarel Chapter No. 3, Order of the Eastern Star was organized in 1880, he became a member, and took an active part in its affairs. In 1885, he was elected as a representative to the State Legislature, and served two terms. He was elected to the State Senate in 1890, and served two years.

Tod Cameron was 37 years of age when he married Mary (Mollie) Krause. She was the widow of Frank Krause, who had been editor of the *Oregon Sentinel*, a Jacksonville newspaper, in the 1870s and 1880s. They were married on March 3, 1892, by Justice of the Peace William Plymale. Mollie had three children: Lavilla (Ella), age 12; Otis, age 10; and Margarite (Maggie), age 8.

They purchased a family home on south Oregon Street in Jacksonville. A son, Charles Donald, was born to them on February 10, 1893. He was called Donald and was to live a long and interesting life. Tod Cameron was left to raise his son alone, when Mollie died unexpectedly on March 19, 1904. He never remarried. He took an active part in the management of Jacksonville municipal affairs and served on the city council several terms. As old age took its toll, he made property settlements to his brothers at Uniontown.

The post office was closed on September 14, 1891, and after that business declined rapidly. Soon the store closed, but the Cameron brothers continued farming and attending to their families.

Theodoric Cameron died on June 9, 1914, at the age of 85.

Officers and members of Warren Lodge No. 10, A.F.&A.M. conducted his funeral. He was buried in Jacksonville Cemetery beside his parents and other family members.

WILLIAM CAMERON

William Cameron worked more closely with his brother Tod than Zack or Robert. They centered their energies on farming and stock raising. At first William was involved in mining projects, but he soon gave this up to tend Tod's store. He built a frame house for himself. He started keeping a diary of each day's activities. This was kept in a small, commercially printed date book. The first entry began Jan. 1, 1864: "Spent the day shingling stable for Chappell...weather disagreeable...rained most all day...spent the evening reading, casting accounts...eating apples...."

He continued this practice until 1878. (1872-1873-1874 missing.) These simple entries give an authentic picture of a pioneer life as lived by these people.

He described his work in taking care of the store while Tod was away. He told of making frequent trips to Jacksonville for supplies, then hauling supplies to the various mining camps in the area. He went to Sterling, Buncom, Logtown and Jackass Creek, and made each round trip in one day. He had a fish trap in the river and peddled fresh salmon to the miners at 25 cents each.

The Camerons were friends of the Herling family, and frequently went there to dances and card parties. The womenfolk often visited each other, riding with someone, or driving their own horse and buggy. In his 1866 entries, William mentioned frequent visits to the home of Squire (Melvin D.) Sturgess, a neighbor adjoining his property to the north. Among Squire Sturgess' children was his teenage daughter, Emma. William worked steadily on his house during the fall and winter of 1866. The house was not quite ready when he and Emma Sturgess were married on February 1, 1867. In his diary he wrote:

Thursday, January 31, 1867: Went up Jackass [creek] before noon. Went to Jackson[ville] in the evening.
Friday, February 1, 1867: Got a team in town, went home, got Emma, went to Jackson[ville] and was married. Stayed overnight at Horn's.

The wedding was performed by U. S. Hayden, Justice of the Peace. It took place in the home of Louis and Mary E. Horne.

According to the diary, the next day they went up the Bear Creek Valley over bad roads in a steady rain, and spent the day at Dad Wells'. (The Wells family were relatives near Ashland.) Monday they drove home. Tod took the team to town. William slept in the store with James Fryer. Emma remained at the home of her parents because the house was not ready. They moved into the new house on February 8th. "Emma scrubbed," he wrote, and "Mrs. Chappell and Mrs. Eddy called to see us."

Their first child was born December 23, 1867. They named him Wilbur. Over the next thirteen years, six more children were born to William and Emma Cameron. Vernon was born April 8, 1869. He died five years later. The others were: Maude, 1871; Harvey, 1872; Ada, 1875; Carrie, 1878; and Russell, 1880.

Emma's health failed and she died on November 28, 1883, at the age of 33. She left six children. The youngest, Russell, age 3, died a week later, December 8. William was left with five children between the ages of five and sixteen years. The eldest daughter was Maude, 12. She took over as best she could and William hired some help. He never remarried. Wilbur, at sixteen, helped his father with the farm work.

In due time, the girls grew up, married and left home. Harvey did not marry, possibly because he was crippled. As a young man, he was seriously injured in a fall while carrying a deer. When the injury healed, his spine remained severely curved.

He lived with his father for many years, helping as best he could, and had a fairly useful life.

WILLIAM CAMERON'S CHILDREN

William Cameron's oldest son, Wilbur, married Dora Bostwick on Oct. 31, 1888, at the court house in Jacksonville. Witnesses were his sister Ada Cameron and Max Muller, a county official. Wilbur and Dora had no children. In time he took over William's farm and in later years rented it out. They lived in Jacksonville. He died in 1954, Dora died in 1955.

MAUDE CAMERON KUBLI

Maude Cameron married Henry D. Kubli on May 25, 1887, in the house of the groom's father, Kasper Kubli. They made their home on the pioneer Kubli ranch on the Crescent City-Jacksonville road about 2 miles east of the Applegate Crossing. They had three boys, Chester, Harold and Edward, and one daughter Edith.

ADA CAMERON

Ada Cameron married Benton Pool and they made their home on a farm on the east side of the river about two miles from the Cameron Bridge. The ranch was at one time part of William Cameron's property.

They had a daughter, Maude, called Maudie, born December 27, 1907. She grew up, went to Uniontown and Beaver Creek schools, then attended Jacksonville High School. She lived at home with her parents and wrote a rural news column for the Medford *Mail Tribune* for over 20 years. In the 1950s it was called "Rural Reflections." On March 23, 1944, she married William Ziegler, a forest worker. They had one son, Robert, born Jan. 6, 1945.

Benton Pool died March 26, 1946, and Ada Cameron Pool died Aug. 15, 1953. They were buried in the Jacksonville Cemetery.

Maude and William Ziegler inherited the ranch and continued to operate it until William's death in 1979. Robert Ziegler married Madge Barker and they have two sons, Sheldon and John.

CARRIE CAMERON

Carrie, the youngest of William Cameron's children, married Fred Offenbacher some time after the turn of the century. They had three children: Leon, Lance and Catherine. Carrie died on October 2, 1912, leaving Fred with the three small children.

Ma Wilcox became his housekeeper. The boys grew up, married and started homes and farms of their own nearby. Eventually Fred married Minnie Walter and they had one son, Fred Jr., called Fritz. He inherited his share of the estate and presently operates it with considerable success. He has road building equipment and does contract work in the area. Fred has been married twice and has an adopted son.

William, known in his declining years as "Uncle Billy," lived in his own home taking care of his handicapped son, Harvey, who died in 1923 at the age of 51. William sold the house and surrounding farm land to James T. Buckley in 1919 for $7,000.00 (Vol. 120 p. 620-21, Deed Records).

This news article from the Medford *Mail Tribune* was found in an old scrap book:

1926 Pioneer Home Lost in Fire is Replaced

APPLEGATE, July 1. The house on the James Buckley place,

which was destroyed by fire a short time ago, is to be replaced by a new construction, which will be erected under supervision of William Peckham. The building, which was swallowed up by the flames was about the last of the original houses of old time Uniontown, which has withstood the test of time to the present day. It was built by a well-known pioneer of this section, Uncle Billy Cameron, after his arrival in this state from Iowa in the early 60s [1864]. In spite of many long years, it was practically as substantial when overtaken by the ravages of fire, as when first built.

A few months later another article appeared in the same newspaper, the headline had been removed and was not in the scrap book:

APPLEGATE, Nov. 6. Those who have a feeling of concern for the passing of landmarks will be interested in knowing that the familiar shop at old-time Uniontown, at which place James Buckley and family now reside, is being torn down and lumber being used for other purposes. The old building, which was about the last landmark to stand at the pioneer settlement since the Buckley house burned last spring [*sic*.]. It was in existence 60 years ago as a saloon when Wm. Cameron, well-known pioneer of the valley, purchased it after his arrival from Iowa.

After he sold his home and ranch, William made his home with daughter Ada, her husband, Benton Pool, and daughter Maudie. He lived with them about 12 years. About 1932 he sustained a broken hip in a fall. He stayed a few days at the home of his other daughter, Maud Kubli. He died on June 23, 1932, at the age of 90 and was buried in Jacksonville Cemetery.

ZACK CAMERON

Some historians and a few of the records have his name as Zachariah, or Zachery. He was known to family and friends just as "Zack." He was married to Rena (Verena) Kubli of Missouri Flat on October 18, 1882, at the home of her father, Jacob Kubli. The ceremony was by J. H. Huffer, Justice of the Peace. Witnesses were Ellen and Kaspar Kubli.

They had one daughter, Corrine, called "Cora," born in 1883. Corrine was married twice, first to Guy Lawton and then to Oren Murphy. She had no children. She worked all her adult life as a bookkeeper for Nichols and Ashpole who operated a butcher shop and a mercantile business in Medford.

Zack Cameron built this house in the 1870s at Uniontown. The house has been remodeled frequently and is still occupied in 1989. (Author photo)

Zack Cameron and his wife lived out their lives at Uniontown. Their frame house is the only original Uniontown structure standing in 1989, on the Upper Applegate Road.

Zack did some farming and helped in the store when needed. He seemed to have been the quiet one. Not much is known about him or his last years.

ROBERT CAMERON

His full name was Robert James and he was the second son of Robert James and Emeline Cameron. He was called Bob.

He came with his brother Tod to Jackson County by wagon train in 1852 (Walling, p. 502).

He made two round trips back home by sailing vessel, between 1856 and 1858. When he returned to Oregon by wagon train in 1863, he brought with him his 16-year-old bride. Her legal maiden name was Hester Le Fevre. The family called her "Het." Many records have her name as Esther. (This writer will use Esther.)

The Gideon B. Davidson Donation Land Claim joined Cameron's land to the southeast and was located along Little Applegate
River. It had already changed hands twice when Robert Cameron
purchased it in 1865. He acquired other lands adjoining, upstream
on Little Applegate River, giving him control of about one and
one half miles of land for farming and the creek for mining.
The D.L.C. claim was 320 acres. He paid $2,400.00 for it to U.
S. Hayden on Nov. 4, 1865. (Vol. 4, p. 207, Deed Records.)

Since he was more of a farmer than a miner, he leased the
mining ground to a Chinese mining boss, Gin Lin. On June 6,
1887, a lease was signed for mining rights for 6.67 acres on the
south of Little Applegate Creek [*sic.*] (River) for the sum of
$500.00. Rules were listed as to the size of the ditches, etc. The
contract stipulated that Gin Lin's miners pipe the tailings into a
long continuous bank on the north side of the creek to protect the
farm lands from possible flooding. These banks, overgrown with
trees and brush, remain today. Contract release was granted on
Sept. 12, 1894. (Vol. 13, p. 654, Deed Records.)

Robert built his home on the west side of the road, a few yards
from the intersection of Little Applegate and Upper Applegate
roads. It was a large two-story house, with landscaped yard and
big trees. It was eventually destroyed by fire. Not even one of the
trees remain. A modern ranch-style house now occupies the site.
Across the highway from this house are two large hay barns,
which were part of Robert Cameron's farm buildings. In 1989 the
barns are in use, and in fairly good condition.

Robert and Esther Cameron had six children, two boys and four
girls. They all lived to adulthood. They were: Frank, 1864; Helena
(Lena), 1866; Clara, 1868; Anna, 1871; Bernice, 1875; and
Warren, 1879. Frank worked with his father on the ranch, raising
cattle, which were pastured with other ranchers' cattle on the high
ranges of the Siskiyou Mountains. They raised hay and grain and
carried on general farming.

Frank married Melissa Combest. They had one daughter,
Virginia, born in 1910. She grew up on the ranch, attended
Uniontown School, then graduated from Medford High School in
1930. She married Ernie Holbrook, a mechanic. They made their
home in Medford. The couple had no children. Ernie died in 1959,
followed by Virginia in 1960.

Robert Cameron died on May 6, 1910. Esther spent her last
years in Medford. She lived until January 17, 1937.

Lena Cameron married Lee Jacobs, a Medford businessman.

Robert Cameron property near Uniontown. The house and outbuildings are gone but the barns remain as of 1987. (Author photo)

They had a son, born January 18, 1894, who died in infancy. Their daughter, Eula, never married. She worked at Mann's Department Store in Medford most of her adult life. All three of the Jacobs family were buried in the I.O.O.F. Cemetery in Medford.

ANNA CAMERON

Anna Cameron grew up on her father's ranch, and after finishing high school she went to college in Omaha, Nebraska. She married George Cater, a widower, who had a daughter, Gladys. Mr. Cater was a businessman. They lived in Houston, Texas, and Los Angeles for many years. In the 1940s, George Cater died and Anna moved back to the Rogue Valley. She bought a house on Hillcrest Street in Medford and lived there until her death on April 15, 1963. She was 91.

Anna was a devoted member of Adarel Chapter No. 3, Order of the Eastern Star, in Jacksonville. She was Worthy Matron in 1934 and kept her membership during the years when she lived elsewhere. She became active again when she returned to southern Oregon to live. In 1964, Warren Lodge No. 10, A.F.&A.M. was planning a major remodeling of the Masonic Temple. The downstairs hall was to be redesigned into a kitchen and dining room. Also, an addition was built on the rear to house a storage vault, a ladies' dressing room, and rest rooms. Anna was very much aware of the need for these downstairs facilities. Before she died, she arranged a bequest of $5,000.00 to Warren Lodge with the stipulation that it be used for construction of a ladies' dressing room and a downstairs rest room. The Lodge accepted her gift as specified. This project was completed in 1964. A plaque has been mounted above the entrance to the facilities: "This addition made possible through the generosity of Anna Cameron Cater, 1964."

CLARA CAMERON HANLEY

Clara Cameron was always an outdoor girl. She rode with her father and brothers gathering cattle from the ranges every fall. She could handle a horse as well as any man. All activities on the ranch were familiar to her. Her education was the same as her brothers and sisters: high school and a year or two of college. On July 6, 1892, she married William "Bill" Danforth Hanley, son of Michael and Martha Hanley, who lived on a fine ranch near Jacksonville. Bill Hanley had been trained in the ranching and livestock business by his father while still in his teens. At age 17, his father sent him to Harney County with large herds of cattle to manage. Bill did so well he was able to buy his first ranch there. By the time he married Clara, he owned two ranches and he was one of the most successful cattlemen in Harney County. Right from the start Clara was an ideal wife. Always at home out-of-doors, their honeymoon journey was by buggy from the Rogue Valley all the way to Harney County, where they would make their home on the high desert. The two became great cattle barons, during which time they rubbed noses with cattle king Peter French. Although they had no children, their home was always open to visitors, oftentimes young fellows from Portland who worked summers on their ranch. The ranch, by 1912, was at its largest, 20,000 acres. Many details of their cattle ranching affairs, and Bill's entry into politics, are in George Brimlow's *Harney County, Oregon and its Range Land*.

Bill's health failed in the early 1930s and he died on September 17, 1933, while in town for the Pendleton Roundup. His wife, Clara, continued to manage the ranches and their business interests for another fifteen years. She died in March 1954 at age 85. Clara left a houseful of antique furniture to her sister, Anna.

Among other bequests were several lots at the edge of the City of Burns that she gave to the Harney County Historical Society for the purpose of establishing a museum. There were also funds to help build it. The new Harney County Museum and Pioneer Club buildings were dedicated on August 2, 1960, and Clara Hanley's sister, Anna Cater, was an honored guest. Later, Anna donated Clara's antique furniture to the Harney County Museum. (This was noted in Anna's will.)

Robert and Esther Cameron's fourth daughter was Laura Bernice, called Bernice. There is no record of her education beyond high school, but she was a career woman ahead of her time. She served overseas in World War I. When she returned, she took a position with the Postal Telegraph Company in Medford and remained with that firm for over thirty years. She never married. The inscription on her marker in Jacksonville Cemetery is:

L. Bernice Cameron
July 30, 1875—January 19, 1959
Oregon
C E, USNRF, WWI

WARREN CAMERON

Warren Cameron, the youngest of the family, graduated from Medford High School and enrolled in the College of Physicians and Surgeons in Chicago to become a doctor. After graduation, he practiced in North Dakota a year or two before returning to Grants pass and Medford. He married Catherine Vail and they had one son, Lloyd. Their son died while serving as an apprentice seaman on June 20, 1917. Dr. Cameron eventually gave up his medical practice. His wife, Catherine, died on November 15, 1917, just six months after losing their son. Warren was affectionately known as "Doc." He was regarded by the people of the community as a good man struck down by misfortune. He lived at Uniontown until his death on October 20, 1936.

Robert Cameron's ranch was inherited by his three daughters, Anna Cater, Clara Hanley and Bernice Cameron, and granddaughter Eula Jacobs. In June 1944, they sold the entire property to Ben C. Gerwick, a professional engineer from San Francisco. Gerwick made some changes, and one of his daughters made her home on the ranch for a few years. As of 1989 the farm lands are leased for pasturing cattle.

The 1959 Oregon Centennial historical marker for Uniontown

is, in 1989, still in the front yard of the present owners of Zack Cameron's house. It is weather-worn and reads:

Uniontown, once a bustling mining camp
Middle of the 1850s

Regrettably, the author of that inscription errs. Uniontown was not established until 1862. It was a trading center for the nearby mining camps.

The Camerons were an important part of the community for over 50 years. □

Chapter 5

SETTLERS, RUCH TO UNIONTOWN

Among the early settlers who were neighbors of the Camerons between Ruch and Uniontown, was Melvin DeWitt Sturgess and his family. He was born on a farm in Allegheny County, New York, on Dec. 15, 1825. His parents moved to Illinois in 1837 where he grew up. He crossed the plains to Oregon in 1847. Arriving in Polk County near Dallas, he took up a 320-acre land claim and built a one-room cabin on it. He joined the gold seekers to California in 1849, where he mined on the Feather River for about a year.

He married Eliza Burbank in March 1849. In the spring of 1850, they returned to the land claim in Polk County where they lived until 1857. Three children were born to them during these years: Emma, February 4, 1850; Alonzo L., 1855; Wallace, 1857.

Sturgess moved his family to Wilbur in Douglas County in 1857, where he operated a general store and hotel until 1859.

He was attracted to Jackson County and settled on a 105-acre land claim along the Applegate River in 1859. He received the patent to it in 1880. Eliza Sturgess died in January 1861. Five years later, Melvin married Almira McKee, daughter of Joseph and Almira (Hutchinson) McKee, who lived in the area. Three children were born to this second marriage: Orville, 1868; DeWitt, 1869; and Oscar, 1875.

In addition to general farming, Sturgess raised sheep and goats. His son DeWitt,, at age 11, was an experienced sheep herder. Oscar, by age 5, was a goat tender. Oscar died when he was 16 from an accidental gunshot. He was buried in Logtown Cemetery. Melvin Sturgess was appointed Justice of the Peace, and performed many weddings in the area. He came to be called Squire Sturgess. A mountain to the east of his property was named Squires Peak in his honor. He and his wife lived out their lives on the ranch and are buried in Jacksonville Cemetery.

In 1910, the M. D. Sturgess's 105-acre ranch was owned by a Charles Schafer, and he had it for sale.

Charles A. Smith, his wife and family, who had been looking for property, bought it for $6,500.00. With it were water rights and irrigation ditches.

The Smiths came to Jackson County by train from Kansas in 1908. They had three sons, Rolland, Harold and Clayton. Smith gave up trying to farm in Kansas on account of the drought conditions so he sold out and moved to Oregon. They lived in Ashland two years, where Mr. Smith worked for wages, while looking for a farm to buy. Charley Smith, as he was called, and his sons farmed the ranch for many years. They raised white navy beans for a cash crop. The story goes that every fall he would set out with horse and buggy, peddling his beans to housewives all around the valley. Rolland Smith took over the ranch, and operated it, with his wife Clara until 1945. They sold out and moved to another ranch up the Little Applegate River. In 1989 the property is subdivided and has several rural residences across the old farm fields.

LYMAN CHAPPELL

Another neighbor in this area was Lyman Chappell. He came to the state in 1854 and to Jackson County in 1858. He had a wife, Sarah, but no children. He took a homestead of 167 acres near Melvin Sturgess and engaged in general farming. William Cameron mentioned the Chappell family frequently in his diaries. He worked for them and they often exchanged visits. Lyman Chappell sold out sometime in the 1880s and moved down the Applegate River in Josephine County, where he operated a hotel and stopping place along the Jacksonville-Crescent City Road. (Walling, p. 508).

JOHN CANTRALL

Among the miners who came to the Jacksonville area in the late 1850s was John Cantrall. He worked with his brother, Andrew, and others on Sterling Creek during the boom years. He married Sarah A. Newlin on June 15, 1862. She was from a pioneer family who settled near Eagle Point in 1857. John and Sarah were to be the parents of twelve children, but unfortunately not all of them lived to adulthood. During the three years they lived on Sterling Creek, babies born were Adaline, 1863, and Malinda, 1864. Both died in infancy. Omar was born in 1865 and he lived to be 80.

John Cantrall left Sterling Creek in 1865 and took up an 80-acre land claim across the river from Uniontown. He moved there with his wife and family. He owned mining claims and continued mining as well as farming for the next twenty-five years. The patent to the land claim was granted in 1887. (Vol. 7, p. 546, Deed Records). He also purchased land adjoining. Children born here were James, 1867; Miles, 1869; Ida, 1870; Roscoe, 1873; Amy, 1875; Andrew, 1878; Jessie, 1883; and John Jr. 1888. Six children grew to adulthood on this place: Omar, James, Miles, Roscoe, Amy and John Jr.

John Cantrall died in 1890 at the age of 54. Sarah is said to have managed the ranch for a few years with the help of her sons. Eventually she moved to Jacksonville. The property was later owned by Frank Preston in the 1930s, and Martin Grier in the 1970s.

Widely known as Grandma Cantrall, she lived out her life as an honored member of the Southern Oregon Pioneer Society. She took a special interest in its meetings and the association with other pioneers. She died in 1935 at the age of 91.

One by one, the Cantrall children married and had families of their own. James (Jim) married Verlinda Buck, Dec. 3, 1890. Their children were: Evert, Vernie, Leonie, and Maude.

Amy Cantrall was trained as a teacher and taught school at Sterling and Uniontown several terms. She married Robert Dow on Sept. 30, 1903. They had no children. She owned and operated a grocery store and lunch counter in Jacksonville during the 1920s and 1930s. Her establishment was called Amy's Place.

John Jr. married Ossie Saltmarsh on December 31, 1907. They had two boys, Emmett and Truitt, and a daughter, Norma. John Jr. was drowned in Squaw Lake with a companion, Frank Howard, of Medford, while fishing from a small row boat. It sank unexpectedly and the two men, in their heavy clothing, went under and were lost. Another man with them, Gilbert Robertson, made it to shore and summoned help from a farmer at the end of the lake. It was the next day before the bodies were recovered. The accident was reported in the Medford *Mail Tribune* on November 1, 1936.

Roscoe and his wife Nana (Ankeny) had one son, Edward. Not much is known about Omar Cantrall. He had a son named Gene, who was married to Isabell Dorris of Alturas, California, in 1927. Omar died in 1945 and is buried in Sterling Cemetery.

Miles graduated from Jacksonville High School in 1887, when it was only a two-year course. After graduation, he applied for, and was granted, a Jackson County scholarship to attend University of Oregon. He enrolled there in the School of Education to become a teacher. His first position was principal of

North High School in Ashland. He left there to become vice principal of Jacksonville High school. He also attended the College of San Francisco, where he took a business course.

JOHN DEVLIN

This Irish emigrant, John Devlin, came to Jackson County in the 1860s, and took up land near Ashland, where he engaged in farming and stock raising. He was married to Anna Murphy on June 14, 1868, in the Catholic Church in Ashland. He was age 32, and she was 29. They were the parents of these children: Mary, born 1869; John Jr., 1871; Agnes, 1873; and Peter, born 1874.

The eldest daughter, Mary, was educated in the public schools of Ashland, and attended St. Mary's Academy in Jacksonville.

In 1888, John Devlin sold his Ashland property, and purchased a 375-acre ranch located between Ruch and Uniontown on the Applegate River. It was some of the best river bottom land in the area, and most of it was cleared and under cultivation. The land extended from the river to the hillsides above the Uniontown road. The owner was William H. Bostwick, who had farmed it for several years. The price was $5,000.00. The deed was signed on October 20, 1888, and the Devlin family moved to their new home the next spring. (Vol. 16, p. 549, Deed Records).

According to information from grandson Harlan Cantrall, they lived in a small log cabin near the river the first year. In the winter of 1890 the rivers of Southern Oregon staged a tremendous flood and waters of the Applegate forced the family out of their home where they fled to the barns on higher ground. After the flood, John Devlin had a large two-story house built further away from the river.

MILES CANTRALL

The Devlin and Cantrall families had known each other about eight years when Miles Cantrall and Mary Devlin were married on October 28, 1896. Three children were born to them: Otto L., Jan. 1898; John Leland, Sept. 1899; and Miles Harlan, June 1908.

John and Anna Devlin lived out their lives on the ranch, cared for in their last years by Miles and Mary Cantrall. Miles raised hay and grain on the ranch. He also had beef cattle, horses, hogs, and dairy cows. He was interested in politics and served as a State Representative in 1902. Later he was a member of the Ruch school board and helped plan the new school building constructed in 1914.

Otto Cantrall, the eldest son, graduated from Oregon State College as an electrical engineer and made his home in Atlanta, Georgia. He had one son, Otto Jr., born in 1929. Leland was a mechanic. He died in 1931 of pneumonia in Klamath Falls. His wife, Aletha, was a telephone operator. She operated the Jacksonville exchange until dial phones were installed in 1939, then she continued to work for the telephone company until her retirement.

HARLAN CANTRALL

Harlan was nine years younger than his next oldest brother, so he grew up more or less as an only child. He attended Ruch School and graduated from Jacksonville High School in 1926. The next year he was a student at Southern Oregon Normal School in Ashland, where he received a teaching certificate. He taught school at Ruch—all 8 grades in one room—during the 1928-29 school years and again the following school year. His salary was $100 per month.

To enhance his earnings, he joined with his father in farming. Soon, he married a former high school classmate, Cheryle Smith, of Jacksonville. They had no children and the marriage eventually ended. Harlan's mother, Mary, died in 1939. His father, Miles, lived until 1946. They were both buried in Jacksonville cemetery.

Harlan was a progressive farmer. He participated in programs sponsored by the Jackson County Extension Service to help farmers during the Depression. One of these programs was an experiment in raising sugar beets for seed. Under a government contract, Harlan raised beets for several years with considerable success. When the contracts were discontinued, he raised grain and hay for his herd of beef cattle. He was a member of the Applegate Stockmen's Association. He ranged his cattle with other stockmen of the valley on the low ranges in the spring and the high ranges in the summer and fall. Cattle raising was fairly profitable because of the expanse of open range, which cost little or nothing in the early days. Even after the Forest Service started issuing permits and charging fees, it was still possible to make a little money on cattle, most years.

In 1942, Harlan married Margaret Thomas, a registered nurse from California. She had a pre-teen-age son, Robert, from a former marriage. Together they had three daughters: Suzanne, Mary Ann and Joanne. Tragically, they lost Suzanne at age three in 1952. Mary Anne, Joanne and Robert attended Ruch School and Medford High School. They were active in 4-H projects, raising fine registered sheep, and dogs for the Seeing Eye program.

In 1949, Harlan sold 76 acres fronting on Upper Applegate Road to Lance and Stella Offenbacher. They built a house on a knoll facing the road, under some existing trees. Lance farmed this place for several years until they sold out and moved. In 1989, this acreage is the Valley View Vineyard, with a winery operated by Ann Wisnovsky and her sons.

Tragedy again struck Harlan and Margaret on the night of June 10, 1961, when the historic house, built by Grandfather Devlin, caught fire and burned to the ground. At 5:00 a.m. a State Forestry fire warden, with a marine pumper, arrived to put out the smoldering remains. It was later determined the fire had started in the attic from overloaded electric wiring. It burned so fast the family did not have time to save very much. A new house was built on the site, shaded by the big trees, which survived the fire.

Harlan was a member of the Oregon Farm Bureau. He served on the board of directors of the Jackson Soil and Water Conservation District for many years. He was on the Ruch School board several terms and was a member of the Upper Applegate Grange. His daughter, Mary Anne, was honored as Farm Bureau Sweetheart in 1968 when she was a senior in college. Her work in the farm youth programs was outstanding. After college she made a career of raising and training prize-winning sheep for a commercial grower in the Willamette Valley. Unfortunately, Margaret's health began to fail and she died on July 1, 1970. Harlan continued to farm the ranch for several years. Eventually he married Pearl Jordan. They sold the ranch and retired to a quiet home in Jacksonville.

In 1989, there is a large new log home on the ranch, adjoining the older house. There are stables and corrals for raising horses. A sign at the gate reads "Crane's Arabians." The historic Devlin-Cantrall ranch is still being farmed and is as beautiful as ever.

THE OLD SWIMMING HOLE
CANTRALL-BUCKLEY PARK

In the river on the Cantrall property is a natural rock-rimmed swimming hole. This pool has been popular with local residents since pioneer days. The riverbank was not very wide, and there was no beach, but there was room for several picnic and swimming parties at a time. Cars parked on the shoulder of the road. Popularity of the Cantrall's swimming hole grew steadily during the 1940s and 1950s, but at times there were troubles which were disturbing to the family. A solution came in 1960, when the Bureau of Land Management proposed to build a bridge across the river, just above the swimming hole, to gain access to their tracts of forest land on the slopes of Nigger Ben Mountain and Offenbacher Point. Harlan cooperated by donating the right of way and the bridge was built as planned. A plaque on it reads:

Cantrall Bridge, 1960
U.S. Department of the Interior
Bureau of Land Management
This bridge is named in honor of the pioneer
Cantrall family and is dedicated to the
coordinated management of all resources of
farm and forest.

The bridge made it possible to develop a large park on the west side of the river. In 1962, the Jackson County Parks Department purchased 45 acres, and over the next few years built a park and picnic facility to accommodate large crowds. In honor of the neighboring Buckley family, the park was named Cantrall-Buckley. It continues to be enormously popular every summer.

HENRY H. BROWN DONATION LAND CLAIM

Located between John Cantrall's homestead and John Devlin's ranch on the Applegate River was a 160-acre Donation Land Claim, which lay in two townships and on both sides of the river. The best river bottom land was on the west side of the river, and there were three river lots totaling 70 acres that went with it. This claim was settled by Henry H. Brown in July, 1854. He was on the land less than five years and had some improvements on it, when he sold it to P. J. Ryan, a Jacksonville merchant, for $500.00. (January 25, 1859, Vol. 2, p. 256, Deed Records).

The property changed hands four times in the next four years. Finally, it was sold at sheriff's sale on April 6, 1864, for $200.00. A man named Reuben Armstrong purchased it. (Vol. 3, p. 738, Deed Records). One month later, May 6, 1864, Reuben Armstrong sold it to Albert W. Sturgis for $1,000.00. (Vol. 3, p. 767, Deed Records). As described in Chapter 3, Albert W. Sturgis, with his wife and family, lived on the ranch about 14 years. He built an irrigation ditch which was fed out of the Applegate River to provide water for the west side fields. The house and farm buildings were on the east side of the river, reached by a long lane from Uniontown road. The Albert Sturgis family were good friends of the neighboring Melvin Sturgess family, Lyman Chappell and the Camerons at Uniontown during those years. William Cameron's diaries mention frequent visits and exchanges of work.

All this came to and end in 1878, when Albert Sturgis and his wife, Mary E., were divorced. She was awarded the ranch in the divorce settlement. She continued to live there and farm it for almost ten years, with her sons, Winter and Fred. She was well known enough to be listed in Walling in 1884: (p. 507)

> Mrs. M. E. Sturgis; lives near Uniontown on Applegate [River]; is a farmer; was born in Quincy, Ill.; came to state in 1860; was married in 1861. Maiden name, M. E. Talley. Children: Winter, Albert (deceased), Fred T.

She was married to George Reaves (Reive) on July 10, 1887. Four months later, M. E. Reaves and her husband, George Reaves, sold the entire 160-acre ranch, with the river lots and the irrigation ditch rights, to Samuel B. Hamilton. The price was $4,750.00. (November 2, 1887, Vol. 14, p. 557, Deed Records).

THE HAMILTON FAMILY

Samuel B. Hamilton was born in Tennessee in 1833. His family moved to Iowa and Missouri, where he grew up. He made his first trip across the plains in 1853, arriving in Jacksonville, where he mined for three years. He spent the year of 1857 in the Yreka mines, and then returned home by way of Panama. He was married to Mary Catherine (Katherine) Martin in Missouri in 1858, and brought her by wagon train to Watsonville, California. They lived there until 1864, when they moved to Ashland. He took up a homestead. Five children were born to them: William, 1862; Enoch, 1863; Charles, 1865; Jesse, 1878; and Elsie, 1883. Sam Hamilton sold his Ashland farm in 1887. He was attracted to the Applegate Valley, where he purchased the Henry H. Brown Donation Land Claim, and moved his family there to farm it. His son Charley was 22 years old, and younger brother Jesse was nine. Nothing is known of the two older boys. They all had a common school education. Charley had been apprenticed to a carpenter when he was a very young man. He became skilled in the use of poles to frame big hay barns and other outbuildings. He rebuilt and repaired the house and barns on the ranch, and worked at the farm with his father. On March 17, 1895, Charley married Mary S. Matney at the home of her father, Carroll Matney, about two miles west of Ruch. He brought her home to live with his parents, Sam and Mary Hamilton. This was a unique situation as there were now two Mary Hamiltons in the same house! Exactly what the feelings were about this does not seem to be recorded; nevertheless, this arrangement was not to last very long. Six months later, his dad gave Charley a 99-year lease on ten acres "more or less" of the Henry H. Brown D.L.C., all unimproved, so Charley and Mary could set up their own place.

This was located on the east side of the road. The lease was dated September 10, 1895, and was to run until September 9, 1994. The terms:

> Said Charles Hamilton is to improve the same by building a house, barn and other outbuildings, fencing, etc.... He is to have enough water to water a garden from my interest in the Farmer's Ditch. In consideration of $5.00, I, Samuel Hamilton, place said Charles Hamilton in possession of the above-described land. The object of this lease is to give Charles Hamilton a home.

This document was signed by Sam B. Hamilton with his mark and witnessed by his wife, Mary and son Charley. A third signature was R. W. Kennedy. (Vol. 77, p. 607, Deed Records).

Charley accepted the lease and complied with its terms. He built a comfortable board and batten house, a woodshed and a barn. The house lasted until the late 1970s and the barn is still standing. Six children were born and grew up in that house. They were: Bryant, December 1895; Hazel, 1897; Ruth, 1899; Boyd, 1901; Mary and Margaret (no dates available). Charley earned his living by working as a barn builder and carpenter around the community. Several of his barns are still standing in 1989. He was a member of the Ruch School board, with Miles Cantrall and Horace Venable, when the new concrete block school hose was built in 1913-1914. With the help of his family, he cultivated his small tract of land intensively, raising fruit trees, garden produce and some high quality alfalfa hay.

As Sam Hamilton was approaching old age, he turned the ranch over to his wife, Mary Catherine. He made out a deed to her on June 5, 1901. (Vol. 42, p. 247 Deed Records). The legal description gave the full 160 acres and the three river lots, and included the water rights in the Farmer's Ditch. He died in 1904, and was buried in Logtown Cemetery.

A little over a year later, Mary Hamilton deeded the ranch to her son Jesse, with certain stipulations:

> Jesse Hamilton is to come into possession of said lands and premises, so long as he complies with the following agreement: To furnish his mother, during her natural life, a comfortable room in which to live, plenty of good wholesome food to eat, a good bed and bedding, sufficient wearing apparel to render her comfortable, to provide medical care and nursing care in case of sickness or physical disability; a Christian burial at the time of her death; and in default of Jesse Hamilton complying with any of these requirements, the agreement shall terminate and become void, and the property shall revert to Mary Catherine Hamilton without intervention of law.

The document was dated November 21, 1905. It was signed with her mark and witnessed by T. W. Miles and Silas J. Day. (Vol. 61, p. 125, Deed Records.) She lived two more years. She died on September 4, 1907, and was buried in Logtown Cemetery beside her husband.

Jesse Hamilton was married to Goldena J. Sears, eldest daughter of William and Mary Sears, on February 3, 1909. The Sears family lived on a farm near Jacksonville. She was 17 years old and he was 31. Less than a year later, Jesse and Goldie Hamilton sold the Henry H. Brown Donation Land Claim to Henry H. and Florence Taylor, whose family were to own it and farm it for over 30 years. (December 22, 1909, Vol. 76, p. 112, Deed Records). Nothing more has been found about Jesse Hamilton and his family.

THE TAYLOR FAMILY

In 1900, Henry H. and Florence Taylor had six children ranging in age from 10 months to 16 years of age. They were: Jesse, Leon, Stella, Edwin H., Florence and Johnnie. When they moved to the Brown D.L.C., Edwin was 19 years old, and his brother, Jesse was 25. They farmed the place with their father as long as he lived. Eventually, they took over the ranch. Jesse established a home on the south half, and Edwin had the half with the original house and barns, and the best cultivated fields across the river.

One of the most common sources of a small but steady income

for farmers in the 1920s and 1930s was dairying. Every family had a milk cow or two for their own use. Some people had several cows, separated the milk, and sold the cream to the creameries for butter making. The skimmed milk was fed to calves and pigs.

In the fall of 1931, Edwin Taylor and his wife, Mildred, went into the dairy business in a big way. He had built a modern dairy barn and milk house with concrete floors, along with complete equipment for producing Grade A milk. Included was running water and a cooling vat. They were milking between 16 and 20 cows, which produced about 45 gallons of milk each day. The milk was delivered daily to the Gold Seal Creamery in Medford where it was bottled for the retail trade. Milking machines were to be added later. (See article in the Medford *Daily News*, November 3, 1931.)

Edwin Taylor was a man who knew an opportunity when he saw one. In 1935, the County was rebuilding the Cameron Bridge across Big Applegate River, on Upper Applegate Road. Edwin made a deal with the County officials to donate his labor on this

House on Taylor property and remains of dairy barn. (Author photos)

project in exchange for the old bridge timbers and planking. He moved this material to his ranch and built a sturdy bridge across the river to his farm fields. Ever since this property was settled, access to the fields across the river had been troublesome. Every bridge built was lost in a flood. This one lasted until the big flood of 1955, but this was after the Taylors had moved away. By this time, there were several families who had homes across the river thus the bridge was quickly replaced.

Another opportunity attracted Edwin Taylor in 1936, when he began raising onions for the food services in the Civilian Conservation Corps camps in Jackson and Klamath counties. He raised 35 tons of onions that year. He became involved with a businessman named Carold J. Parker, who had a potato chip factory in Medford. Parker was also a distributor for snack type foods, including pickles and relish. Somehow they came up with the idea of establishing a pickle factory on Edwin Taylor's ranch. In 1937, he planted 20 acres of cucumbers, 5 acres of onions, 7 acres of potatoes, and 8,000 cabbage plants. The dairy buildings were remodeled, and equipment for making pickles was installed. It was ready by the time the cucumbers were harvested in 1937. Recipes for dill pickles, sweet pickles, and relish were developed. The brand name chosen was "Taylor Maid." The product was a success. By 1940, "Taylor Maid" products were being distributed in seven counties in southern Oregon and northern California. The Taylors were planning to expand the plant and add new equipment. (Medford *Mail Tribune*, September 25, 1940).

During World War II, when Camp White, north of Medford, was in full operation, the Taylors had a contract to supply the Army Food Services with huge quantities of carrots, potatoes and onions for several seasons. About this time Edwin Taylor decided to trade farms with Fred and Ethel West, who were farming an acreage in the Table Rocks area. This location was only a "stone's throw" from Camp White so hauling time and expenses (gasoline was rationed) would be cut way down. He believed the fine soil on the West's farm would be more suited to his cucumbers and other vegetables than his Applegate land. The Wests agreed. They moved to the Taylor place and set up to operate a small dairy. The Taylors moved to Table Rock, pickle factory and all. The first crop of cucumbers was all right, but they found that the water used in the processing plant was different. The pickles turned soft and had to be discarded. By the time this challenge was solved, business began to decline. "Taylor Maid" pickles ran into stiff competition from the big grocery chains which were under contract to sell only certain brands in their markets. Thus the colorful years of "Taylor Maid" pickle farming came to an end. Ed Taylor retired from active farming. He went into politics and was elected a County Commissioner where he served several years.

Fred and Ethel West operated a successful dairy on the Henry H. Brown Donation Land Claim until 1960. They sold out and moved away. Eventually this land was subdivided, and in 1989 has a number of rural homes on its acreage.

The road to the ranches along the river was called Taylor Lane until about 1960, when it was officially named Hamilton Road. It is two miles in length from the intersection of Highway 238 and the intersection with (Upper) Applegate Road.

THE BUCKLEY FAMILY

The neighbor to the north, adjoining the Cantrall-Devlin ranch, was James D. Buckley and his brother John. They came to the United States from Ireland in the 1850s. They crossed the plains to California, mostly on foot, occasionally being offered a ride with a wagon train. After several years of working in the mines in California, they made their way to Jacksonville, where they mined along Poormans Creek and Jackass (Forest) Creek.

A settler named Willard Spencer had taken up a 320-acre Donation Land Claim in 1852, which was bisected by Jackass Creek, and extended along the Jacksonville-Crescent City Road about a mile from the river. Located between this land claim and the John Devlin ranch was a 160-acre parcel of river bottom land available for a homestead. It was Donation Land Claim No. 37, which had been taken up and abandoned by Jacob Toffelmier. John Buckley purchased it from David L. Hopkins on April 15, 1863, for the sum of $3,000. (Vol. 3, p. 551, Deed Records). He received the patent in 1872. James Buckley bought the rights to a 160-acre parcel of land adjoining his brother to the east. The patent to this was issued in 1875. Together, they owned about 350 acres of good farm land, which extended from the river to the hills above Upper Applegate Road. The Buckley brothers developed and farmed this large acreage together for about ten years.

James Buckley found a loving wife in 1871, when he married Margaret (Maggie) Riley, a 17-year-old Irish girl. She was living at the home of her uncle, Thomas McAndrew, east of Medford, with other members of the Riley family. She was the daughter of Irish

The Buckley house was built in the 1880s and still stands. It is easily identifiable because of the wood-framed antique water tower. (Author photo)

immigrants, James and Mary Riley, and was born in Trenton, New Jersey, in 1852. She was brought up by her grandmother, Rosa Riley. The two of them came to Oregon by sailing vessel around the Horn in 1869. (Interview with Lewis Buckley, June 11, 1989).

James and Maggie Buckley became the parents of seven children, six of whom lived to adulthood. They were: Rose, 1872; John, 1873; James Thomas (Jim), 1874; Mary Catherine (Kate), 1877; David, 1881; and George, 1884.

The first house on the Buckley homestead was destroyed by fire. A new house was built in the 1880s and is still standing in 1989. It is T-shape in structure, with classical revival style, clapboard siding, a gabled roof, and a corbeled brick chimney. A wide veranda across the front had boxed columns. At the rear of the house was a wood-frame water tower. The youngest Buckley child, George, was born in the new house in 1884. According to grandson Lewis Buckley, he was the only one to be born in it. The Buckley house is one of the very few historic houses remaining in the Upper Applegate area.

JAMES BUCKLEY'S CHILDREN

The daughters, Rose and Kate, were educated at St. Mary's Academy in Jacksonville. Kate graduated in 1889 and later qualified for a teaching certificate. She taught several terms in the area schools. She enrolled in St. Mary's Hospital in San Francisco to become a nurse, and graduated in 1901. She worked in the Bay area for a time and eventually returned to live at home with her family. During World War I, she served as a nurse overseas. When she returned home, she was often called on to see cases of serious illness or accidents by people for miles around. She was widely known and highly respected.

James Thomas (Jim) Buckley married Emma Ulrich, of Jacksonville, on January 1, 1905. Three boys were born to them: Francis, 1906; Lewis, 1912; and Lawrence, 1914. A baby girl died in infancy.

George Buckley remained single until 1922, when he married Elizabeth Poe. She had a son, Carell, by a former marriage. George and Elizabeth lived in a small house on the ranch. He worked at farming with his brothers.

In 1907, James Buckley was approaching his 80th birthday so he deeded the ranch over to his wife. (Vol. 68, p. 44, Deed Records). He lived two more years until October 30, 1908. Maggie took over supervision of the ranch, and with the help of her sons, carried on general farming as long as she lived. Her daughters, Kate and Rose; her sons, John and David, never married. They lived out their lives together in the big house. The first to go was Maggie, February 15, 1933, followed by John, December 26, 1933. Next was David, 1949; Rose, 1960; Kate, April 1963; and George, November 1963.

In 1919, Jim and Emma Buckley and their children left the family ranch and bought a place of their own. It was William Cameron's ranch at Uniontown, as described in Chapter 5. Jim Buckley farmed this ranch successfully for about 30 years. They lost their oldest son, Francis, in 1927, a victim of polio, and Lawrence died in 1936. After high school, Lewis attended the University of Portland and graduated in 1937 with a degree in Business Administration. He served in the enlisted ranks in the United States Army during World War II, and saw France, Italy and Africa during his tour of duty. After the war, Lewis came home to help his father with the ranch. His mother, Emma, died in 1942. In 1945, Lewis married Helen Oman of Grants Pass. They adopted and raised three children, Jim, Mary and Anna. His father, Jim died in 1959, and the ranch was sold. The house, built in 1926, after the fire, is still standing and in good condition. Lewis inherited the Buckley ranch and farmed it until 1967 when he sold it. He reserved 20 acres along Upper Applegate Road, where he and his wife, Helen, built a comfortable retirement home. New owners farm the fields, which have not, in 1989, been subdivided.

JOHN AND MARY BUCKLEY

John Buckley took a wife who had been married before and had several children. Her name was Mary Billups when they were married on August 27, 1873, at the court house in Jacksonville. Mary Buckley and her children were to become permanent settlers in the Ruch area. They owned parts of three Donation Land Claims and two homesteads. They were successful farmers for three generations.

She was born Mary Terrio in Illinois in 1831. She grew up without schooling and married very young. Her first husband was Joseph Zelmore, a miller from France. They had three daughters, Mary Louisa, Margaret, and Susan. They came across the plains by ox cart to Oregon in 1851, and spent the first winter with other settlers on Sauvie Island in Washington County. Joseph Zelmore died the next year. Mary, being left alone with three small children, married Marcus Lafayette (Lafe) Enyart. Three children were born to them: Alex, 1859; Josephine, 1861, and one infant who died. Not long after the baby died, Lafe Enyart died and left her with five small children. She stayed with relatives on Sauvie Island. Peter Enyart, Marcus' brother, had settled in the booming mining town of Jacksonville. Mary, her children, and other families went to Jacksonville together. They arrived in 1862. Among them were the Enyarts, Louisgnonts, and Smiths, Benjamin and Elijah. Mary's daughter, Margaret, had married Elijah Smith. They all settled around Forest Creek and Ruch.

On July 1, 1863, Mary married a miner named William (Billy) Billups. He was working in the famous Steamboat mine. They had two children, Sarah and an infant daughter. By 1866, Mary was a widow again when Billy and the infant daughter died in a smallpox epidemic. They were buried in the same grave in Logtown Cemetery. Sarah died when 17 of consumption (tuberculosis). She too was buried in Logtown Cemetery.

Mary's next husband was Benjamin Smith, who was from New York. He had a wife, Lucy, and five children. Lucy divorced him and married Lafayette Allen of Grants Pass. Mary married Benjamin Smith on February 23, 1867. One son, William Henry, was born to them on November 18, 1868. Their marriage ended in divorce in December, 1869. She signed the divorce papers with her mark, and requested that she be allowed to keep Billy Billups name. It was more like an annulment than a divorce, making it possible to marry a man of the Catholic faith.

On the very same day of their marriage, August 27, 1873, deed records show that John Buckley turned over his homestead to his brother James, who had a large family (Vol. 6, p. 321 Deed Records). According to grandson Lewis Buckley, this ended his farming partnership with his brother. John and Mary made their home on the east half of the Willard Spencer Donation Land Claim, which he had purchased in 1866 from George Stephenson. (Vol. 4, p. 444, Deed Records). In December 1873, he bought the west half of the Spencer D.L.C. from Martin Drake, thus he became the owner of the entire 320-acre claim.

Martin Drake and his family came to Jackson County in 1860. He purchased this Donation Land Claim from the original settler, Willard Spencer, for $3,500. (Vol. 2, p. 498, June 13, 1860). Spencer had settled it in 1852 and had lived on it about six years.

The Drake family lived on the farm until the early 1880s. As he had other business interests, he hired others to do the farming. He bought and sold land and had a mercantile business in Ashland. He is best remembered for his interest in the local school district. He was instrumental in having a frame school house built in 1873. As a member of the school board, he had considerable influence in the community. The school came to be called Drake School, even after the Drake family moved to Ashland.

Martin Drake again became the owner of the west half of the Spencer D.L.C. in 1876, when John and Mary Buckley sold it back to him. In turn, he sold it to Samuel Phillips of Buncom. Other owners over the next 20 years included W. H. Bostwick, John A. Mushette, and Albert W. Sturgis, who bought it in 1902. It remained in the Sturgis family over 70 years.

John and Mary Buckley lived out their lives at their home on the east half of the Willard Spencer Donation Land Claim.

MARY BUCKLEY'S CHILDREN

Three of the younger children made their home with John and Mary until they finished grade school and grew up. They were William Henry Smith, Alex and Josephine Enyart. In later years Alex made his home in Josephine County. Josephine was married twice: W. F. Ford and Abraham Rhoten. She had a family and lived near Jacksonville most of her life.

On October 5, 1872, the eldest daughter, Mary Louisa Enyart (Zelmore) married William Ray. He was born in Butler county, Pennsylvania, and came to Jackson County about 1857. He purchased a 319-acre Donation Land Claim which was located across the Jacksonville-Crescent City Road, on the north side, from the Willard Spencer Donation Land Claim. Thus Louisa and William Ray became neighbors of her mother and step-father, Mary and John Buckley.

The settlers who had taken up this land claim were Xavier LaClaire and his wife Rachel, in 1854. They were from Canada, and came to Oregon in 1846. He was called "the Frenchman," but he became a naturalized citizen in 1855, in order to qualify for the title to the claim. He sold it in 1859 to W. J. Matney for $500. (Vol. 2, p. 305, Deed Records). Matney sold to R. W. Benefield, 1863; Benefield sold to James Barnes, 1867; and he sold to William Ray, for $1,000 in gold coin. (Vol. 25, p. 27, Deed Records, March 2, 1869).

William Ray built a two-story board and batten house and other buildings at the site where the road drops down toward the river. The locust trees they planted towered over the house in later years. The best farm fields were between the river and a bench to the east. Four children were born and grew up on the Ray farm. They were: William, Jr. (Bill), 1875; Robert (Bob), 1877; Mary Belle (Mollie), 1879; and Matthew (Matt), 1881.

William Jr. was the only one to marry and have a family. He married Maud Murry on December 29, 1896, in the United States Hotel in Jacksonville. They had two daughters, Rita and Frances. Rita married Edward Kubli and they had one son, Norman. Frances married Gene Mee. They had a son, Russell, and daughters Eleanor and Patricia.

The Ray family came into possession of the 160-acre east half of the Willard Spencer D.L.C. in 1883 when John and Mary Buckley sold it to William Ray, her grandson, for the sum of $2,400. (Vol. 10, p. 282, Deed Records, April 3, 1883) John and Mary continued to make their home on the place until John's death in 1890. Mary sold the remainder of the property to William Ray for a transfer fee of $5.00. John was buried in the Jacksonville Cemetery. Mary's children took care of her in her last days. She died in 1917 and was buried in Logtown Cemetery among her children and grandchildren.

William Ray and his sons farmed the two places for many years. After William Ray died in 1906, William Jr., Robert and Matthew took over the farming. They raised sheep in addition to cattle. William Jr. and his family lived on a 40-acre farm across the road, which was part of the Spencer D.L.C. Robert and Matthew lived with their sister, Mollie, who kept house for them. They lived out their lives on the farm. William Jr. and Robert died in 1942, Matthew in 1948. Mollie lived until 1956.

Two descendants of William Ray live on the property as of 1989. Russell Mee and his wife Genevieve have a modern home overlooking the valley. The old house and other buildings were taken down. Some of the trees are still standing. Russell's sister, Patricia Garrison, has a home on a small acreage nearby. Russell owns 112 acres of the best farm land and farms it himself. He sold the hillside acreage as a subdivision and rural homes occupy the area where formerly sheep and cattle grazed. The Ray farm has been in the family for 120 years, and is the only one in the area still owned and operated by a direct descendant.

MARGARET AND ELIJAH SMITH

Mary Buckley's second daughter, Margaret and her husband Elijah Smith, took up a homestead adjoining James McDonough near Ruch. They had five children live to adulthood. They were: Mary Ann, 1864; Lillie, 1866; Silas, 1870; Joseph, date unknown; and Edward Alexander, 1883. Mary Ann married Thomas A. Stevens. Lillie married James McDonough, and Joseph left the area. Silas remained single and lived with his mother, Margaret, in her last years. Elijah died in 1908 and Margaret died in 1928. They were buried in Logtown Cemetery.

Edward A. Smith married Elva Law on December 23, 1898. She was the daughter of Catherine (McKee) and Alfred Law who lived on a mining claim across Forest Creek from Logtown. There were five children in the Law family: Andrew, 1875, died in infancy; Emma, 1878; Fred, 1879; Elva, 1881; and Sarah, 1884.

After his marriage, Ed Smith worked for wages wherever he

could get a job on a farm or in a mine. Their first child, Lester, was born in 1901, Everett, 1904, and Glenn William in 1908. In February, 1908, Ed Smith and his brother Silas purchased the east half of the Spencer D.L.C. from the heirs of William Ray for the sum of $1,500. The heirs involved were Mary Louisa Ray, widow; William Ray Jr., and wife Maud; Mollie and Matthew Ray. There was a 40-acre tract in the north east corner reserved to the heirs, but it was not legally described. (Vol. 63, p. 104, Deed Records, February 12, 1908). Ed and Elva and their family made their home on this place for many years. A daughter, Jessie, completed the family in 1917. She and the boys attended Ruch School, and helped their father on the farm. Lester and Everett attended Applegate High School from 1922 to 1924. Everett Smith graduated with a class of seven students in 1924. Glenn attended Applegate in 1925, and went to Jacksonville High School in 1926. He quit school and joined the United States Navy on August 10, 1926. He returned home in 1930 and took up farming with his father. He was married to Ruth Peebler on July 23, 1935. Her family lived near Ruch. Glenn and Ruth made their home on an acreage across the road from his parents, which they purchased from the Barnum family. Glenn built a small house of used lumber for his family. Five children were born to them: Esther (Kennedy); Sonja (Swinney); Emma Jean (Weinhold); Stanley and Gary. Esther became a legal secretary, Sonja and Emma Jean became teachers. Gary became a carpenter and cabinet maker, and owns a cabinet shop in Medford. Stanley is a plumber, and owns his own business in Medford.

Ed Smith died in 1952, and Elva made her home with Ruth and Glenn until she retired to a nursing home. She died in 1959. She was buried beside her husband in Logtown Cemetery.

Glenn established a Grade A dairy, which he operated for about fifteen years. He was active in the Dairymen's Association. He was a member of the Ruch School Board, the Jackson County School Boundary Board, and the Masonic Lodge in Jacksonville. He served on the board of directors of Logtown Cemetery for over 50 years. He retired from the dairy business in 1962, sold the farm, and with his wife Ruth moved to a subdivision home east of Jacksonville.

WILLIAM H. (BILL) SMITH

Mary Buckley's son, Bill Smith, married Emma Law on January

21, 1894. Emma was a sister of Elva Law and they were to be neighbors and friends all their lives. Within months after she was married, Emma's father, Alfred Law, died, and her mother, Catherine, turned over her home and property on Forest Creek to Bill and Emma. There was a frame house, barn and other buildings, a few acres of farm land and mining claims. They moved in and Bill went to work as a miner for Albert Sturgis. Three children were born here: Clifford, 1894; Clyde, 1896; and Lee Fred, 1897. They attended Forest Creek School in 1902, 1903 and 1904.

Bill Smith was ahead of his time in restoring land after placer mining. When the muddy water flowed downstream during the mining operations, he built brush dams and directed the water over leveled tailings so that soil was gradually deposited deep enough for crops to grow. Over several years, he developed about ten acres by this method.

Many years later, a gold dredging operation mined out the Smith farm fields, and all that remains is a homesite.

In 1916, Bill Smith purchased a 30-acre farm from Charles Buman. It was located on the Applegate River about one half mile west of the Hamilton Road intersection on the Jacksonville-Provolt Highway. The price was $4,000 but it was good river bottom land, and had a water right from the Applegate River. (Vol. 112, p. 633, December 16, 1916). There was a typical one-story board and batten house, a barn and other buildings, all on the south side of the road. In later years, Emma built a second story on the house.

The farm prospered and Bill acquired more land until he owned 300 acres, all planted in grain and alfalfa. He also had cattle, sheep and pigs. (*Farmer's Exclusive Directory*, p. 130, Jackson County, Oregon, 1921-22). Their sons grew up, married and started families of their own. The first to marry was Clyde when he and Mildred Sweet exchanged vows on April 20, 1920. He worked for the Forest Service at Crater Lake, Soda Springs, and was lookout on Tallowbox in 1955. Their children were: Naomi, 1921; Leah, 1924; Clair, 1927; Catherine, 1929; Carroll, 1935; Clyde, Jr., and Stephen Henry, 1943.

Lee Fred married Mary Ryan in 1924. He worked at various jobs in the area. They had no children and the marriage ended in divorce. In later years he married Wilma Messenger. He died in 1975 and was buried in Logtown Cemetery.

Clifford remained on the farm with his father and built up his own herd of cattle. He first married Lucile Hyde but they were later divorced. They had no children. His second wife was Wanda Heinze, who taught school at Thompson Creek School in 1937-38. They had three children: Larry, Leland and Linda. A change in their lives took place in 1941 when Clifford died from complications of a leg injury. Some time after his estate was settled, Wanda married Bill Byrum. They moved to eastern Oregon.

In the summer of 1943, Clyde and Mildred, with their family, moved home to take charge of the farm. Although the country was in the middle of World War II, farmers had certain priorities for machinery and other materials. Accordingly, when Clyde applied to the War Production Board for lumber to build a farm house, his application was approved. They built a small house on the hill across the road from Bill and Emma's home. The older girls grew up and left home. Clyde continued farming for about fifteen years. His mother, Emma, died in 1948. His father, Bill, made his home with them until he died in 1951. Emma and Bill were both buried in Logtown Cemetery. Family ownership of the farm came to an end after Clyde died in 1957. Mildred sold the farm and moved to Jacksonville. The old house was owned in the 1970s by Harlan and Marie Bosworth. It is still standing in good condition and is owned by Marie Geizer in 1989.

William and Emma Smith house is owned in 1989 by Marie Geizer. (Author photo)

CHINA GULCH

On the hillsides above the Xavier LaClaire Donation Land Claim is a little valley called China Gulch. At one time there was some mining along the creek, but this was never very intensive. During the railroad boom in southern Oregon, there was a survey made for a railroad through the Applegate Valley to Crescent City. Bertha Barnum of the Barnum family railroad in Jacksonville,* bought a piece of land near China Gulch Road to build a depot.

This scheme, like several other plans to build a railroad to the coast, came to nothing. The land was eventually sold for farming.

THE COUNTRY CHURCH

At the intersection of the China Gulch Road and the Jacksonville-Provolt Highway, there was once a small church. In the winter of 1890, a group of neighbors, under the direction of Jeff Matney, got together to build the church.

Services had been held in the schoolhouse for years, but sentiment was strong for a building of their own. The group selected trustees from the community and organized under the Southern Methodist denomination. Membership and attendance grew for several years. Older members died and some families moved away. By 1910, only occasional Sunday School meetings were held. Eventually, even this was discontinued and the building was left vacant.

Glenn Smith bought it from the Ray estate in 1935 and took it down, board by board, to use in building his house nearby. By 1989, the China Gulch area has been subdivided and has rural residences along its entire length.

The peaceful Applegate Valley is home to many satisfied residents, most of them unaware of the exciting history of their properties. □

---

*This was the Rogue River Valley Railroad that operated for a number of years between Jacksonville and Medford.

Chapter 6

BUNCOM, STERLING AND
LITTLE APPLEGATE VALLEY

The ghost town of Buncom is probably the best-known pioneer site in Jackson County, as it is the only one with buildings still standing.

The original settlement was located at the confluence of Sterling Creek and Little Applegate River where the road to Sterling Creek intersects Little Applegate Road.

Soon after gold was discovered in Jacksonville, miners came to work on these creeks. A mining district was organized on Sterling Creek in 1854. The Buncom mining district was formally organized in 1867. Mining claims were held by whites who leased them to Chinese mining companies. The Chinese were experienced miners, as many had earlier worked the California gold fields. They did hard work and paid royalties to the owners. The Chinese

These are the last buildings standing from the town of Buncom. Shed said to have been cookhouse at Federal Mine then moved to present site by Hukill family. False front store (right) was post office and store in early days. (Author photo)

lived together in a camp of tents and shacks near this site. The camp began to be called Buncom. There are conflicting stories about the origin of this name. The most logical one is that it came from some pioneer slang meaning "not worth much." The name stuck long after mining was discontinued and settlers took up land to establish homesteads.

Samuel Phillips was the earliest known permanent settler in Buncom. He came to Oregon and Jackson County in 1853. He was a miner, but he soon turned to farming. With the help of Chinese labor, he built two mining ditches to bring water from the Little Applegate River to his mining claims and farm fields. He purchased a 173-acre homestead by cash entry and received the patent to it in 1871. (Vol. 8, p. 378, Deed Records). His brother, Riley Phillips, took up a homestead adjoining him upstream on Little Applegate River. They worked together to develop the farms.

Samuel Phillips was married to Mrs. Elizabeth J. Finley on January 1, 1868. She had four children by her first marriage: Lucinda, William, Henry and Grant Finley. A daughter, Adaline, was born in 1871, and a son, Charles Raymond, was born in 1875. Adaline and Raymond (Ramie) grew up, married and had families in the Beaver Creek area. Adaline married Oliver Dews, an early settler, and Ramie married Edna McKee, daughter of A. D. (Deb) McKee. Their children were Ora Vernon, Emmet R., Leona and Fern. Elizabeth Phillips died and Samuel married Minerva Bell in 1892. He sold his farm at Buncom to W. H. Bostwick in 1889. (Vol. 18, p. 277, Deed Records). Records show that he frequently bought and sold properties in the area. He owned part of the Bishop D.L.C., the Spencer D.L.C. and a D.L.C. of his own, which he let revert to the government.

Other settlers came into the area. Jacob Parks had a homestead to the north, adjoining Ansil Gilson and family. Jacob Parks was the first postmaster at Buncom, when a post office was established in 1896. It was in a house below the road facing the intersection of Sterling Road. In 1907, William Garrett became postmaster. He served until 1915, when Harley Hall was appointed. During his term, the house burned to the ground. He resigned.

A man named Allie Ingles was appointed postmaster on January 25, 1917. He built a small board and batten store building with the typical false front, on the site of the burned house. He had a few staple groceries and supplies for the settlers, but the post office was most important and was his main interest. Mail days were

Tuesday and Friday.

During Harley Hall's term as postmaster, his mother, Annie Hall, drove the mail route with a horse and buggy. The route was south from Jacksonville on the old road through Sterling to Buncom, then to the road to Upper Applegate, terminating at Watkins post office.From there, the carrier returned to Jacksonville by the same route, by-passing Ruch. This plan was continued when Buncom post office was closed on December 15, 1917. Allie Ingles moved away, and the little store building was vacant for many years.

In 1947, O. E. and Lillian Hukill purchased the property from Maggie West. (Vol. 287, p. 352-3, Deed Records, November 8, 1947). They moved the little store building across the road to its present location and built a new house on the site. Eventually, this house, too, was destroyed by fire. The Hukills moved into a mobile home further up the hill.

In an interview with Lillian Hukill in 1984, she stated that the other two buildings at the location were moved there from the old Federal placer mine on Little Applegate River. The building above the road was the cookhouse for the miners, and the one beside the store building was a bunkhouse. The only original Buncom structure is the small building which was once the store.

Buncom was never a large or colorful settlement compared to Logtown or Sterlingville, but it has served as a landmark in the Little Applegate area for over 125 years.

STERLING CREEK (STERLINGVILLE)

The discovery of gold on this stream, which flows into Little Applegate River, is credited to James Sterling.

He arrived in Jackson County in 1852 from Illinois with his mother, his brother Richard, and his sister Lucinda. He took a Donation Land Claim in Eden Precinct near Phoenix, and began to lay out a farm in partnership with Aaron Davis. In the fall of 1854, James and his partner found their way over the divide south of Jacksonville to do some prospecting along a small creek. They found gold enough to excite them into returning home for supplies and equipment. On the way, they stopped at a place where a group of settlers were having a house raising. Somehow, the news of their discovery was allowed to slip. Before Sterling and Davis returned to stake their claims, other miners had found the stream and staked claims from one end to the other. This, of course, embittered Sterling considerably. He returned to farming and later moved to Cottonwood Creek in Siskiyou County, California. He took up a homestead there and lived out his life. The creek where he discovered gold was named for him and seems a just reward.

The development of the settlement of Sterlingville, after the discovery of gold, was fairly typical of many other "boom and bust" mining camps in the west. Businessmen set up shops, usually in tents, within weeks. A general merchandise store was started by Gustav Karewski of Jacksonville in the fall of 1854. Theodoric Cameron operated a bakery. Soon there were gambling saloons, boarding houses, a blacksmith shop and a livery stable. By 1856, there was a population between six to seven hundred people scattered through the camp and along the narrow valley. The most easily worked ground was exhausted in less than five years. A few of the miners remained and turned to farming, which kept the community alive. Some of these were George Yaudes, A. B. Saltmarsh, Joe and Sylvester Saltmarsh, Ancil Gilson, Reuben Armstrong, Sam and Riley Phillips. A few determined miners kept their claims and had success when there was a good water year. Water was only available during the winter, and some years water was in short supply. Several times miners tried to build ditches to bring water from the Little Applegate River. The first to succeed in this project was a group under the direction of W. W. Gallagher and his brother, J. A. Gallagher. Their ditch was about four miles long by 1860 and brought a steady flow almost year-round. When the gold was mined out, the water rights to the Gallagher ditch were sold to farmers for irrigation.

In the 1870s, a company was organized under the direction of former governor of Idaho, David P. Thompson. His plan was to build 23 miles of ditch around the hillsides to bring water from the Little Applegate river to the upper mines of Sterling Creek. This was a tremendous project and required two years to complete. The first water was delivered in the fall of 1877. The mine operated at full capacity for about five months. This clean-up of the old mines yielded almost $27,000, with expenses of $7,000. There was no mention of the expenses of building the ditch; however, labor in this period was inexpensive by today's rates. Thompson and his backers were not interested in operating mines. What they wanted to do was development then seek a buyer. They found one in Captain A. P. Ankeny of Portland. He was a wealthy and successful merchant, who owned a full block of business buildings in Portland, including a popular theater. In 1879, he made a deal with Thompson to trade this property in Portland for the Sterling

Mining Company. An experienced miner named Frank Ennis was hired as superintendent. The mine prospered until 1884 when Ennis retired due to failing health.

Captain Ankeny had a son, Henry E., and a daughter married to Vincent Cook. There was also an adopted son named Levi. After Ennis' retirement, Henry, his wife and family, came to make their home at the Sterling mine. A two-story frame house was built for them in 1888. Their children were: Cora, Nanie, Frank, Dollie and Gladys. They attended Sterling School and grew up in the community. Captain Ankeny died in 1891 and he remained enthusiastic about his Sterling mine to the very end. Henry operated the mine with varying degrees of success until 1905 when he sold out to Fred J. Blakely, a promoter from Roseburg. This ended about 25 years of Ankeny family ownership of the Sterling mine.

By 1910, mining was no longer profitable and the property was taken over by Spencer S. Bullis and T. N. Barnsdall of Medford, as a speculative venture. Mr. Bullis had some success in reopening and operating the mine. He died in 1928. His heirs did not pay the taxes so Jackson County took it over.

The Depression in the 1930s brought about a revival of mining in southern Oregon if for no other reason than here was a way for men literally to dig out a little money for subsistence. County relief agencies sent many of the unemployed into the hills with county-provided gold pans and simple tools to work the old Sterling mine tailings. A report filed in 1933 showed nearly one hundred people were mining there and along other creeks. (In Jacksonville, folks dug up front yards and under buildings as well as under city streets seeking gold. They found some and often left huge caverns, some of which caved in decades later. The most recent street cave-in was when a car passed over the pavement on Fourth Street a few feet south of California Street on October 14, 1982.)

The Sterling Mining Company eventually paid the back taxes and redeemed the property.

The Bullis and Barnsdall interest was purchased by Yarra Engineering Company of Jersey City, N.J. Acting for this company was D. Ford McCormick. The next year, 1934, McCormick was operating under the Quercus Corporation. He proceeded to take charge of the mining in a big way. He had a concentrating plant built using water from the existing reservoir. Big earth-moving machinery and trucks were brought in to remove

Hydraulic mining brought a terrific force of water at pressures of hundreds of pounds per square inch through giant swivel-mounted nozzels. The jet of water broke down the soil which was then washed through lines of sluices. Operating costs were so low that working even poor ground was generally profitable. (Top, author collection. Lower, photos by author)

the topsoil, then haul the gravel to the plant for processing. The project ended in failure, mainly because the gold was no longer where the men worked. In the fall of 1937 McCormick returned the machinery, which he had on loan, and hired a caretaker for a few months.

Paul Pearce was a dedicated miner with an instinct for finding gold. He mined this claim alone using a hydraulic giant nozzle every season until 1957. Pearce was one of very few miners who made a good living at it all his life.

The property has changed hands several times in recent years and has many new rural residences. All traces of the settlement of Sterlingville, except the cemetery, have long since disappeared. The mine tailings are overgrown with trees and brush but they are still there. Portions of the famous Sterling Ditch bank have been recently developed into a hiking and horseback trail by the Bureau of Land Management.

Sterling Cemetery is located on a knoll about one fourth mile from the Griffin Lane intersection with Sterling Creek Road. A board of directors takes care of the cemetery and holds an annual meeting and clean-up day. Over the gate is a sign: Sterlingville Cemetery—Sterlingville, Oregon—1863. A historical marker similar to the one at Logtown Cemetery was installed by the driveway in 1976 by the Applegate Bicentennial Committee and the Southern Oregon Historical Society. Text of the anodized aluminum plaque:

STERLINGVILLE 1976

James Sterling and Aaron Davis located a rich gold strike here in 1854. Miners poured in and Sterlingville grew to 1,200, including Chinese. The site became famous in Oregon for placer mining. There was a bakery, saloons, stores, butcher shop, gambling house, dance hall, two boarding houses, livery stable, blacksmith shop, hotel, school and post office in use four years. Prominent names included: George Yaudes, Joseph Saltmarsh, Ted Cameron, Capt. A. P. Ankeny, U. S. Hayden, David P. Thompson, Fred J. Blakeley, and Seth Bullis. The mine was last operated by Paul Pearce.

JOSIAH CRUMP FAMILY

Another early settler in the Little Applegate Valley was Josiah Crump. He came to Oregon with his wife, Rebecca, and several children in 1864. They arrived in Jackson County in 1867, where he took up a 40-acre homestead on the divide between Sterling

Creek and Poormans Creek. Josiah and Rebecca were the parents of twelve children: William, Thomas, John H., Elmira, Firman, Josiah F. (Frank), Clara, Charles, Perry E., Olive, Ethel and Harry. Nine of them lived to adulthood. They attended Sterling School and grew up on the homestead. Josiah Crump died in 1881, but his widow continued to farm the homestead as one by one the children married and left home.

Frank (Josiah F., Jr.) was married to Cora Ankeny in 1893. Their children were Vivian, Harold and Jack (John).

In 1899 he purchased a 160-acre homestead from Phil Gleaves at the confluence of Yale Creek with Little Applegate River. (Vol. 34, p. 489, Deed Records). Already on the ranch was a hewed log house, a barn and other outbuildings. Frank remodeled the house by raising the roof and building a second story. The outside was covered with drop siding and the inside was finished with cloth and wall paper. A big fireplace and chimney, of homemade brick, provided the main source of heat.

In 1904 Frank Crump purchased a 160-acre ranch from James Cantrall. He also bought an adjoining parcel of land from Miles Cantrall on the same date, March 16, 1904. (Vol. 49, p. 259, Deed Records).

The farm fields were all on the hillsides but there was ample irrigation from four ditches out of Yale Creek and the Little Applegate River. Frank and Cora and their sons farmed the place and raised cattle for many years.

Jack left home after he finished school and went to work for the Forest Service. He married Fern Leroy, who had two boys, Merton and Malden, by a former marriage.

Harold married Irene Hughey, a local school teacher. She taught at Little Applegate School during the 1923-24 school year and lived with the Crumps.

After she and Harold were married, she taught grades one and two in Jacksonville from 1928 to 1931.

Harold and Irene had three children: Rolland, Janet and Dale. In 1944-45 she returned to teaching at Ruch for one year.

After Frank Crump died, Harold continued to run the ranch and Irene taught school. They became interested in bulb farming at Brookings and moved to the coast. Cora decided to sell the ranch.

Rolland Smith and his wife Clara were farming his parents' ranch near Ruch, but they had their eye on the Crump ranch for some time. The purchase was accomplished on Dec. 22, 1945.

(Vol. 271, p. 560, Deed Records). This gave them more hay and pasture land and was closer to the high ranges. They sold their place to a man named Baily, who operated a dairy there.

The Crump house was remodeled by installing wall board on the interior. The fireplace was closed off and a wood stove was placed in front of it, using the old chimney. This proved to be a mistake, for on the night of November 26, 1971, fire erupted around the chimney. Rolland and Clara were awakened by the frantic barking of their dog, to find fire growing rapidly up the walls. By the time help arrived it was too late. Another historic house was reduced to ashes.

The Smiths replaced the house with a comfortable mobile home and a utility building. They continued their cattle raising operation until Rolland's health began to fail in the early 1980s. He died in 1987. Clara sold the ranch to a California family and moved to Jacksonville, ending a 42-year period of successful operation of the historic ranch.

THE SALTMARSH FAMILY

Among the miners attracted to the Sterling mines were Joseph B. Saltmarsh and his brother Sylvester. They came from the Willamette Valley with their families.

Joseph was the leader of a small group of miners who established claims in the mid-Sterling Creek area. Folks began to call him "Cap" Saltmarsh. The result of this venture was like a yo-yo. They had "up" years and "down" years, but they stayed at it.

In 1870, Joseph Saltmarsh and his wife Mary E. had four children between the ages of six months and eleven years. They were Arzie, Arthur B., Lilly J., and Edward G. While living in the Willamette Valley they had suffered the loss of five children.

During the 1870s five more babies were born and died in infancy. The mother of this large family died in 1878, and was buried beside her babies in the Sterling Cemetery.

Joseph married Ella Pool Cameron on November 24, 1881. She was the eldest daughter of Arthur and Aletta Pool, who were early settlers in Eagle Point and Little Butte Creek area. She had two daughters by her former marriage, Ola and Mary J. (called Mamie).

She made a home for her husband's children and her own. Together they had a son named Madison, born in 1882. The toddler died when he was two.

They lived on a 140-acre homestead on Sterling Road which he had taken up in the 1860s. The patent was issued in 1872. (Murray Abstract Co., Medford, Oregon Abstract of title No. 5350.) The Saltmarshes operated their mining claims every winter and farmed in the summer.

The Sterling Mining Company held claims both above and below the Saltmarsh properties. A situation involving the deposit of the tailings finally became overwhelming for the Saltmarshes, and they gave in to the mining company. On May 21, 1881, a deed for ten and one half acres of mining claims was made out to Sterling Mining Company by the following: George and Anna Yaudes, J. B. Saltmarsh, Reuben Saltmarsh and M. Saltmarsh, his wife, Sylvester Saltmarsh and Annette Saltmarsh, his wife, C. R. Klum and Lucinda Klum, his wife. The price listed was "$1.00 and other considerations." This was an accepted method of concealing the purchase price in the public records. (Vol. 9, p. 291-292, Deed

Barn on Saltmarsh ranch was built in 1895 by Jason "Jay" Hartman, at very top of frame. Others unidentified other than Bill Anderson, lower left and Benton Pool far right. (Photo from author collection)

Arthur Bird Saltmarsh home on Little Applegate River built about 1891-1892, burned 1929. Left to right: Ossie, "Bird" (father), Dean (baby), Dora (wife), Lee. (Author collection)

Records, May 25, 1881).

Joseph B. Saltmarsh lived on the homestead till 1898 when he sold to W. H. Venable. He died in 1906. As Arthur Bird (A. B.) grew up on his father's homestead, he only worked as a miner when it was necessary. He knew that mining was very hard work with uncertain returns. He took up a homestead on the Little Applegate River and became a farmer. He married Dora May Pool, a sister of Ella Pool Saltmarsh, on April 10, 1886. They lived for a couple of years at Lakeview, where a baby was born and died. Their other children were Lee, Dean, Ossie and Glen. They grew up on the Little Applegate homestead. Lee died young.

Dean told the author he was sixteen years old when he took over farming on his father's homestead. He later worked in the woods, logging, and for the Forest Service. He married Flora Manke on June 24, 1924. Their children were: Earl, Hazel, Richard, Melvin and Curtis.

Dean's sister Ossie married John Cantrall and they had Emmett, Truitt and Norma. His brother Glenn married Vieva Hamilton. They had no children. Glen stayed on the ranch and his widow inherited it. After her death in 1987 it went to her relatives.

CHARLEY DUNFORD

Less than one fourth mile past the Saltmarsh place was the home of Charles F. Dunford, a bachelor who owned it for many years.

His parents, Charles F. Dunford Sr. and Emma (Trefern) came to Jackson County in 1894. they had four boys: Charles Jr., Oscar (O. W., Ike), Alvin, and Vernon; and two girls, Flossie and Mrs. B. Simmons.

Charles Dunford Sr. operated a freighting business in Jacksonville and purchased a 240-acre ranch on upper Poormans Creek. The boys and their sisters grew up on this place. After their father died, Charley and his mother made their home in Jacksonville. During this time Charley became a member of Warren Lodge No. 10 A.F. & A.M. He was to remain a member for over 50 years. He never married. His mother died in 1912. Soon after that, he purchased a 10-acre parcel of land on Little Applegate River from Frank Crump.

He had a few cattle at first and gradually built up his herd. He ran his cattle with Kleinhammer, Saltmarsh and others on the high range under the Forest Service permit system. Because his home ranch was so small, the Forest Service officials put a limit on the number of cattle allowed on his permit. He was very angry about this. His first reaction was to purchase a 320-acre ranch about a mile up Yale Creek which gave him the required acreage for his range permit. The ranch was purchased from Mary Pursel in 1939. He lived by himself in the big ranch house.

Charley was unique in other ways. When the horse and buggy was replaced by automobiles, he did not learn to drive so he did not buy one. But all his neighbors did. He walked or rode with other people as long as he lived on his ranch. He was very thrifty— actually frugal. When rural electrification came up the river he had his house wired but seldom used his lights.

He worked for wages whenever the local ranchers needed extra help. As the years went by and old age set in, Charley sold his properties and went to live in Jacksonville.

He died October 15, 1970, aged 86. In his will, among other

beneficiaries, was Warren Lodge No. 10, Jacksonville, which received $1,000.00.

THE KLEINHAMMER FAMILY

A well-known farmer and stockman in the Little Applegate Valley for about eighteen years was Arthur Kleinhammer. He was the son of Claus and Frances (Saltmarsh) Kleinhammer. Claus had come to Oregon in 1851, and to the Sterling mines in 1853. He owned and operated rich claims at Sterling for several years. Arthur was born at Sterling in 1870 and grew up in the area. He had brothers, Fred and William, and sisters Catherine, Ida, Augusta and Frances.

He was married to Mary E. (Molly) Anderson on August 8, 1900. They had three children: Esther, Doris and Claus T.

In 1899 he purchased a 160-acre homestead from Thomas A. Gilson about seven miles up the river from the intersection of Little Applegate Road and Upper Applegate Road. He and his wife lived there about eight years.

He had big plans to expand his ranching and cattle raising business. There were two 160-acre ranches near Buncom which he decided to buy in 1907. The original settlers were Samuel and Riley Phillips. In 1907 these properties were owned by Andrew and Annie Cantrall.

Arthur Kleinhammer sold his 160-acre ranch to Ralph Jennings on October 30, 1907, for $6,500.00 (Vol. 61, p. 549, Deed Records). On the same day, the deed for the two 160-acre homesteads plus a 173-acre parcel adjoining them was signed by Andrew and Annie Cantrall (Vol. 61, p. 547, Deed Records). By this transaction he became the owner of over 490 acres of the best farmland on the Little Applegate River, complete with three water rights. The property extended from Buncom to the Saltmarsh homestead, a distance of about three miles. The price was $12,000.00. Most of it he borrowed from two banks.

He chose a site about 5 miles up Little Applegate to build a large two-story house, barns and other buildings. The house had a porch across the front and a two-story porch across the rear. On the second story was a screened sleeping porch opening from the upstairs bedrooms.

A gravity water system from a big spring supplied the house with running water. Hot water came from coils in a wood-burning kitchen range. A brick fireplace in the living room and a

Dave Jones family in yard of house at intersection of Sterling Road and Griffin Lane. The house, now gone, was built in 1880s. (Paul Jennings collection. He lived here as a boy.)

woodstove in the dining room kept the big house warm in winter.

In later years, Arthur installed a water-powered electric generator and had the house wired for electricity. Eventually the water wheel was replaced by a gasoline engine to run the generator. It was still in use in the 1940s. Commercial electric power did not reach Little Applegate until after World War II.

To operate the ranch, Arthur had several men hired full time during the growing season. The irrigation system took two men who did nothing else. Haying, riding the range to look after cattle as well as other chores kept some of the men busy all year. He insisted that everything be done *his way*. This seemed to be a good method to keep personal control of this large operation. He was running about 500 head of cattle. Art Kleinhammer was the leading cattleman of the Little Applegate area and became a legend in his own time. Other permit holders on this high range were Emmett Beeson from Talent, Ralph Jennings, Edwin Taylor, Paul Anderson and Frank Randleigh. At roundup in the fall, Art would organize the drive so that sections of the range would be systematically covered. There were three holding corrals complete with cabins and sheds. One was called "Freezeout" on the northwest slopes of Wagner Butte. Another was "Jacks Flat" on Seven Mile Ridge. A third was called "Brick Pile" on the northern tip of Seven Mile Ridge. When the cattle were gathered, each owner separated out his own and with dogs and helpers trailed them home. Some buyers came right to the ranches to buy steers. When steers sold they were driven to the loading pens on the railroad near Medford to be shipped to market. When beef prices were high the ranchers made a profit. But if prices were low, some faced serious trouble.

A major financial disaster took place in 1921 when a Jacksonville Bank went broke. It affected almost everyone, farmers, cattlemen, business people; fraternal orders, and townspeople. It was many years before the bank examiners made any restitution and then it was only ten cents on the dollar.

Arthur Kleinhammer was among those who lost money in the bank failure, thus he was not able to make his mortgage payments.

The First National Bank of Ashland was the holder of the Kleinhammer mortgage. By 1925 he had not been able to make the payment or even pay the taxes. Records show that he and his wife, Mary E., simply turned the ranch over to the bank by giving them a deed which included 490 acres with all water rights complete. The deed was subject to a $10,000.00 mortgage in favor of the Federal Land Bank of Spokane. (Vol. 156, p. 278-279, Deed Records, August 26, 1925).

In order to protect their interests, the bank permitted them to continue living on the ranch for several years. Their son Claus took over farming part of it. The bank leased parts to other farmers.

In 1950 Arthur and Mary moved to Jacksonville and lived in the Noonan house. Claus and his family also moved to Jacksonville.

Their daughter Esther was married and living in Ashland, so Arthur and Mary moved to Ashland to be near her. They lived out their lives there and were buried in one of the Ashland Cemeteries.

After the Kleinhammers left the ranch, it was leased in separate acreages to people who continued to raise hay, grain and a few cattle.

Fred and Ethel West lived in the main house and operated the place on a work-lease agreement with Henry Enders of the First National Bank of Ashland for eight years in the late 1930s and early 1940s. They left soon after the ranch was sold to William T. Grant in 1942. He named it the "Circle G" and carried out a number of changes and improvements. The house was remodeled, the barns and other buildings were painted red with white trim. Other owners were Robert Waugh and Arman Richter.

The historic Kleinhammer house was destroyed by fire in the early 1970s. The new owners built a modern house and landscaped the knoll where the original house had been located.

The part which was the original Sam Phillips ranch was purchased by a developer in the 1970s. To make the best use of the river frontage, this developer had the county relocate the road across one of the largest and best farm fields. Handsome rural homes were built along the river and on the hillsides overlooking the valley. Several of these residents carry on some hobby farming with horses, a few cattle and other animals. The farm fields which remain provide hay and pasture. This is still a beautiful area to visit any time of the year.

THE PURSEL FAMILY

The Pursel family were residents of the Upper Applegate and Little Applegate Valleys for four generations and they made a significant contribution to the development of the area.

The original settler was Charles C. Pursel. He was born in 1857 in Pennsylvania to Clinton W. and Christina (Snyder) Pursel, one of eight children. They lived in Michigan and Kansas where the children grew up and went to school. Charles made his way to Oregon in 1880 and settled in Jacksonville.

He acquired a threshing machine and steam tractor and did threshing for farmers in the area. He met his future wife at a ranch where she was cooking for the threshing crew. Her name was Mary A. Louden (Lowden). They were married October 19, 1882. Witnesses were Charles Basye and Henrietta Knutzen. Five children were born to them between 1884 and 1894. They were: Nelson, 1884; Charley, 1886; Della, 1887; Esther, 1892; and George, 1894. They went to Jacksonville School when the teacher was Gus Newbury. Charles worked at various jobs, mostly carpentry. He built a house on North Fifth Street which is still standing. He served as Town Marshal at one time. George was born in Jacksonville in 1894. Shortly after that Charles moved his family to Upper Applegate. He leased a ranch from William Cameron up the river above Star Gulch. He became involved in operating a sawmill on land owned by James M. Dews. The location was on the east side of the river, across from the mouth of Palmer Creek. Charles moved his family to the mill site and cabins were built for other families who came there to work in the mill and to carry on with the logging in the woods. A small settlement developed. There was a store for basic supplies. A post office named Pursel was established on February 11, 1898, and was active till 1904.

The mill was powered by a steam engine. Logging was done with oxen. The Pursel family raised and trained their own oxen. Timber was cut on government land as well as private properties. The government allowed settlers living in or near the forests $50.00 worth of free timber. The mill prospered for several years.

By 1906 Charles Pursel was looking for another site for his mill. He found that Frank Crump on the Little Applegate River was willing to sell 360 acres of good timber land and cultivated fields which lay up Yale Creek. This property had been homesteaded by James and Miles Cantrall. They sold to Crump in 1904. (Vol. 49, p. 259-60, Deed Records). The deed from J. F. Crump to Charles C. Pursel was signed on February 26, 1908. The price was $6,000 and included two water rights. (Vol. 103, p. 457-58, Deed Records).

Nelson Pursell logging with oxen at his sawmill on Yale Creek about 1910. (Author collection)

It took several months to dismantle the mill and move it to the new location, using their oxen, horses and heavy lumber wagons. Dean Saltmarsh was just a little kid about seven years old. Many years later he told Kay Atwood that he had never seen oxen until Pursel's double yoke came plodding up the road past his place pulling a steam boiler on a lumber wagon. He thought "that was a very big thing." (Atwood, p. 156.)

There was a log house on the place which burned in 1910 and was replaced with a two-story frame house which was built on a hillside above the mill. It is still standing. Barns, corrals and other buildings were constructed later. The site was about one mile from Little Applegate River.

Charles' oldest son, Nelson, was 23 years old at this time. Charley was 21 and George was 13. They had worked with their father in the mill from the time they were able to handle the lumber and other tasks. They farmed, raising hay and grain for their livestock.

Nelson Pursel was acquainted with a young school teacher named Ina Stoker, who came to teach the Beaver Creek School in 1907. She and her mother, Mrs. R. S. Birchard, who was also a teacher, had come to Jackson County in 1906. They were originally from Council Bluffs, Iowa, where Ina had graduated from high school and attended Iowa State Teachers College. She had taken summer courses at the University of Chicago and taught school in Iowa.

Ina taught a spring term at Little Applegate School in 1908 and stayed with the Pursel family. She and Nelson were married on August 26, 1908, in Jacksonville. They made their home on the ranch for a year or so. A daughter, Ethel, was born March 9, 1911, in a little house near the mill. Then Nelson purchased 40 acres up Muddy Gulch off Little Applegate Road. (Vol. 96, p. 67, Deed Records, May 15, 1911). They moved there and worked very hard to farm the hilly land and make a living.

Nelson worked for the Forest Service on fire crews, and seasonal work for the farmers in the area. He helped his father in the mill occasionally. Ethel went to Little Applegate School until she was in the fifth grade.

Charles Pursel continued to operate the mill on his Yale Creek ranch. People came from miles around to buy lumber to use in building barns, houses and other structures. Heavy beams were usually hewed from small logs. Roofing was of hand-split shakes from big, straight-grained sugar pine trees. The mill did not run on

Ina Stoker came from Iowa to teach in Beaver Creek School and married Nelson Pursel in 1908. Ina operates "trolley" (which was stout enough to carry passengers) across Applegate River, there being no bridges. (Author collection)

a daily schedule. When a neighbor or a farmer needed lumber, he ordered it. Nelson and his brother went up in the woods, felled the trees and skidded them to the mill. Then they sawed the lumber to fill the customer's order.

Times changed and the mill was shut down about 1917. It was sold and moved elsewhere. Charles sold the ranch to Thomas G. Dews in 1919. The price was $15,000. The agreement called for a $2,000 down payment, followed by yearly payments of $1,000 through the year 1934. The deed was placed in escrow in the Bank of Jacksonville. (Vol. 133, p. 575, Deed Records, December 9, 1919).

In 1918, Charles and Mary moved to Medford. The next year, Nelson and Ina moved to town, too. They lived in adjoining homes on the west side. Ethel attended Washington School, which was located at West Main and Oakdale streets. During those years Ina worked as a bookkeeper for Hutchinson and Lumsden Department Store. Nelson and Charles worked on farms, orchards, and in a sawmill.

Ethel graduated from Medford High School in 1928 and attended business college a few months.

Charles and Mary moved back to the ranch in the mid-1920s, when Tom Dews was unable to make the payments. Their son Charley and his wife Edna, lived with them and operated a dairy on the ranch. Charles Pursel Sr. died there in 1927. Mary continued to make her home on the place.

Ethel Pursel married Fred West March 13, 1929. He was one of twelve children born to Joseph Alexander and Maggie Belle (Hinshaw) West. Joseph West brought his family to Jackson County in 1918.

They had come from northern Idaho by way of California, seeking a more healthful climate for Maggie. They traveled with a team and wagon, camping along the way. Wherever there was work in farming or construction, they would camp near the job while it lasted. When they arrived in Jackson County, they stopped near Phoenix and the children went to school there from 1918 to 1923.

The children were: Oren, who died young; Edna, Agatha, Fred, Laura, Archie, Louetta, Glenn, Raymond, Lydia and Ina Belle.

Louetta married Louis Straube, of Upper Applegate. Lydia married William (Bill) Barker. They lived on Upper Applegate many years.

Joe was a farmer who made a living on rented farms in several areas of the Rogue River Valley. They lived in the Table Rock district when Ina Pursel taught school there. They were among her pupils. The author rode the bus to Medford High School with them in 1927-28 when they lived in the Dewey School District northeast of Medford.

Joe and Maggie, with their family, settled on Little Applegate in 1929, where they purchased a hillside ranch located across from the mouth of Yale Creek. This was less than a mile from the Pursel ranch. The ranch was purchased from Milford Hopper. (Vol. 224, p. 331, Deed Records). It had been owned by Cyrenus and Celia Combest in the 1920s. The West family lived on this place several years. The baby of the family, Ina Belle, was born in January 1930. They moved to a place above Buncom off Sterling Creek Road in 1935. They bought it from Arthur S. Palmer. Joe West died on December 10, 1940. Maggie sold out to O. E. and Lillian Hukill in 1947. In 1989, it remains in the Hukill estate.

Nelson and Ina Pursel moved back to the ranch in 1929 where Mary was still living. Nelson made plans to rebuild the sawmill. He acquired a 24-horsepower diesel engine from an irrigation company. The other machinery was purchased and set up by the end of 1930. Pursel's mill was once more in operation.

Fred and Ethel West made their home on the ranch. Fred worked in the mill. A daughter, Colista, was born to them on December 21, 1930. Eight years later, Gary was born November 7, 1938.

Nelson operated the mill five years on the ranch. By this time, most of the mill-size timber had been cut, thus the need for more timber was urgent.

There was a small ranch with good timber about a mile on up Yale Creek owned by William (Billy) Anderson, a bachelor. He named it "End of the Trail" when he bought it from Harley Hall in 1930. Nelson and Ina purchased this ranch in 1935 and moved the sawmill up there. The old house was remodeled for the family members who worked in the mill. Nelson built a new two-story house, which is still standing and in good condition.

Nelson operated the mill and planer for several years. In 1938 he leased it to Saylor Bailey of the Green Springs Mountain area. Mr. Bailey and his family moved to Little Applegate. He and Nelson had a contract to saw railroad ties. (Medford *Daily News*, March 26, 1938.) The next year Vern Cox leased the mill but he was not successful in this venture.

Mary Pursel decided to sell the ranch. Members of the family considered buying it, but she was persuaded to sell it to a race horse promoter from southern California. His name was Noel Richardson. The contract was signed on September 10, 1938. The price was $7,654.00. There was to be $500.00 down payment and $500.00 in sixty days. The balance was to paid semi-annually at 4% interest. A stipulation was that if the payments were delinquent, the contract would be canceled. (Vol. 223, p. 478, Deed Records).

Apparently Richardson changed his mind. He gave his lawyer power of attorney on September 29, 1939, to cancel the deal. A Quit Claim Deed was made out to Mary A. Pursel on November 8,

1939. (Vol. 223, p. 480, Deed Records). She then sold it to neighbor Charley Dunford on November 8, 1939. (Vol. 223, p. 481, Deed Records). He was to own it for many years.

Nelson continued to operate the mill during the 1940s. It was finally shut down in 1947. A man named Sanderson purchased the mill and moved it to the Butte Falls area. This ended almost forty years of operation of Pursel's sawmills in the Upper Applegate Valley.

The ranch was sold to Amos Bishop in 1947 (Vol. 287, p. 457-58, Deed Records). Ina and Nelson moved to be near Fred and Ethel on the Taylor ranch.

Ina Pursel taught school a total of 57 years, over forty in the Upper Applegate Valley. In the 1930s she taught at Little Applegate, Watkins and Ruch-Sterling. She was at Uniontown in the 1940s. The small schools were consolidated with Ruch in 1950 and she taught at Ruch, mostly first grade, until 1958. She was honored with a retirement party attended by over 200 people, many of them her former pupils. She and Nelson had a few more years together. He died in 1964.

Fred and Ethel retired from farming in 1969. A home in Jacksonville was purchased for Ina and after she was settled, Fred and Ethel moved to Jacksonville.

Ina enjoyed nearly twenty-five years of retirement. She was active in the Little Applegate Sewing Club, the Applegate Garden Club, Upper Applegate Grange, Retired Teachers Association and the Sacred Heart Catholic Church. She died on June 4, 1980, age 93, and was buried in Jacksonville Cemetery beside her husband.

Her devotion to her family, her pupils, their parents and the entire community was deep and sincere. She is remembered as one of the most outstanding teachers in the Applegate Valley.

There were many other families who lived in the Sterling-Little Applegate area over the 125 years since first settlers arrived. Some of them were renters, others worked in the mines or on ranches. A few owned small acreages. A partial list includes: Josiah Crump, Sr.; Bill Davis; Horace Farley; J. D. French; Clyde Fields; Ed. Graupner; Joseph Ginet; Ansil Gilson; Albert Nelson; Hollis Parks and his sisters Ella, Edna and Mattie; George Yaudes; George and Grace Brownlee; Cyrenus and Celia Combest; Clifford and Abbie Dunnington and their nieces, Ileane and Donna Brownlee; Lawrence Dunshee; Glen and Mary France; Milton Houston; Glen and Marvie Lawrence; William Jennings; Paul Jennings; J. J. Munsell; James Rhea; Grace Hall Sharp; Willis and Anna Scott; Oscar Wolfe; Frank Dutton and Sam Reynolds. □

Chapter 7

SETTLERS: LITTLE APPLEGATE CROSSING TO STEAMBOAT

Before any settlers arrived in the Upper Applegate Valley, Indians had a summer encampment at the confluence of Little Applegate River and Big Applegate River. They had huge drying racks for fish where it was easy to catch and prepare the fish for the winter food supply. The first explorers through the area reported finding this encampment and the drying racks. Indians lived well in the valley with its abundance of acorns from the oak trees and numerous edible plants. They left with reluctance.

The Upper Applegate Valley lies generally north and south from Little Applegate Crossing to the California border, a distance of about 15 miles. Tributaries that flow into the river along this stretch from the west include: Lime Gulch, Star Gulch, Flumet Gulch, Palmer Creek, Billys Gulch, Kenny Creek, Kanaka Gulch, Grouse Creek and Carberry Creek. On the east are Murphy Gulch, Neds Gulch, Squaw Creek and Manzanita Creek.

The best and most level land was settled by homesteaders before 1875. There were no Donation Land Claims in this area.

Among the first to take up land for agriculture were John Wright, Kinder Boaz, Nicholas Wright, Mark Watkins, and Oscar Collings (Collins). There were numerous miners in the area as well.

A road up the river to serve these settlers was surveyed and opened in the summer of 1876. There were no bridges. Where it was necessary to cross the river a ford was used. One was at John Wright's homestead where the road crossed to the west side. Another was near the mouth of Palmer Creek, crossing to the east side. The 1876 road terminated at the homestead of Nicholas Wright. A year later, 1877, a road was surveyed and opened from Nicholas Wright's to Mark Watkins' homestead and Squaw Creek. A pack trail from the mouth of Squaw Creek to Steamboat was over Collings Mountain until the 1920s. The road to Steamboat was up Thompson Creek in the early days. The Forest Service built a road up Carberry Creek in the early 1920s, linking Upper Applegate with Thompson Creek.

114

Hat stores were kept busy in these days as men played baseball and women watched the game nearly all wearing hats. But the ladies usually just talked as they sat behind the men and couldn't see the game anyway. Pictures made about 1918. (Harry Bostwick collection)

THE STRAUBE RANCH

The 160-acre homestead taken up by John Wright in the 1860s eventually became a very productive ranch. This property has been in the Straube family for 60 years. It is located about three miles from Little Applegate Crossing on the East Side Road.

John Wright was already over 60 years of age when he came to the Applegate Valley as a miner. He did the work to prove up on his homestead, but the hard labor took its toll for a man of his age. Records show he sold two-thirds interest to Lydia Suiter of Dewitt, Saline County, Nebraska, for $900.00 on March 18, 1877. The other one third interest was sold to the Jackson County Board of Commissioners for $400.00 (Vol. 7, p. 562-567 Deed Records). Both documents were signed with his mark on the same day. In the 1880 census, he is listed as a resident of the County Hospital, age 80. He died on March 27, 1881, and was buried in Jacksonville Cemetery. John Wright is best remembered for the ford across the river at his homestead.

Theodoric Cameron acquired John's homestead by purchasing the one third interest from the county for $66.66. The other two thirds he bought from Lydia and Frank Suiter for $200.00 (Vol. 12, p. 676, Deed Records). The patent was filed and recorded September 6, 1883, under the act of 1820. (Vol. 10, p. 546, Deed Records). Theodoric Cameron owned the Wright property for about six years. In 1892, Cameron sold this land to a newcomer, Patrick "Pat" Swayne.

PATRICK SWAYNE

Pat Swayne paid $1,000.00 to Cameron for this property. (Vol. 26, p. 79, Deed Records). Swayne was born in Ireland in 1862. He was one of twelve children. He came to America, arriving by way of Canada in 1864.

He worked on farms in eastern Canada, but later moved to Massachusetts where he became a stonecutter. He made his way to Oregon and came to Jackson County in 1891. After he purchased the Wright homestead he made numerous improvements. He enlarged the farm acreage by clearing trees and brush. He also sought gold along the river on two mining claims which adjoined the ranch. John Wright's Ford across the Big Applegate River became known as Swayne Ford.

Pat was a hard worker, but he often did poorly on business deals. He once purchased a trainload of Mexican steers and turned them out on the range, where these wild steers became even wilder. When it came roundup time very few were ever found. They simply left the country. He accepted this as part of the cattle business.

During the first decade after he bought the ranch, he had numerous financial concerns. In an effort to succeed, he bought and sold various adjoining properties, but he lost money on many of them. Regrettably, he was one of those involved in the failure of the Bank of Jacksonville in 1921.

In 1899 he married Mary Barbara Herberger of Jacksonville. Their children were all girls: Hazel, Josephine, Mildred, Lois, and Jennie. Jennie died at age 26.

A large two-story house was built about a quarter mile from the road. In 1907 Pat Swayne sold the ranch to Miles Cantrall, who in turn sold one half interest to his brother Andrew.

Gus Newbury, a Medford attorney, purchased Andrew Cantrall's one half interest in the place in 1913. The place was known as the Cantrall-Newbury ranch. A manager, H. P. Sellars, was hired to operate the ranch. His wife and two children, Mary and Lawrence, lived there with him. A large acreage was planted to alfalfa which produced high quality hay for beef and dairy cattle. Eventually Newbury went into sheep raising.

Pat Swayne's house on the Straube Ranch. (Author photo)

In 1930 Newbury sold the ranch to Fred Straube of the Central Point area. There were 215 acres of farm land, 700 head of sheep and the wool for 1930. Farm machinery included mowers, rakes, hay bucks, four head horses and a mule. A Central Point ranch was exchanged in the deal. The total price was $32,000.00.

FRED STRAUBE

Fred Straube was the son of John and Christina Straube, who came to Jackson County in the 1870s. The parents were German born. Fred was born in Oregon in 1869. He married Sophia L. Clark on November 11, 1908. They made their home on a farm in the Willow Springs area west of Central Point. Their children were John William (Bill), Louis, and Lola. Bill married Catherine Fletcher. Their children were: Bill Jr., John and Donna. Lola married Ray Vogel in 1941. They had no children. Louis married Luetta West and their children were Fred and Robert.

After Pat Swayne sold his ranch to Miles Cantrall, he purchased another about 10 miles upstream on the Applegate River at the mouth of French Gulch. This ranch was owned by John Louden when Pat Swayne bought it on November 7, 1910. It was 320 acres and had some improvements. Irrigation was supplied by the Hanley ditch out of Squaw Creek. (Vol. 83, p. 560, Deed Records).

Pat and his family lived on this ranch till 1927. The girls went to Watkins School. Hazel took nurse's training in the Sacred Heart Hospital School of Nursing in Medford in the 1920s. She continued in the nursing profession until her retirement. She never married.

Pat sold the ranch in 1927 to V. J. Emerick and moved to Medford and later to Klamath Falls. (Vol. 165, p. 230, Deed Records).

His health failed after he suffered a stroke in March 1929. Hazel brought him to the hospital in Medford. He lived until May of 1930. His funeral was attended by many of his old friends of the Upper Applegate Valley. He was buried in Jacksonville Cemetery. He is remembered by a small park at the Applegate Dam called Swayne Point.

KINDER BOAZ

Among the many miners who came to the Upper Applegate and remained to become farmers was Kinder Boaz. He arrived in

118

Jackson County before 1860, and was active in mining in the Little Applegate area. When he first came, there were numerous Chinese miners living along the river. Kinder had a small boat which he used to ferry the Chinese across the river for 50 cents apiece. The Chinese called him "Captain" Boas. (Lee Port, "Notes on Historical Events, Applegate Ranger District," p. 5, 1945.) The nickname stuck. He took up a 160-acre homestead about four miles from Little Applegate Crossing on the east side of the river.

He and Laura Jane Wells were married on February 10, 1861. Boaz built a two-story hewed log house for his family. He covered the logs with exterior siding which was allowed to weather without paint. Floors and partitions were made of twelve-inch pine boards a full inch thick. The logs had been carefully notched to fit tightly and were laid up four feet above the floor of the second story. Poles were used for rafters. The roof was of hand-split sugar pine shakes.

The upper story was all one big room, used for sleeping. The lower floor had a front room, two small bedrooms and a kitchen-dining room. One side of the kitchen was completely filled with a huge fireplace built of river boulders and clay mortar. Other buildings were a springhouse, smokehouse and woodshed. There was a barn and corrals.

Kinder and Laura had six children born between 1863 and 1874, who grew up in this house. They were: Mary (May), Emma (Emily), Laura, Nicholas, Clara and William Cody. The mother of these children died while they were small. Boaz took a second wife on September 26, 1877, when he married Eda Elizabeth Newman. The two older Boaz girls married men of the same surname. Mary married J. F. Sargent, January 3, 1881. Emma (Emily) married A. L. Sargent on July 30, 1882.

They made their homes in the area. Children of A. L. Sargent were listed on the Beaver Creek school census in 1898 along with Cody Boaz, age 19.

In 1903 Kinder Boaz and others petitioned the county for a road by his place from Swayne Ford over the summit of Dead Horse Hill, past the open fields of Deb McKee's place and terminating at the California border. (Vol. 3, p. 256, Road Records). This made it possible to avoid fording the river during the winter.

The ford at Palmer Creek was eliminated when the McKee covered bridge was built in 1917. About the same time a covered bridge was built about a mile downstream from Swayne Ford. The right of way was on William Cameron's property thus it was known as Cameron Bridge. This bridge was replaced twice, the most recent was in 1954 with a concrete structure.

In 1903 Kinder sold his homestead to T. J. Kenney of Jacksonville for $3,000.00. (Vol. 48, p. 10, Deed Records, July 22, 1903).

The Boaz family moved to Jacksonville where Kinder died in 1909. He was buried in the Jacksonville Cemetery. His widow, Eda Elizabeth, married Andrew J. (Jack) Marvin on March 18, 1910. They had about 10 years together. He died in 1920. She died in 1921. They were both buried in Logtown Cemetery.

Kinder Boaz and his family are best remembered by Boaz Gulch and Boaz Mountain which was named for him. The mountain rises to 3,500 feet elevation and is in the south part of Twp. 39 S., Range 3 W. McArthur reminds that the name is sometimes spelled "Boaze" in records.

The Boaz homestead changed owners several times in 1903. T. J. Kenney sold it to James T. Buckley for $2,500.00. The deed was signed July 28, 1903. Next day, James T. Buckley sold to Pat Swayne for the same price. (Vol. 54, p. 101, Deed Records).

Pat Swayne had the place three years. He sold to Benton Pool in 1906 for $2,500.00. (Vol. 54, p. 591, Deed Records).

Benton and Ada Cameron Pool lived out their lives on this ranch. Their daughter, Maud, inherited it. After she married William Ziegler on March 23, 1944, they made their home in the old log house. A son, Robert, was born January 6, 1945. The house was damaged by fire around the kitchen chimney in the summer of 1958. The Ziegler family saved the house by forming a bucket brigade of neighbors from the irrigation ditch in the front yard. After thinking it over, the decision was made to take down the house and replace it with a mobile home. William Ziegler died in 1979. The ranch was sold, reserving the home site and a small acreage for Robert Ziegler and his family.

THE BUCK FAMILY

In 1907 Charles C. Buck purchased a ranch from Pat Swayne on the west side of the river at the mouth of Star Gulch. (Vol. 59, p. 29, Deed Records). The house, barns and corrals were located at the intersection of Star Gulch Road and Upper Applegate Road.

Charles C. Buck was one of seven children of William R. and Matilda Buck, who came to Jackson County from California in 1874. The other children were: William T., Verlinda, Mordecai, Bruce, Catherine and Campbell. Mordecai, who was called

"Maud," (M. R.) married Edna Parks on June 3, 1892. They made their home on a ranch on Little Applegate Road just about a mile from the intersection of Upper Applegate Road. Their children were: Otis, Ernest, Vernie and Grace. The children grew up and the parents lived out their lives on the place. Otis Buck owned it for many years. The ranch was famous for wild blackberries. People came from miles around to pick them. In the 1920s, crews picked large quantities for a cannery in Medford.

Charles C. Buck married Metta A. (Mattie) Parks on November 19, 1892. Metta and Edna were the daughters of Jacob Parks and grew up on the Parks homestead near Buncom.

The children of Charles and Metta were Clarence and Aletha. She married a man named Clark. Clarence never married. He stayed on the ranch farming and raising cattle with his father. In later years they purchased adjoining land.

Charles buck died in 1951, and Clarence continued to operate the ranch, making his home with his mother. He died in 1961 and left the ranch to his sister, Aletha Clark. In 1964 she sold to young Fred Straube. The historic house was taken down and a new house built overlooking the river. In 1989 Fred raises beef cattle and farms the ranch.

Original office and mule barn at Star Ranger Station, both now moved from original sites. (Author photo)

STAR RANGER STATION

Adjoining the Buck ranch on up the river is Star Ranger Station of the U.S. Forest Service. It has been in that location since 1911. From the 1850s to the 1890s, all government land was considered public domain. Settlers could purchase land for $2.50 an acre or file for a 160-acre homestead for a small fee. There were other benefits for settlers such as some free timber for their own use and open grazing for their livestock.

Much of the best land in Oregon was settled and privately owned by 1890. This included many square miles of virgin forests. Members of the Forestry Association, Will G. Steel, Judge John Waldo, B. E. Furnow, and others, became concerned about protecting the forests from fire and various abuses. They were instrumental in having legislation enacted by Congress to set aside certain areas for forest reserves.

This legislation was vigorously opposed by groups of cattle and sheep men. They had been able to use the range freely and were outraged about this so-called closing of the public lands.

President Grover Cleveland believed in forest protection and was well-informed on the subject. He refused to modify the plans for the establishment of the forest reserves.

A proclamation was issued by the President on September 28, 1893, formally establishing the Cascade Range Forest Reserve in Oregon. It extended from the Columbia River almost to the California border and contained 4,500,000 acres. This region was divided into three sections: Bull Run was in northern Oregon; Cascade Range Reserve was central Oregon, and Ashland Forest Reserve was southern Oregon, mostly Jackson County.

The districts were organized with a superintendent in charge. Working under his direction were supervisors and rangers. Standards of training for personnel were set up and put into practice.

Regulations were adopted. Gradually, over a number of years, the public accepted the Forest Service and its activities. These include building roads and trails, fighting forest fires, issuing grazing permits, guarding against poaching and other abuses, and providing recreational facilities.

In 1905, the Bureau of Forestry in the U.S. Department of Agriculture was renamed the U.S. Forest Service. Administration of the Forest Reserves in Oregon was taken over by the Forest Service in 1907. The Ashland Reserve was expanded and renamed

Crater National Forest with headquarters in Medford. At this time, plans were submitted for a resident ranger's cabin in the Applegate area in 1908. It was built and was made ready for occupancy by the summer of 1911. There was a 10-acre pasture and a barn for the horses and mules. It was called Star Ranger Station as it is located near the mouth of Star Gulch. The first ranger to be stationed there was Ira Tungate from Butte Falls. Another ranger station was established at Hutton near the California border. The first ranger there was William Fruit. He worked for the service for many years. Fruit Mountain and Bill Fruit Trail up the middle fork of the Applegate River were named for him.

The ranger who served the longest at Star was Lee Port. He was working as a fire guard out of the Ashland Station in 1913 when he took the ranger's examination and received his appointment in 1914. He came to Applegate as ranger at Hutton in 1917. A year later Ashland and Big Applegate districts were combined to form Applegate Ranger district. Port was placed in charge of the new district with headquarters at Star Ranger Station.

He was married to Maude A. Peachy of Ashland on December 24, 1912. A son, Lee Jr., was born in 1916 and a daughter, Frances, in 1920. They attended Beaver Creek School through the eighth grade and went to high school in Ashland. Lee Jr. joined the Oregon State Forestry Department after he finished college and made it a career. Frances became a teacher.

Lee Port retired in 1945. He and Maude lived at Ruch for several years and remained active in community affairs.

Many changes have taken place in the Forest Service over the years. The name Crater National Forest was changed to Rogue River National Forest in 1932. The Star Ranger Station has always been an important part of the Upper Applegate community since its establishment. An expanded administration building was completed in 1989. The work of the Forest Service continues in the traditions for which it was founded.

THE COPPLE RANCH

Adjoining the Ranger Station buildings was a small acreage which was the home of William Copple, his wife Annie (Matney) and daughter Avanel. Avanel attended Beaver Creek School from 1909 to 1914. An old photograph of the Star Ranger Station buildings, shows a large barn under construction on the Copple place. As of 1989, the barn is still standing. The adjoining property has been subdivided.

LANCE OFFENBACHER

The next ranch upstream from Star Ranger Station was part of the William Cameron estate and had been owned and farmed by his son Wilbur for many years. In 1929 Lance and Stella Offenbacher purchased the ranch from Wilbur and Dora Cameron. They took possession December 1, 1929. (Vol. 180, p. 364-367, Deed Records). Lance was the son of Fred and Carrie (Cameron) Offenbacher and grew up on his father's ranch about three miles west of Ruch on the Jacksonville-Provolt Highway (State Highway 238). He married Stella Layton on September 5, 1924. Their children were: Rosella, Walter and Wesley. The children attended the Beaver Creek School through the eighth grade and went to high school in Jacksonville.

The old house was destroyed by fire in the early 1930s. A new modern home was built on the same site and in 1989 is still standing, shaded by mature trees and surrounded by a landscaped yard.

In 1949 Lance and Stella sold the ranch. The new owners subdivided the ranch into small acreages. Most have pasture for a few livestock.

Lance and Stella moved to a 76-acre parcel of land purchased from Harlan Cantrall near Ruch. After living on this place several years, they sold it and moved to the original Offenbacher ranch. Here they built a new home and retired from farming.

A. D. (DEB) McKEE

The oldest son of John and Maryum McKee of Logtown was Adelbert D., known as "Deb." He grew up at Logtown and went to school with his brothers and sisters, about two miles down the road. He worked with his father in the blacksmith shop, helped with the farming and mined in the winter. He married Leila DeLong on December 25, 1875. They made their home on mining claims for several years. They became the parents of thirteen children between 1876 and 1904. These were: Bert, Arthur, Edna, Zelpha, Verna, Jimmy, Fort, Wilda, Luella (Lila), Leonard, Doris and Dorothy. Ernest died in infancy.

In 1900 Deb and his family were living in the Watkins School District where he was a member of the school board. Two years later he bought two mining claims on the east side, across the river from the newly-built Beaver Creek School. The owner was James McLaren and the price paid was $200.00 September 22, 1902. (Vol. 60, p. 114, Deed Records). Deb built a two-story house close to the new East Side Road. His barns, corrals and other buildings were nearby. A field was cleared for farming. Since the school was on the opposite side of the river from their place and there was no bridge, a cable was suspended across the river near the house. The cable was fastened to big trees and anchored to boulders. A box, large enough to carry up to four people, hung by pulleys from the cable. The crossing was made by pulling the cable by hand. The McKee children and their friends rode this device for years without accident. Eventually a swinging bridge was built for foot crossing.

With so many children from this family in Beaver Creek School, it became commonly called McKee School. Some people called it Palmer Creek School.

When the school building was put up it was on government land. Deb later filed a homestead on the land and donated the site to the school district. Classes were held here until 1913 when operations were moved to a new building about a mile up the road and across the river.

The patent to his 148-acre homestead was issued on November 18, 1920, and signed by President Woodrow Wilson. (Vol. 154, p. 199, Deed Records). The children grew up, married and left for homes of their own. Edna married Ramey Phillips. Their children were: Orie, Emmet, Leona and Fern. They took up a homestead above Upper Squaw Lake where they lived for several years.

Verna married Cary W. Culy. Their children were: Helen, Louis, Omar Jr., and Leora. They lived on a ranch at the mouth of Kinney Creek on the west side of the river. Louella married Thomas Dunnington. They had one son, Thomas Jr. Dorothy married Albert Hackert and they had two children, Delbert and Myrna. Doris married Riley Norris. Their children were Eilene, Kenneth and Jean. These three families lived in Jacksonville. Bert married a widow named Lillie Carroll in 1924. She had five children between the ages of three and fourteen. They made their home in the area until 1929.

BLUE LEDGE MINE

A large copper mine was developed on Elliot Creek just over the California border. It was first located and explored by the Blue

Ledge Mining Company in 1898. Mining equipment was installed and the work began in 1906. Ore was hauled by team and wagon to Medford to be shipped to a smelter in Washington State.

Deb McKee drove a stage from Jacksonville to the Blue Ledge Mine using his own ranch as a stopping place. The mine was operated until 1908 when prices declined. During World War I, the mine was opened and ore taken out for the war industries for a short time. By 1919, everything was dismantled and the Blue Ledge became a mining legend.

McKEE BRIDGE

In 1917, Jackson County made a road change near Deb McKee's ranch. A large covered bridge was built across the river adjoining his property. The West Side Road intersected the East Side Road at the end of the bridge. However, the west side road continued on up the river past the mouth of Palmer Creek as there were several miners and settlers in that area. The bridge was built by master bridge builder Jason Hartman and his sons, Wesley and Lyle, who worked for the county for many years. The bridge was named for the McKee family and has served as a landmark in the area ever since. Efforts to preserve it are ongoing. A historical marker was installed in 1976 by the Applegate Valley Bicentennial Committee and the Southern Oregon Historical Society. Text of the marker:

McKEE BRIDGE

THIS BRIDGE WAS BUILT IN 1917 BY JASON HARTMAN OF JACKSONVILLE. THE SITE WAS DONATED BY ADEL-BERT (DEB) McKEE, A RANCH OWNER TO THE SOUTH, WHOSE HOUSE HAD SERVED AS A STAGE STATION AND HALFWAY POINT BETWEEN JACKSONVILLE AND THE BLUE LEDGE COPPER MINE WHICH WAS OPERATED BETWEEN 1906 AND 1919. RELIEF HORSES WERE KEPT FOR THE SIX AND EIGHT-HORSE TEAMS HAULING ORE FROM THE MINE; LODGING AND BOARD WERE PRO-VIDED FOR TRAVELERS. THE BRIDGE WAS DECLARED UNSAFE IN 1956; IT HAS BEEN MAINTAINED BY COM-MUNITY GROUPS AND LEFT FOR ITS HISTORICAL VALUE AND THE USE OF PEDESTRIANS.

The road was changed in 1956 and a new bridge spans the Applegate near where the old rope-and-pulley "trolley" crossing was located. Deb McKee died on September 23, 1920. His wife,

Leila, stayed on the ranch several years eventually moving to Jacksonville where she lived near her daughter and son-in-law, Albert and Dorothy Hackert. She died on August 9, 1938, and was buried beside her husband in Logtown Cemetery. Deb McKee's home site is marked with a tall pine tree, an oak tree and several apple trees.

DEVELOPMENT OF THE McKEE BRIDGE AREA

The first few years after the bridge was built, people came to swim in the river, picnic and camp on the bank nearby.

Property near the bridge on the west side of the river changed hands in the early 1930s. Albert and Selma Young and Lee Port, Jr., purchased small acreages. The Youngs built a house and lived there while Albert worked for the Forest Service. The Great Depression was underway, and the Upper Applegate community was to be benefited by the government programs established to relieve the economic distress of the nation. One of these was the

McKee Bridge in 1989 is enjoyed by pedestrians and photographers. Highway now bypasses old covered bridge on a concrete span. (Author photo)

Civilian Conservation Corps. It was organized in Jackson County in May 1933.

Medford was headquarters for 18 camps accommodating 4,000 men to be situated on Crater Lake National Park, the Rogue River, Fremont and Deschutes National Forests. Each camp was directed by officers of the Regular Army and contained about 200 men. They were not under regular army discipline, but were required to be healthy and able to do physical labor. Division of authority and responsibility was carefully specified. The Army took care of housing, feeding and clothing the men. The Forest Service planned and directed the work to be done.

Camp Applegate was established in the summer and fall of 1933. It was located at Seattle Bar on Big Applegate River near the California border.

One of the first projects of the men of Camp Applegate was improvement of the campground at McKee Bridge. A rustic picnic shelter building was constructed which featured an enormous fireplace of river boulders. Over fifty years later it is still standing in fairly good condition.

Other projects accomplished by the C.C.C. were the improvement and building of roads and trails, construction of more buildings at Star Ranger Station, manning lookouts and fighting fires. In 1935, the Forest Service and the C.C.C. built a new consolidated telephone system from Jacksonville to Hutton Guard Station. The local farmers' phone line was taken over and improved without cost to the shareholders.

The C.C.C. was active in the Applegate area for eight years until World War II broke out in December 1941. Many of the projects remain in use in 1989.

UPPER APPLEGATE GRANGE

Recreation in the early days was not considered as essential as it is today. People worked hard, but they had good times among themselves when the work was finished. There were card parties and dinners for friends and neighbors. Little Applegate had a ladies' sewing club which met regularly at members' homes. Dances were held wherever there was a hall or other building large enough for a crowd. In 1935, the only large hall was at Applegate, next to Pernoll's store. Applegate Grange met in that hall. They were a very active group, putting on plays, dances and other entertainment for the community. Among the members were several people from Upper Applegate who decided to start a Grange closer to home. They were: John and Pearl Byrne, Bert and Christine Harr, and Lottie McKee. After several meetings held at the Beaver Creek School, Upper Applegate Grange was organized on October 12, 1935. There was a total of 45 members when the charter was closed two weeks later. Meetings continued to be held in the Beaver Creek School. The first Master of this new Grange was Valoris Haskins. Plans were immediately underway to build a hall. Albert and Selma Young, who owned property adjoining McKee Campground, donated one acre for the hall. It was decided to use local materials—small logs set on end stockade style—with poles for joists and rafters. The sills were to be laid on native rocks, eight feet apart. The building was to be 30 by 70 feet. The roof was of hand-split shakes. Each member family was to provide 12 small logs, peeled and cut to the right size, plus two larger logs for joists and two rafters. Everyone cooperated and soon logs were delivered to the site. The master carpenter was Wallace Haskins. He directed a crew of volunteers, both men and women, during the spring and summer of 1936. The C.C.C. helped also. The members had a big Fourth of July celebration and dance in the almost-completed hall.

The first regular meeting in the new building was held August 8, 1936. The next year, they built a kitchen and dining room addition. The C.C.C. boys made a large rustic sign and installed it over the entrance. Formal dedication was held by State Grange officers on June 8, 1938. State Grange Master Ray Gill conducted dedication ceremonies before an audience of almost 200 people. He was lavish in his praise of the unique hall with its varnished log exterior and knotty pine interior trim. He paid sincere tribute to the members who had worked for almost two years to accomplish the project.

Unfortunately, the Grange members and the community were to enjoy this hall only seventeen years. On the evening of September 7, 1955, it was destroyed by fire. Members had been cleaning the hall that day, but the cause of the fire was never determined.

Members set about rebuilding at once. After some controversy about locating closer to Ruch, a site about one mile from Little Applegate Crossing was agreed upon. Mr. and Mrs. Frank Preston, who owned the land, generously donated two and one half acres on a narrow strip of land between the road and the hill.

It took the members two years to build the new hall. It was to be of fire resistant materials, 100 by 35 feet in size. The walls were to

Members of Upper Applegate Grange, 1938. The building burned in September 1955 but a new modern building was ready for use in 1957. (Top photo by author. Lower photo author collection)

Upper Applegate Grange. 1938

Front Row. L to R.	Center Row	Back Row
Gladys Byrne	Cary Culy	Bert Harr
Pearl Byrne	Verna Culy	Bill Norris
Maude Port	Osie Norris	Frank Bowman
Fred Dorn	Grace Buck	Lee Port
Albert Young	Thelma Young	Louis Culy
Jim Winningham	Clara O'Brien	Morris Byrne
Ed. Finley	Albert Collings	Hiram Head
Floyd McKee	Alma Collings	Dow Lewis
Wallace Haskins	Meta Buck	
John Byrne	Val Haskins	
Harry Malott	Helen Haskins	
Christine Harr	Amos McKee	
Mamie Winningham	Lottie McKee	
Omar Culy	Florence Byrne	
Eva McKee	Mr. Royce	
Rosalie Culy	Bertha Haskins	
	Evelyn Byrne	
	Clara Faye McKee	
	Helen Thomas } teachers	
	Mary Esther Davis }	

Identified by Pearl Byrne
May 23, 1978 for
M. Black

be pumice block with concrete floors and composition roof. The heating system was electric forced air units. The first meeting in the new hall was held on June 7, 1957. Over the years Upper Applegate carried out many projects for the betterment of the community. Among them were installation of a relay station on Squires Peak for television broadcasts, commercial trash collection and improvement of the county road. Members faithfully attended meetings of the Rogue Basin board and supported plans for a flood control dam on the Applegate River for years before it became a reality. Members continue to carry on the traditions of social benefits and public service, despite the changing times.

McKEE BRIDGE STORE

The McKee Bridge area became more of a community center in May 1938 when Harold Reed of Jacksonville opened a store in the small building he had built across the road from the Grange hall. He put in a stock of basic groceries which included picnic supplies. In summer he kept a cooler, which he loaded with ice and soda pop, just outside his front door. A little later he installed a gas pump. The store building has been remodeled with changes of owners many times since 1938. In 1989 it continues to function as the McKee Bridge Store, now operated by Tim and Bonnie

McKee Bridge Store and Cafe is operated by Tim and Bonnie Connolly in 1989 continuing a service that started in 1938. (Author photo)

Connolly (since 1987). A cafe, in the same building and part of the store, is enjoyed by visitors as well as by local residents. The McKee Bridge Mobile Home Park is nearby. It opened in 1960.

THE AMOS McKEE FAMILY

Another son of John and Maryum McKee of Logtown made his home on the Big Applegate River about a mile upstream from his brother, A. D. (Deb) McKee. Amos married Lottie Pence, a neighbor girl, on March 18, 1886, at Logtown. They lived in a cabin below the road, where their first child, Ernest, was born in 1888 and the second boy, Floyd, in 1891. About that time they moved to Big Butte Creek with John and Maryum to help run their new ranch. Pearl was born there in 1894. They returned to Applegate and lived at a mine on Palmer Creek where Clara was born in 1904. Amos and Lottie had been married twenty-two years in 1908, when they decided to buy a ranch of their own. They purchased a 160-acre ranch from Manuel and Margaret Silva on May 5, 1908. The price was $3,000.00 to be paid within three years with interest at 8%. The house was located on the east side of the river and part of the land was across the river. It was well irrigated by ditches formerly used in mining.

Manuel Silva and his wife, Mary, came to the Upper Applegate in the 1870s. During the 1880s they had several children. Mary Silva died while they were young. Manuel married Mrs. Maggie Fore on December 31, 1888. Two of Manuel's boys, Frank and Manuel Jr., lived with them. Three girls were born to them during the 1890s: Teresa, Esther and Ruby. They attended Beaver Creek School from 1899 until 1907. Frank Silva married Esther Pursel and they lived on Little Applegate several years.

Amos and Lottie McKee moved into the small house, which was just a shack of rough boards. It was given a thorough cleaning to make it livable. They only lived in it a year or two, when it caught fire and burned to the ground with the family losing everything. A new modern frame house was built on the hill overlooking the road and fields. This house, too, was destroyed by fire, after Amos and Lottie had retired and the place was occupied by renters. Floyd, Ernest and Pearl attended Beaver Creek School through the eighth grade. Clara was eleven years younger than Pearl so she grew up more-or-less as an only child.

Ernest was the first to marry. He married Allene Raye Kingsbury on July 3, 1913. Next was Pearl. She married John S.

Byrne on July 18, 1914. John's parents lived up Squaw Creek in the early 1900s. After the boys and Pearl left home, Clara became her father's helper on the ranch. The cash crop, for several years, was red Mexican beans. These had to be irrigated and cultivated, then threshed and cleaned before sale or trade. Clara learned to handle horses and cattle, as well as raise a garden and help in the house. She finished eighth grade at Beaver Creek School and stayed one more year under teacher Eva Collins, who coached her in advanced subjects. Mrs. Collins had come to teach at Beaver Creek School in 1920. With her was her small daughter, Leah. They stayed with Deb and Leila McKee. She taught three years at Beaver Creek School. She married Floyd McKee on June 5, 1923, in Yreka, California, then taught school one more year before becoming a mother and homemaker.

Eva and Floyd had two boys, Douglas and Richard, who grew up with Leah as their sister. Leah was married to Maurice Ritchey in the old Upper Applegate Grange hall on March 9, 1938. They made their home in Colorado. Two girls were born to them, Anita and Sharon. In later years, they moved back to the Medford area. Leah and Maurice celebrated their fiftieth wedding anniversary on April 24, 1988, in the new Upper Applegate Grange hall. A large crowd of family and friends came to this party.

Amos and Lottie's youngest daughter, Clara, married John (Jack) O'Brien on October 10, 1923. They had one son, Donald. Eventually this marriage failed. In 1937 Clara married Rolland (Sandy) Smith. They made their home on his father's ranch near Ruch.

John and Pearl Byrne built a home on part of Amos McKee's ranch on the west side of the river where they lived for many years. Their children were Morris, Evelyn and Gladys. In 1947 Evelyn married Clarence Williams, who later served as Jacksonville postmaster. They had two girls, Valinda and Janeen. Gladys married Glen Williams in 1949 and they had one son, Gary. They lived in Medford. Morris was married twice and had Catherine, Dennis, Rita, Larry and Jimmie.

Amos and Lottie lived out their lives on the ranch. Lottie became ill and died in 1944. Amos lived till 1950. At first, his daughters Pearl and Clara looked after him, then he spent his last days in a nursing home in Jacksonville. Morris Byrne acquired part of the ranch in 1989 and still farms it with his other acreage.

John and Pearl Byrne's home was on the west side of the river on Palmer Creek Road shown as it appeared in 1969 before modernization. The property is presently owned and occupied by Phyllis Haseltine who loaned this photograph.

JAMES M. DEWS

The next settler adjoining Amos McKee upstream (south) was James M. Dews. He took up a homestead in the 1870s and received the patent to it March 13, 1893. (Vol. 43, p. 470, Deed Records). He was son of Thomas G. Dews who brought his family to Jackson County in the 1860s. His occupation was a teamster. His children on the 1870 census listed as James M., age 16; Nancy, 13; Eliza, 9; and Thomas J., 5. Oliver was 14. James M. Dews married Teresa DeLong on January 1, 1887, and they made their home on his homestead. In later years, they adopted a son, who was named James Merrit Dews. He was called Merrit. He attended Beaver Creek School in 1906 and 1907, when the teacher, Maude Harr, stayed at their home. James had helped to organize the school district and served as clerk. Soon after Pursel's sawmill was moved from Dews' place to Yale Creek, James Dews sold his ranch to Henry and Frank Stephenson, share and share alike, for

$2,000.00. The deed was signed January 6, 1908. (Vol. 62, p. 411, Deed Records).

NICHOLAS B. WRIGHT

One of the earliest settlers in the Palmer Creek area was Nicholas B. Wright. He was a farmer who had a 160-acre homestead across the river above the mouth of Palmer Creek before 1860. In the 1870s, his ranch was a stopping place for miners and packers on the way to the Steamboat and other mines. He had a small store with basic supplies. A post office named Wright was in existence from April 25, 1878, to December 22, 1888, which he served as postmaster. He had a wife, Florence, and a daughter, Ida. She was married to William H. Lewis in 1889 and they moved to Pleasant Creek in northeastern Jackson County. Nicholas Wright was 65 years old in 1880 so he turned the property over to his wife, Florence, on April 21, 1893. (Vol. 26, p. 404, Deed Records). The patent was issued on April 24, 1884. (Vol. 23, p. 493, Deed Records). Nicholas Wright is remembered for the post office and stopping place at his ranch. It was also the terminus of the 1876 road, and the starting point for the later road on up the river. The Wright place has changed hands many times during the years.

As of 1989, Morris Byrne owns and farms the fields. He raises cattle. His hay fields and pastures are healthy and green with dependable irrigation from the Applegate Dam.

OLIVER B. DEWS

James M. Dews had a brother, Oliver B. Dews, who took up a 160-acre homestead adjoining Nicholas Wright's ranch upstream (south). The largest farm fields were on the west side of the river. It was irrigated by a ditch out of Kinney Creek, built by Oliver Dews. The buildings were on the east side of the river. It had to be forded to get to the fields on the west side.

Oliver Dews married Adaline Phillips on May 13, 1884. She was the daughter of Samuel and Elizabeth (Finley) Phillips, who lived near Buncom in the 1860s. Her brother was Charles Raymond (Ramey) Phillips. Oliver and Adaline had two children, Oliver Edmund and Ella. They were born on the homestead. The patent to the homestead was issued on February 14, 1893.

When Beaver Creek School District No. 82 was organized in 1898, Oliver and James were active in choosing a site and putting up the schoolhouse with Charles Pursel and others. Oliver Edmund, age 5, was on the school census in 1899.

Oliver and Adaline Dews sold the homestead to Charles Raymond Phillips in 1901. The price was $450.00. The two water rights, one from Mule Creek and the other from Kinney Creek, were included. (Vol. 45, p. 3, Deed Records, October 26, 1902).

Oliver moved his family to Ashland, where Adaline died on July 16, 1902. She was buried in Hargadine Cemetery. In 1903, Oliver married Mrs. Hattie Jones and they moved to Klamath Falls. Oliver spent his last years in Ashland. He died on June 20, 1951, at the age of 91 and was also buried in Hargadine Cemetery which is in Ashland.

Ramey Phillips and Edna McKee were married on November 20, 1899, and two years later they were owners of the Dews ranch. Ramey farmed the place for about ten years. He sold fifty acres on the west side of the river to Cary W. Culy on November 12, 1910. Cary's wife, Verna, and Ramey's wife, Edna, were sisters, daughters of A. D. (Deb) McKee. This transaction was within the family.

Cary and Verna McKee were married in 1905. They raised four children on this ranch: Helen, Louis, Omar and Leora.

Cary built a board and batten type house for his family across the fields close to the hill. His barn and corrals were nearby. He planted the main field to alfalfa, cultivating the top soil carefully to avoid rocks and stumps. With adequate irrigation, the alfalfa produced a good quantity of hay for his own beef cattle.

There was no road up the west side until later years. The river had to be forded, so a swinging bridge was built for foot traffic. After automobiles came into use, Cary built a garage near the bridge on the east side of the river. It was about one fourth mile walk to the house. The children went to Beaver Creek School through the eighth grade. Helen married Ernest McIntyre. They had children whose names were Russel, Ronald and Luella. They lived in Jacksonville.

Louis married Rosalie Madsen. Their children were Lucille, Charles and Mary Lou. Louis worked for the County Road Department for many years. Omar married a nurse. They had no children. Omar was also a County Road Department employee until his retirement in the 1970s. Leora attended Central Point High School and Southern Oregon Normal School in Ashland, then she taught school for about thirty years. She was married to Edward Pease. They had an adopted daughter whom they named Sonja.

137

After their children left home, Cary and Verna sold the ranch and retired to Jacksonville in the 1940s. Subsequent owners of the ranch include Gail Buffington, Bruce Merickel and W. E. Chinn. The acreage on the east side of the river was farmed by Edward and Viola Finley. The house was near the road but the barn was some distance away against the hillside. In 1989 the barn is still there, but the house has been removed. The fields are being farmed by new owners.

THE DORN FAMILY

The next settler up the river past Oliver Dews' was William Fredrick Dorn. He was a miner who came to the area in the 1870s. He had a wife, Annie, and one son, David, born in 1878. In 1887 he entered into an agreement with Henry Klippel and the Squaw Lake Mining Company to acquire 20 acres of mining ground near the mouth of Water Gulch. He made a home on this claim and became owner of additional land for a small farm (Book A, p. 541, Miscellaneous Records, June 14, 1887). Five more children were born to William and Annie Dorn during the next twenty years. These were: Frederick William (Fred), Laura, Caroline (Carrie), Addie and Ernest. They attended Squaw Lake (Watkins) School District No. 68 in the 1890s. Carrie died in 1902 at the age of fifteen and was buried in Logtown Cemetery. Addie was married to William Louden on August 15, 1910. (F. W.) Fred married Bessie D. Lewis on February 8, 1904. They made their home on the family ranch. They had one son, Billy, who left the area after he grew up. After his father, William, died in 1930, Fred inherited the place. David Dorn purchased part of the James M. Dews ranch from E. D. Stephenson in 1914. He never married and lived there many years. He served as supervisor of the area road district. In later years he moved to Jacksonville where he operated a wood yard. He died in 1956 and was buried in Logtown Cemetery.

About a mile on up the river (south) was the mouth of French Gulch where Pat Swayne had his second ranch. Subsequent owners of this property were Jennie Barr (1930s) and A. R. Street (1950s).

SQUAW CREEK AND SQUAW LAKES

The next tributary up stream (south) on the east side of the river is Squaw Creek. This stream is about six miles long and drains many square miles of steep, rugged country. At the headwaters of the creek are two lakes, one much larger than the other. They are called Squaw Lakes from the days when the Indians camped and fished there. These lakes may be considered man-made in a way, because the dam was raised in order to impound more water for irrigation. The land around the lakes was taken up by homesteaders and the area became popular for camping and fishing in the early years.

There was a group of homesteaders who took up land on both sides of the Applegate River in the area of Squaw Creek and lower Carberry Creek. They were: Mark Watkins, Oscar Freeman Collings, Terrence Byrne, John Harr, Sylvester Arrasmith, Ed Langley, Ezra Arnold and others.

THE WATKINS FAMILY

Mark Watkins was an Englishman who came to Jackson County in the 1850s. He was born in 1831 and was about 26 years old when he arrived. He took up mining along the Upper Applegate River. On April 3, 1876, he married Martha Maria Langley, who was the daughter of neighboring miner, Edward Langley. Their children were: Mark Anthony (1899) and Robert (after 1900). He took up a homestead and built a house for his family on the west side of the river. The patent was issued December 28, 1889. (Vol. 23, p. 358, Deed Records). He acquired other lands in the area, where he carried on mining and farming, as his family grew up.

In 1891, Mark cooperated with other settlers to organize a school district, which was first called Squaw Lake District No. 68. The other settlers were: Oscar F. Collings, William Dorn, Sylvester Arrasmith, Sanford Carter, Newton Haskins and Mrs. M. Silva. Within a year or so the name of the district was changed to Watkins No. 68.

A post office called Watkins was established on March 25, 1893, with Mark Watkins as postmaster. He operated this office in his house. He served eight years (see Chapter 10).

The Watkins children attended the Watkins School and grew up on the ranch. Anthony was the first to marry. He married Polly (Winningham) Bond on November 29, 1912. They lived on part of the Watkins property at the mouth of Carberry Creek. He built a large two-story hewed log house, barn and other buildings. Polly was unfortunate in her childbearing. She lost two babies while she was married to Robert Bond and two by Anthony. One son, Guy, grew up and remained at home. He never married. Anthony,

Guy's father, died in 1930 and Polly lived until 1937. They were both buried in Logtown Cemetery.

Pearl Watkins married Vernie Stephenson. They moved to Butte Falls, where they raised a family.

THE WINNINGHAM FAMILY

Mamie Watkins was married to James B. Winningham Jr. on December 31, 1915, in Jacksonville. He was born on Trail Creek in the Upper Rogue area, April 21, 1892. His parents James B. and Mary Jane (Hatten) came to Jackson County in the 1860s. They had four small children, John J., Almira (Almeda), Mark and Calvin. Seven more children were born on the Upper Rogue

The hewed log house built by Anthony Watkins for his family. Left to right: Anthony Watkins, wife Polly, woman in white unknown, Martha in chair holding Helden Smith, Albert Collings. (Author collection)

homestead: Sallie A., Martha J., Pollie, Jemima, Ella, Pearl, and James B. (Jim).

In 1900 Mary Jane was a widow and was living on Forest Creek. With her was son John and the three youngest children, Ella, Pearl and James. Her son Mark had a wife, Nancy, and four small children: Mary, Meada, Robert and William. Calvin and his wife had a baby named Vernie. They formed a family group. The men were all miners. The children attended Forest Creek School from 1898 until 1904.

Soon after Jim and Mamie were married, he went to work in the Blue Ledge Mine. For some years they made their home wherever Jim had work. He joined the Forest Service in 1929 and stayed until his retirement in 1952. During 1944, Jim and Mamie were fire lookouts atop 5,023-foot elevation Tallowbox Mountain. The mountain is 16 miles southwest of Medford and 4 miles south of Applegate in the Siskiyous. Mamie continued as summer lookout until 1948. The Oregon State Forestry Department continues to man Tallowbox to the present time during fire seasons.

In the 1920s Mamie was postmaster at Copper, Oregon. They had two daughters, Valera and Dorothy. Dorothy was married twice and had several children. She left the area. Valera married a man named Merrit and had a daughter named Eugena. In later years, Valera married Chester McDonough of Ruch.

Jim and Mamie spent their retirement years in a small home at Ruch. She died in 1974. Jim made his home with daughter Dorothy until his death in 1976. They were both buried in Logtown Cemetery.

THE COLLINGS FAMILY

Oscar Freeman Collings came to Oregon in a wagon train in 1852 at age 23. He worked in the mines until he took up a homestead near the mouth of Squaw Creek in the 1870s. He married Sophia Lewis on February 10, 1878. They had seven boys and one girl between 1880 and 1896. They were: Albert, John, Mary, George, Francis (Frank), Zebulon, Walter and Oscar. The children all attended Watkins School, where, among other things, the boys learned to play baseball. One of them, Frank, got into professional baseball and was also a professional boxer. After years of travel and various types of work, Frank returned to live near his father's homestead in 1932. His wife, Mary, died in 1968. His brother Albert and wife Alma had an adjoining ranch for several years. Frank lived to celebrate his one hundredth birthday on August 13, 1986, in Jacksonville. The Collings family are remembered by Collings Mountain near the old homestead, which was named for them.

SYLVESTER ARRASMITH

Among the miners who worked along the Upper Applegate in the Squaw Creek area were Sylvester Arrasmith and his brother Ira. They came to Jackson County in the 1870s. Sylvester had a wife and two daughters. The girls were Anna, age two, and Harriet, age four, in 1880.

He purchased a forty-acre parcel of school lands from the State of Oregon in 1887 for $80.00. Two years later he purchased another eighty acres of school lands adjoining his forty. The price was $100.00. (Vol. 14, p. 480, and Vol. 25, p. 597, Deed Records). Children born on this place were: Matilda (1881), Irene (1889), Lavinia (1892) and Willie (1896). They all attended the Watkins School and were on the census until 1914. The ranch was later owned by Mark Watkins, Sophia Collings, Frank Collings and Albert Collings.

THE BYRNE FAMILY

Terrence P. Byrne was an Irishman who brought his family to the Applegate in the late 1880s. He and his wife, Katie, and four children: Stella (1878), Carroll (Carl) (1880), Maude (1883) and John (1887). Katie, Jr. was born in 1892.

Terrence worked in the placer mines on Forest Creek in 1893 and 1894. The children attended Forest Creek School. He moved to the Squaw Creek area and filed on a 160-acre homestead adjoining Sylvester Arrasmith. He proved up on the homestead and the patent was issued on December 17, 1900. (Vol. 43, p. 424, Deed Records). The children attended Watkins School. Terrence served as a director on the school board. When John and Carroll were in about the fifth grade, they were sent to board with the O'Brien family and attend the Applegate School. Stella Byrne was married to Emmet O'Brien in 1902, then they moved to California. Maude married Frank H. Watson in 1910. They also moved to California. Carroll Byrne was killed in a quarry explosion just outside Jacksonville on June 6, 1912. He was one of four men who died in this disaster. It was reported that a drilling crew made a mistake and the dynamite went off prematurely. Four other men in the quarry were seriously injured. The coroner's jury verdict was that unskilled workmen and company negligence caused the accident. (For detail refer to *Siskiyou Sites and Sagas*.)

Terrence Byrne died in 1904 and John took over the ranch, operating it for his mother. His sister, Katie, lived at home until 1914 when she married Floyd McKee. They had one daughter, Florence. After John and Pearl McKee were married in 1914, they made their home on the ranch. His mother went to California to live near her daughter Stella. Katie followed her and died at the home of her mother from complications following tonsil surgery.

John and Pearl left the ranch about 1920. They had a daughter, Aletha, who died in childhood. Morris was born in 1916, Gladys in 1918, and Evelyn in 1926. John worked in a mill in Medford until 1930. They moved back to the Applegate, where Lee Port hired him to work for the Forest Service. He was to remain with this job until his retirement in 1970. Evelyn and Clarence Williams retired to a home on Palmer Creek Road, and Pearl Byrne lives nearby in 1989.

THE HARR FAMILY

In 1901 a new family moved to a ranch on Squaw Creek. They were John and Louise Harr, with their son, Bert, and two daughters, Maude and Grace. They were originally from Nebraska, where Maude was born in 1886. George Bert was born in Wyoming (1889) and Grace in California (1891). They came to Jackson County in 1894 and settled in the Willow Springs area west of Central Point. John Harr bought a few cattle and they spent one year at Flounce Rock about 1899. He wintered his cattle at Fort Klamath where there was an ample supply of hay. The next year, 1900, Harr purchased the ranch on Squaw Creek. At this time Maude was 13 years old, Bert was 10 and Grace was 8. They attended Watkins School. Maude graduated from the eighth grade in 1902. She stayed in Jacksonville and finished the two-year high school course in 1904. She wanted to become a nurse, but her parents persuaded her to take teachers' training in Ashland. She received her teaching certificate and was hired to teach her first school at Steamboat in 1905. It was a three-month summer term. She lived at home with her parents and rode a horse over the Collings Mountain trail to school every day. This was the beginning of about fifteen years of teaching, mostly at Beaver Creek, Watkins and Steamboat. She was at Laurelhurst on the

Upper Rogue River and it was there she met her future husband, Frank Ditsworth. She was hired by Central Point Schools in 1909 and taught there for ten years. She and Frank Ditsworth were married on June 9, 1920, then went to make their home on his ranch in the Laurelhurst area on the Upper Rogue River. The Ditsworth ranch was purchased by the Government for the Lost Creek Dam on the Rogue River. Frank and Maude retired to a home in Ashland in 1972.

Grace Harr married Ervin Lewis September 6, 1914. They had one son, Dow. Ervin had grown up in the Beaver Creek area. He was the son of Newton Lewis. Grace and Ervin lived most of their lives in the area. In later years Grace married Gerald Buck and they lived on a place adjoining her parents on Squaw Creek.

Bert Harr grew up helping his father on the ranch. He took up a 40-acre homestead of his own adjoining Mark Watkins along the river upstream from the mouth of Squaw Creek. He met his future wife, Christine Beaver, in 1911 when she came to teach at Watkins School. Her parents lived in Ashland. Her father, John Martin Beaver, was a minister. They came to Ashland in 1910 when Christine was 19 years old. She took a teachers' training course at Van Scoy's Preparatory School and received her teaching certificate. She stayed with the Harr family the year she taught at Watkins. She taught at North Phoenix and Valley View Schools and one more year at Watkins. Bert Harr and Christine Beaver were married in Ashland on April 5, 1914. He jokingly told everyone he had caught a Beaver. He was a great joker and story teller all his life. Two children were born to them, John and Louise. John became a teacher. Louise married James Allen from Alabama where they made their home for many years. Eventually they moved back to the Ruch area.

In the 1960s Bert established a resort at Squaw Lake. The Game Commission agreed to stock the lake with fish if Bert would put in a free parking lot for a certain number of cars. The site chosen was the barn lot of an old homestead. During the leveling activity with a bulldozer a cache of gold coins worth several hundred dollars was uncovered. Several people picked up twenty dollar gold coins from the area with latest mint date 1882. Eventually Bert gave up the resort. The Forest Service acquired the land in 1971, removed the buildings and maintains the area as a natural recreation site.

Christine served as a volunteer weather observer for the Medford Weather Bureau for over thirty years. She was active in local school affairs, and served on the school board. She and Bert were charter members of Upper Applegate Grange.

When plans for the Applegate Dam became a reality, they sold their ranch to the Government. They spent their retirement years near Ruch. Bert died in 1974. Christine died December 6, 1976, age 84. They were buried in Jacksonville Cemetery.

ED LANGLEY

A miner who came to Jackson County before 1860 was Edward Langley, an Englishman. He mined on Kanaka Flats west of Jacksonville. He married Nancy Weakerer in 1859 and their daughter Martha Maria was born at Kanaka Flats June 15, 1860. By 1871, Ed Langley was living near the mouth of Squaw Creek and married Betsy (Bessie) Lewis. They lived in the area over 20 years. He was active in helping build the Watkins School. In 1893 he was elected to serve as director on the school board. In 1908 Ed gave part of his property to his step-daughter, Sophia Collings. He signed the deed with his mark. (Vol. 68, p. 45, Deed Records). His wife Bessie died in 1888. Ed died in 1913. They were both buried in Collings Cemetery. In 1980, eight graves from this cemetery were moved to Logtown Cemetery when the Applegate Dam was under construction. Among them were Edward and Bessie Langley.

THE HASKINS FAMILY

Near the mouth of Beaver Creek on the Upper Applegate Road is a large, well-built log house below the road overlooking the river. This house was built in 1935 by Wallace Haskins for himself and his wife, Bertha. She was a teacher from Illinois. Wallace met her in her home town of Pekin, Illinois, while serving in the army about 1923. They were married in 1924 and he brought her to Oregon to meet his family. She soon had a teaching position near Ashland. Wallace was a carpenter who had a special skill with the use of logs and poles. He learned these skills on the Haskins homestead on the Applegate where he grew up. His grandfather, William H. Haskins, came to Jackson County in the 1860s with his wife, Jeanette, and nine children. They were: Newton, Annette, John, Josephine, William Jr., Mary, Jennette, Gertrude and Valoris. William Haskins was a blacksmith. His son, Newton, married Arzie Saltmarsh on October 15, 1877. They had seven children. Only four lived to adulthood: Wallace, Isalena, Oren and Christina. They attended Watkins School from 1893 until 1910. Other members of William Haskins' family who lived in the

Wallace Haskins, a man with special skills for building log houses, constructed this one for his family in 1936. Photographed in 1989 by the author.

Watkins district include John, who married Lilly Saltmarsh; William, who married Eliza Jennings; and Valoris, who married Etta Jones.

Wallace and Bertha returned to Illinois in 1931 where she taught in the Peoria County schools until 1935. They moved back to Oregon and the Applegate Valley, where he built the log house, and they entered into the life of the community with enthusiasm. She was hired to teach the Beaver Creek School in the fall of 1935. Her teaching career in the schools of the county was to continue another twenty-five years. Wallace worked at carpentry and was much in demand for rustic type construction. Wallace and Bertha had no children of their own, but they had many devoted friends among her students and their families. She died in 1961. Wallace outlived her by several years.

THE NEWTON LEWIS FAMILY

Isaac Newton Lewis and his wife, Ella, lived in the Beaver Creek area in the 1890s. His parents arrived in Jackson County in the 1860s with four children. There were James H., John F., Isaac N. and Ruthabel. By 1898, Newton and Ella Lewis had seven children: Henry Ervin, Ollie May, Bessie (Rosa), Elmer, Orpha, Trueman and Lydia. They grew up in the area and attended Beaver Creek School. Lydia married George Pursel on November 1, 1919. They made their home at Pursel's mill on Yale Creek. Orpha married Fort McKee on December 23, 1915. He died after a brief illness in 1917. Trueman married Lena Arnold on August 8, 1919. They lived in the Beaver Creek area until about 1930.

SANFORD CARTER—EZRA ARNOLD

Two more families remain on the records as early settlers in the Watkins district, Sanford Carter and Ezra Arnold.

Sanford Carter came to the area in the 1870s with his wife Sarah and three small children, Oliver, Danny and John. He took up a homestead at Squaw Lake, but he did complete the proving up on it. The children, who attended Watkins School from 1893 to 1897, were: Danny, John, Milton, Charles and Claude. Some time in the next two years they moved to Forest Creek where Sanford and the older boys worked in the mines. Sanford and Sarah had eight children but only four lived to adulthood. Those buried in Logtown Cemetery were Claude, John, Sarah and Sanford. There is no record of their death dates but it was after 1900.

Ezra Arnold was born in California in 1858. On the 1870 census, he is listed as age 11 with sisters Helen, 19, and Lizzie, 14, living in the home of G. W. Stephenson. By 1880, his age was 22 and he was listed as a woodcutter. He was married to Elsie Bennett on May 7, 1891. They made their home on a homestead near Squaw Lake. Elsie had two children by a former marriage, Alex and Charles Bennett. She and Ezra had four children: Vernie (Venie) (1893), Herman (1895), Lena (1899), and Melvin (after 1900). They attended Watkins School from 1896 until 1904 and later. Melvin grew up on the home place. In 1933 he married Lucille De Wolfe. They made their home at the Arnold Mine. Their children were: Vernon, Lorraine, Joyce and Janet. Melvin worked for the Medford Corporation in Butte Falls for 18 years. He retired in 1967 to a home near Ruch. He and Lucille celebrated their fiftieth wedding anniversary in 1983.

APPLEGATE LAKE

The old homestead sites of Swayne, Harr, Watkins, Winningham, Arrasmith, Collings and the Copper Store and post office are forever preserved beneath the waters of Applegate Lake.

The problem of flood control on the Rogue River and its tributaries has been the subject of concern for over thirty years. In the 1930s a group of farmers, business people and others organized the Rogue Basin Flood Control and Water Resources Association. They carried on a persistent campaign over the long years to have a dam built on the Upper Rogue and its tributary, Elk Creek. A dam on the Applegate would complete the series and provide protection from devastating floods throughout the entire Rogue River Valley.

The Oregon delegation to Congress finally prevailed and the three-dam series was authorized in 1962. The Upper Rogue dam was built at Lost Creek during 1976-1977 and the impoundment was named Lost Creek Lake. Elk Creek Dam was started, but the environmentalists intervened. A court order was obtained to stop the project at about the half-way point. In 1989 there is no work on the dam.

A small group of vocal environmentalists carried on a negative campaign in an effort to stop the Applegate Dam project. Considerable controversy developed. Supporters of the project held a county-wide election and Congressman James Weaver promised to abide by the will of the people in his efforts to secure government financing. The vote was overwhelmingly in favor of the dam, and Weaver kept his promise. Construction began in 1978, with Peter Kiewit Sons' Company as general contractor, under the direction of the U.S. Army Corps of Engineers, Portland. The project engineers avoided some of the problems encountered at Lost Creek. All of the gravel and sand used in the dam was taken from the upper end in the river bottom. In the process of washing and grading the crushed rock, a gold recovery device was installed. The construction company was required to pay a royalty to the government on gold extracted, but was allowed to keep all the rest. No dollar amount was ever revealed publicly as to this gold salvage operation's success, but information leaked that the value was several hundred thousand dollars. Numerous individuals with small suction dredges worked the river downstream of the project. Most had limited success in recovering gold.

148

Applegate Dam blocks the flow of the Applegate River for flood protection and to maintain an even year-around flow in the river assuring good quality water even in dry summer months. The dam is 242 feet high and 1,300 feet long and is 1,994 feet in elevation (National Geodetic Vertical Datum).

Applegate Lake is 4.6 miles long and when full covers 988 acres. There are 12 campsites and viewpoints around the lake's 18-mile shoreline. A hiking trail circles the lake. This U.S. Army Corps of Engineers Project is 23 miles southwest of Medford in the Rogue River National Forest. (Photo courtesy of U.S. Army Corps of Engineers)

The dam was finished in October of 1980, a year ahead of schedule. The gates were closed on December 2, 1980, and the lake started filling. By March of 1981, it was more than half full. In April, names for the view points and the recreation areas were announced. They include Swayne Point, a viewing area, Har-Tish Park, Watkins Picnic Area, Carberry Picnic Area, Tipsu Tyee Camp, Latgawa Camp, Harr Point Camp and French Gulch Camp.

Formal dedication was held at Har-Tish Park on May 27, 1981. The speakers emphasized the purpose of the dam and its impoundment as flood control, water enhancement, irrigation, municipal water supply and recreation, especially fishery benefits. The Rogue River National Forest administers the recreation programs. The Bureau of Reclamation markets the irrigation water. The U.S. Army Corps of Engineers controls the flow of water through the system. A major storm in December 1981 put both Lost Creek and Applegate Dams to a severe test. Flood waters were contained and the rivers remained below flood stage for the first time in history. □

Applegate Lake facing south from top of Applegate Dam. (Photo by author) While this book was in final editing, these data became available. The gravel from the lake bed yeilded 4,481 Troy ounces of gold which was sold for $2,646,763.53 at prices ranging from $202.00 to $668.00/ounce. In addition, there were 589 ounces of silver which was sold for $10,824 as well as $195.00 realized from sale of quicksilver. The government received $572,010.42 with the balance going to the contractor. A separate contract for building the road around the lake, also using gravel from the lake bed, yielded around $50,000.00 in precious metals. Source, U.S. Army Corps of Engineers. Weekend amateur gold seekers continue to strike "pay dirt" in the Applegate and other rivers and streams of southern Oregon.

Chapter 8

STEAMBOAT, THOMPSON CREEK, LOWER APPLEGATE

The area known as Steamboat is about six miles up Steamboat (Carberry) Creek from the Applegate River. Miners worked along this creek in the 1860s and 1870s. Chinese miners worked the tailings after the easiest gold had been taken. Prospectors roamed the mountains searching for quartz gold locations. A promising ledge was discovered in February 1860 by William Billups and Frank Fetterman and others. The location was just below the divide between Brush Creek and Carberry Creek. It was known by two names: Applegate Quartz Mine or Steamboat Ledge. W. W. Fowler and G. W. Keeler became involved. They provided the grubstake for the miners to open the ledge and process the quartz. By June 1860, an arrastra was constructed and the first gold recovered. It was considered to be of high quality. In the first few months the amount of gold increased and an extremely rich pocket was found in February 1861. In one week the crew took out enough to pay all the previous expenses of the mine. Four new arrastras were built, along with other improvements as the mine continued to yield spectacular amounts of gold.

In November 1861, an experienced miner, Samuel Taylor, was hired as superintendent. Under his direction, during the next two years, the mine yielded about $190,000.00. With the previous yield the total was $315,000.00. There was a rival mining company owned and operated by John O'Brien of lower Applegate, who had taken up claims on the other side of the ridge from the Fowler ledge. This company took out about $25,000.00 in 1861. The Fowler Company filed a lawsuit to stop O'Brien's mining activity. After a long and expensive trial, Fowler won. A four-stamp mill was brought in and installed, but paying quantities of ore had diminished. Eventually the owners abandoned the claims. Others filed on them and continued to work and hope for several years. But not much more gold was ever found.

John O'Brien built a 13-mile ditch from a tributary of Carberry Creek to bring water to his mine. The tributary was named O'Brien Creek for him. In later years the water from his ditch was

This house owned in 1989 by Trueman Aubrey is at Steamboat. (Author photo)

diverted for irrigation to the ranches on Thompson Creek.

The mine and the mountain on which it was located were called Steamboat, which was a pioneer term for a disappointing prospect.

GEORGE C. CULY

An early settler in the Steamboat area was George C. Culy. He came from California with his wife, Permelia, and one child, Albert, about 1882. He purchased six mining claims from Jerome Epperson for $700.00 on October 1, 1883. (Vol. 10, p. 619, Deed Records). The mining claims were 20 acres per claim and were situated end to end along a fairly level stretch of the creek, which was then called Steamboat Creek. It was renamed Carberry Creek in later years. This gave George Culy 120 acres of land which he developed into a ranch. He built his house and barns near the site of a Chinese miners' camp. The Chinese miners had set out a small apple orchard, which produced fruit for many years.

George and Permelia had six more children born on this ranch: Cary William (1882), Lora (1885), Neldrett (Ned) (1889), Branch (1891), Frank (1897) and Nellie (1899). The children attended Steamboat School and grew up on the ranch. The boys worked with their father farming and raising cattle. At one time

George had 500 head of cattle and 30 head of horses on the surrounding ranges. The ranch was later owned by Ben Dawson and family. In 1989 it is still a working cattle ranch.

STEAMBOAT CEMETERY

About a mile west of the Culy ranch is a small graveyard called Steamboat Cemetery. It is the last resting place of a number of early day miners and residents. For many years it was forgotten and neglected, just a few markers among the trees by the road. In the 1950s a group of members of the Upper Applegate Grange took on the project of cleaning away the brush, restoring the markers and building a fence around it. The Forest Service cooperated by providing the fencing. A hand-carved sign was made by one of the Grange members and mounted above the gate. There are about fourteen graves most of them without markers.

Burial records include those of: Frances Scherer Scroggins, Albert Dressel, Phillip Dressel, Jace Morgan Williams, Delos Alfred Wright, James Levi Tyson, Andrew Farrier, Charles Garnett, and Frank Ortman. The earliest marker date was 1895. The most recent is 1972.

THOMPSON CREEK

About a mile west of Steamboat Cemetery, the road follows Sturgis Fork of Carberry Creek over the divide into the headwaters of Thompson Creek. This stream, about ten miles in length, flows into the Applegate River near the settlement of Applegate, on State Highway 238.

The original settler was William Thompson, who took up a Donation Land Claim in 1853 at the mouth of the creek. He held 320 acres and included the land on which the store, school and church were later established, as well as rich farm land on both sides of the river. Thompson died August 8, 1856, and was buried in Jacksonville Cemetery. His widow inherited the property. She married Legrand J. C. Duncan, administrator of Thompson's estate, on July 26, 1857. They made their home in Jacksonville, where he became County Judge, and where they lived out their lives.

The land was sold and divided among early settlers: Rial Benedict, Orlando Rose, Peter Majors, the Brown family and others.

Settlers who acquired land on upper Thompson Creek and

established ranches include: James and Thomas Mee, Henry Knutzen, William Jordan, Jasper Darnielle, James Louden, Fritz Ruch Jr., George Hoffman, Herbert Elmore and John and Marion Bingham.

Tallowbox Mountain overlooks Thompson Creek to the east. There has been a forest fire lookout station on its summit for over 50 years. The name, Tallowbox, is said to have come from a party of hunters who killed several deer to obtain tallow for candlemaking. The tallow was packed in small cedar boxes made for that purpose. As the packers had more than they could handle on one trip, they hid some of the boxes on the mountain. When they returned months later to claim their cache, the tallow had melted. While this story is plausible, it is really classed as folklore.

About six miles up Thompson Creek was a stopping place owned by two brothers, Marion T. and John Bingham. They had adjoining ranches and raised hay for beef and dairy cattle. Bingham was not a post office and there never was a store but the name persists on present day maps as a landmark from the early days.

APPLEGATE CROSSING

The original Jacksonville-Crescent City trail through Murphy and Missouri Flat was intersected by a new road built along the south side of the river in 1860. It crossed the river near the mouth of Thompson Creek on a primitive wooden bridge. The two roads joined about 500 yards from the bridge. The area was called Bridge Point.

One of the early settlers was Orlando Rose. He was a farmer who came to the Applegate in the 1860s. He had a wife and three small children. His house and barns were on the south side of the river close to the road and the approach to the bridge. He built a large two-story building with an upstairs hall where dances and other affairs were held. Rose's Hall became famous for miles in every direction. Orlando helped organize the Bridge Point School District in 1872. He was postmaster of the Applegate Post Office in 1895 at which time the post office was in his home. Eventually his property was sold and the buildings removed.

VALLEY PRIDE CREAMERY

Overlooking the river adjoining the site of Rose's Hall is a concrete and wood building which was built for a creamery in

The building that housed the Valley Pride Creamery has undergone many changes and in 1989 is a private residence. This 1987 photograph was made by author.

1912, by James F. Werth and his wife, Cecelia. Dairying was an important part of farming in the lower Applegate Valley before and during the First World War. The farmers brought their fresh milk and cream to be processed into butter and cheese, which was sold in stores around the area as well as in Medford and Grants Pass. The Werths operated the Valley Pride Creamery until 1915. Their son, Donald Robert, and daughter, Cecelia, were born during those years. Every year the Werths were hosts for a community picnic in May for the school children and their parents. In 1915, Oregon Governor James Withycombe attended the picnic. This was considered quite an honor for the local people. The governor's visit was reported in the Medford *Mail Tribune* on May 21, 1915. The Werths sold the creamery in the fall of 1915 and moved to Grants Pass. The creamery was operated by others until the late 1920s. In later years the creamery building was remodeled into a locker-freezer plant. In 1989 it is a private home.

The new 180-foot long steel bridge across the river at village of Applegate was dedicated in June 1934. Applegate Community Church sits on a bench of land just above Highway 238. (Aerial picture by Bert Webber, October 30, 1989)

THE PIONEER BRIDGE

The existing steel bridge spanning the river at Applegate is the third structure since the first one was built in 1860. The second was a covered bridge built in 1860 by Thomas Mee under contract with the Jackson County Commissioners. It was replaced by a similar bridge in 1892. This was still in use in 1934 when the 180-foot steel span was constructed a few yards downstream from the site of the old bridge. Concrete piers of the old bridge may still be seen. The steel bridge was built in four months by Mountain States Construction Company of Eugene at a cost of $32,806.00.

The dedication ceremony was held on Saturday, June 23, 1934. Honored in the program were all of the old settlers of the area who were able to attend. Mrs. Louisa Ray, 87, was chosen to cut the ribbon, formally opening the bridge to traffic. There were two speakers, Dr. Arthur Taylor of Southern Oregon Normal School, Ashland, and C. E. (Pop) Gates of Medford, who was a member of the State Highway Commission. Music was provided by a brass band from Grants Pass and there was community singing. The activities closed with a dance at the Applegate Grange Hall.

A committee of local people raised money to have a plaque made which was installed, free, on the bridge by the State Highway Commission. The plaque reads: Pioneer Bridge. Dedicated to the Pioneers of Applegate Valley, 1934. (Medford *Mail Tribune*, May 21, 1934.)

APPLEGATE STORE

The first store in the area was a temporary trading post operated by W. W. Fowler and his partner, G. W. Keeler, in the 1860s. Another store was established by William W. (Billy) Pernoll on his homestead on the north side road in the 1870s. He had already been in southern Oregon about fifteen years. He was a member of the 9th Regiment of the Oregon Militia and was involved in the trouble with the Indians. After the war, he acquired land on Williams Creek where he farmed until 1874. About this time he moved to a homestead two miles west of Applegate Crossing on the north side. Here he built a frame house and a small store building of hewed square logs. He stocked a supply of basic grocery items, clothing, shoes, hardware, drugs and whiskey. A priceless old photograph shows the buildings, with a sign over the entrance reading, Grang (Grange) Store. He was involved with an early Josephine County Grange, which may be why he called it the

At the Applegate Store in 1931. There was a Grange project for re-seeding grass following the Humbug Creek and China Gulch forest fires. The sacked grass on the Ford truck was *poa bulboea* donated by grower Charley Hoover. Pictured are: Walter Miller (on truck hood), man in front of truck not identified, Jack O'Brien (by wheel), Sid Hansen, (unidentified), Glenn Smith, Charles Elmore, Bernard Andren, Rita Kubli, Clara O'Brien Smith, Charley Hoover (in business suit), Lou Hansen, Edward Kubli and son Norman, John Pernoll (wearing bow tie), Ed Hawkins, Sid Hansen owned the truck. (Picture from Charles Elmore collection)

Grange Store.

In 1876, Billy married Nancy Miller and they had eight children. Seven of them lived to adulthood: John, Martin, Lydia, Myra, Maude, Henry and Alice. They attended Applegate School as they grew up on the ranch. Lydia married Bert Clute. Maude married John B. Herriott, Martin married Bernice Quimby, Myra never married. They left to start homes of their own. John remained to help his father operate the ranch and the store. During the 1890s the business was moved to a new location on the corner which was formed by the intersection of the road to Wilderville and the road to the house of O. E. Rose. The deed records show that John Pernoll purchased a 60-foot square of land on this corner on December 13, 1900. There was also another lot 100 by 200 feet,

Pernoll's store is going home. Billy Pernoll's store in which son John helped with the operations. After a new building was put up, the old store was used for general ranch storage. George McUne acquired it then rebuilt it when he moved it to his Pioneer Village in Jacksonville. In 1989, the Applegate Valley Historical Society has been incorporated and plans to move the historic building back to a site in the Applegate community. (Author photo in 1989)

adjoining it to the west. (Vol. 42, p. 11). On the corner lot, John built a typical western-style board and batten store building with a porch across the front. It was opened and ready for business in the fall of 1901. When John was appointed postmaster, the post office was located in the store. It was a busy and popular place. In 1912, John built a large comfortable frame house on the lot adjoining the store. He married a local school teacher, Laura (Lora) May Couch, on September 18, 1920. They had one son, John Jr. John and Laura operated the store until John's death in 1938. She kept the business open until illness forced her retirement in 1953.

In 1947, Edward Kubli and his son, Norman, acquired property across the road from Pernoll's Store and built a modern store building. They installed gas pumps and limited automotive service. They cleared the land between the store and the river and developed a park and picnic area. It took advantage of a swimming hole in the river nearby. It was called Applegate

Wayside. Edward turned the park over to Jackson County Parks Department for several years. Eventually it was returned to private ownership. Edward Kubli's store changed hands numerous times in the following years. As of 1989, it is known as Applegate Shopping Center. There is a post office substation, a branch library, a lunch counter, a grocery store and gas pumps.

John Pernoll's store building has been removed but in 1989 his house is still standing in good condition. William Pernoll's little log store building is still in existence also, but its future is uncertain. After the new store was built, the log building was put to other use on the Pernoll ranch. Gradually it deteriorated over the years. In the early 1960s, George McUne of Jacksonville was establishing a tourist attraction in Jacksonville, which he called

Pernoll's Store, Applegate, Orgon, early 1900s. Original print given to Jack O'Brien by John Pernoll. (O'Brien collection)

Pioneer Village. He acquired the log building from Bert Clute, who then owned the Pernoll ranch. George took the logs apart one by one, hauled them to Jacksonville and put them back together in his Village. The displays he used in it were authentic and impressive. Pioneer Village was a popular place for over 25 years. In October 1985, the McUne family closed the Village and sold off the buildings and collections in a three-day public auction. The log store building was acquired by the Southern Oregon Historical Society through the generosity of Don Rowlett of the Box R Ranch.

In 1989, the Applegate Valley Historical Society is making plans to return this log building to a site at Applegate for a museum. The Southern Oregon Historical Society has donated the structure and is assisting with legal details of the transfer. William Pernoll's log store is going home.

THE COMMUNITY HALL

On a lot to the south between Pernoll's Store and the river, there was for many years a large board and batten building called the Community Hall. The history of this hall goes back to the first World War. A so-called Socialist Party was organized in the area. This group raised money in the neighborhood and built a meeting hall. It was not a very successful organization and they disbanded in the early 1920s. Three local men, Chester Kubli, Warren Mee and Bert Clute, decided to buy the hall and donate it to the school district for meetings and programs. They organized a Community League which raised money to help pay for the hall. All kinds of activities were held, dances being the most popular. Eventually the school board returned the ownership of the hall to the Community League. The League then gave it over to the Applegate Grange, which organized about 1927. Popularity of the hall continued until the Grange membership declined to a point where the building was no longer needed. They surrendered their Charter in 1955. By then the old building was so dilapidated it was falling apart so it was dismantled. In 1989 all that remains is a vacant lot overgrown with trees and bushes.

APPLEGATE COMMUNITY CHURCH

On the hill overlooking the store, the highway and the river, is the Applegate Community Church. This church was established in 1946 by the Reverend Earl Book, who organized a congregation with ties to the Assembly of God. In 1951 he was succeeded by the Reverend Thornton S. Gapen, who launched a community-wide money raising campaign for a new building. The result, after a few years, is a handsome building with a wing for Sunday School and other activities. Rev. Gapen retired in 1982. The Reverend Kenneth Schubert came in 1980 as assistant pastor. In 1989, now as pastor, he continues his service in the non-denominational church and in the community.

THE BENEDICT FAMILY

The settler who purchased the William Thompson Donation Land Claim was Rial (Royal, Ariel) Benedict. He paid $3,000.00 in gold coin for the 320 acres. The deal was dated January 9, 1871. (Vol. 5, p. 247, Deed Records). He was born in New York State in 1824 and came to Oregon the first time in 1842 where he operated a hotel and stopping place in the Willamette Valley. In 1854 he was in the Applegate Crossing area for a brief time, but returned to Illinois. Again he made the long journey to Oregon, arriving in Applegate Valley in 1859. With him was his nephew, Orlando Rose. Rial built a large house, barn and other buildings about one mile east of the intersection of the North Side Road and the Jacksonville-Crescent City Road. He married Mary Cougle and they opened their home to travelers as a stopping place. Mary died in 1880, and Rial lived with the S. R. Taylor family for a time. He married Louisa Knight of Josephine County. She had a child by a former marriage. Two children were born to Rial and Louisa, Fred and Anna. Anna married Thomas H. Mansfield on December 15, 1907. They made their home on a part of the Benedict place near the school. Fred married Marie Winetrout of Thompson Creek. Fred inherited the home place and they lived there many years. They had two daughters, Carolyn and Georgia. Some time after Fred died, the house was destroyed by fire. It was never rebuilt. Marie sold the ranch and the new owner built a house on the hill overlooking the fields and the river. The barn and other buildings were removed. All that marks the site in 1989 is a huge oak tree by the former yard gate.

THE HERRIOT FAMILY

Adjoining the Benedict ranch, across the road to the northeast, was the property of William Herriot. He was a miner who had mining claims on Carberry Creek in the 1860s. He obtained more land on Thompson Creek in the 1870s. He was a blacksmith who used this skill to build and operate small sawmills in the area. After he was settled on his homestead, he built a dance hall about 1876. This was known as Herriot's Hall. The exact location has not been determined but it was in the neighborhood of his home. William married Amanda Knox, daughter of Thomas Knox of Josephine County. They had a total of twelve children: Minerva, Ida, Katie, Thomas, Edward, Anna, George, Louis, Lola, Nellie, John and Benjamin. They all lived to adulthood in the area except Louis. William helped organize the Bridge Point School District. His hall was the scene of several fund raising dances. The proceeds were to buy furniture and supplies for the school. They eventually married and left to start their own homes except George, who remained on the ranch. He raised hops during the 1930s. He married Laura Darnielle. They had three children: Karl, Eldon and Genevieve. Karl married Daisy Wagner. Their descendants still live on part of the old place. William Herriot died in 1898 but his wife, Amanda, lived until 1908. They are buried beside Edward, George, John and Laura in the Missouri Flat Cemetery.

HUMBUG CREEK

This tributary of the Applegate River flows south about five miles and enters the river on the Thompson Donation Land Claim. Humbug Creek was the scene of much early day mining, but as the gold gave out, farming took over. Between the two occupations, some claim farming was the toughest, but nearly always, weather permitting, there would be favorable results come harvest. Mining, especially working the creeks, was considered back-breaking work with all the bending over. In mining there were rewards almost instantly in the pan, or sometimes no reward at all.

Two of the largest ranches were operated by Herman Walters and the Pittock family. In 1931, a disastrous fire destroyed the forests of pine and fir timber. Some trees and brush eventually grew back over the burned area. In 1989 the old ranches are subdivided and there are many rural residences along the creek.

KUBLI AND BOLT STORE

During the 1870s and 1880s the most important supply center between Applegate Crossing and Jacksonville was the Kubli and Bolt Store. It was located about two miles east of the crossing on the Jacksonville-Crescent City Road. The owner of the site was

Kasper Kubli, a Swiss immigrant who had taken up the land in 1852. He built a two-story frame house on the north side of the road with barns and corrals nearby. The store was in a separate building closer to the road. It had a porch but no false front. As soon as the fields began to produce grain, Kasper purchased and installed a small water-powered mill. Water was supplied by a ditch from the river. It was in use for many years grinding livestock feed and to run a grindstone to sharpen sickles. The waterwheel and a shed stood until the 1970s. Kasper was married to Elinor (Ellen) Newcomb on December 27, 1857. He had come across the plains to Oregon in the same wagon train as the Newcomb family and they were well-acquainted.

Kasper and Ellen had five children live to adulthood: Ellen (Ella), Henry D., Kasper Jr., Louise, and Valine. Two daughters died in childhood.

Kasper Kubli's partner in the store was John Bolt. He was a miner who arrived in Josephine County in the 1860s. He soon became a packer then started a store at Kerbyville. He began to acquire an interest in mining claims from miners who couldn't pay their bills. He sold these claims at a profit and became a well-known promoter and dealer in all kinds of properties. He moved to Wilderville, then to Jerome Prairie where he lived several years. Bolt Mountain in that area was named for him.

In the early 1870s John Bolt acquired a ranch on lower Humbug Creek and brought his family there to live. He had a wife and children: George, Laura, Emma and Lucy. John, Fredrick and Florence were born on the Humbug ranch. Eric and Edward were born after the family moved away in 1885. The Applegate Post Office was located in the store from 1868 to 1871. Kasper Kubli was postmaster. (See Chapter 10.)

The store was operated jointly by Kasper and John until about 1878 when Kasper and Ellen moved to Jacksonville so their children could attend high school. Bolt took charge of the store and continued to carry on numerous land deals in the area for several years. Kasper's son, Henry, returned to take over the store and the ranch when Bolt left.

John Bolt and his family moved to the Gold Hill area, where he opened a store at the mouth of Foots Creek. A post office named Bolt was established on November 11, 1885, with John Bolt as postmaster. The post office was active until December 26, 1896.

Kasper and Ellen lived out their lives in Jacksonville. With his bride, Maude (Cameron), Henry settled into his father's house in

1887. He was appointed postmaster at Applegate that year. The post office was moved back to the store. Henry served as postmaster until 1885 when the store was closed. Four children were born on the ranch. These were Chester (1889), Harold (1894), Edith (1899) and Edward (1902). They grew up and attended Applegate School. They all went to high school. Edith and Edward went on to college. Edith became a teacher.

Henry Kubli was elected to the Oregon House of Representatives in 1906 and served two terms. He was on the school board of the Applegate School when the brick building was put up in 1910. He died a few weeks before it was finished and dedicated. He was honored for his leadership and dedication to the community.

Chester and Harold took over operation of the ranch after their father's death. Eventually they married and moved to homes of their own. Edward married Reta Ray of Ruch in 1922. They made their home on the ranch and operated a dairy for several years. They had one son, Norman. Maude died in 1952.

The ranch was sold and the historic house taken down. The remains of the water-powered mill were removed and its location is overgrown with blackberry bushes. A new modern house was built in the 1950s. A subsequent owner was Roy Kabat who operated an exotic animal facility for a few years. This grew into a training school for Dogs for the Deaf. In 1988, Dogs for the Deaf moved to Sams Valley. One old barn remains at the site of the once-important Kubli and Bolt Store.

EDWARD W. KUBLI

When his brothers, Chester and Harold, left the ranch to live and work elsewhere, Edward took over the ranch and operated it a few years. He was an enthusiastic cattleman. He helped organize the local Cattlemen's Association and served as president several terms. During the 1930s and 1940s he was a state cattle brand inspector. His wife, Reta, died in 1973.

He was an early member of the Southern Oregon Historical Society and served on the board of directors during the time that the museum was developed in the former County Court House in Jacksonville. In later years, he retired from ranching and became a real estate broker specializing in ranches. He was married to Mabel (Mae) Dobbins and they made their home on the Applegate Brangus Ranch near the old home place for several years. After two years of failing health, he died January 1, 1985.

EDITH KUBLI SCOTT

After she received her teacher's certificate, Edith taught a few years in the local schools then she moved to California where she taught school for many years. She was married to Loren Scott on March 5, 1925, in Chico. They returned to the Applegate Valley about 1962 where they built a home overlooking the river on an acreage of the original Kubli ranch. Loren Scott died in 1972. Edith had one son, Chester Lind, who was a teacher in California. He had two sons. Chester returned to the Applegate and was with his mother during her final illness. Edith died July 11, 1987, the last of her generation.

THE O'BRIEN FAMILY

Less than a mile east of the Kubli ranch was a 320-acre Donation Land Claim filed on by John O'Brien who arrived in Oregon on or about October 1, 1852. Records show that he settled on the claim September 23, 1853. He came from Galloway County, Ireland, and was 26 years of age.

The mining boom in Jacksonville and surrounding mountains was just getting underway. John joined the miners on the Upper Applegate and took up claims in the Steamboat area. Even though he lost a major suit and his claims to the rival Fowler mining company, he saved enough money to start improvements on his Donation Land Claim which was on both sides of the river. He married Sarah Barkdull of Williams Creek on March 9, 1862. He built a two-story frame house, barns and other buildings on the north side of the road. His U.S. citizenship was granted on February 7, 1865. An orchard was set out. Then he built a dryer for fruit. He raised hogs in large numbers, selling hams and bacon to the miners. Children born to John and Sarah were: Edward, Robert E. (Emmett), John Jr., James, and Rose. Two more daughters were born in the 1880s, Maud and Anna. James married Flora Offenbacher on December 16, 1897. Emmett married Stella Byrne on January 16, 1902, and Rose married Marshall Baldwin on March 12, 1904. They all made their homes on or near the home place for a few years.

In 1899, John O'Brien lost his life trying to cross the river on horseback carrying a sack of grain in front of him. The horse lost its footing and went down. It was several days before they found John's body. Emmett took over the ranch and operated it for a while. After his marriage, he and his wife moved to California.

166

James (Jim) and Flora had two children, John (Jack) and Beatrice. They attended Applegate School and Medford High School. Jack attended a technical school in California and worked several years. When the big house was destroyed by fire, a new modern bungalow house was built about one fourth mile east of the old site. In 1989 this house is still standing, in good condition. Jack returned to the Applegate and married Clara McKee in 1922. They had one son, Donald. Jack had a small house built across the road from his family. The marriage failed. Both Jack and Clara later remarried but to different spouses. After his mother died in 1942, Jack and his second wife, Harriet, moved into his father's house across the road and took full operation of the ranch. He established a Grade A dairy and had it for twelve years. Then he changed to beef cattle. Jim died in 1956. Jack operated the ranch until 1972 when he sold out and retired to a mobile home park on Thompson Creek Road. Subsequent owners operate a dairy and cattle ranch to the present day.

THE OFFENBACHER FAMILY

The next ranch to the east of O'Brien's is Offenbacher's. They were not covered-wagon pioneers. Valentine Offenbacher brought his wife, Kate, and family to America from Germany in 1881. They came across the country by train, then north from Redding, California, by stage. They had four sons and one daughter. They left Germany to escape compulsory military service for the boys. The boys were: Charles, John, Henry, and Fred, and the daughter was Florentina (Flora). After they arrived in Oregon, Herman was born in 1882 and Walter in 1885. Valentine died in 1885 at the age of 42. His widow, Kate, became head of the household. They were a thrifty, hard-working family. In 1898, Henry, John and Fred jointly purchased the 320-acre George Long Donation Land Claim. Long settled his claim in September 1853, soon after he arrived in Jackson County. He cleared and developed the large acreage into productive farm fields. Other owners further improved it by obtaining water rights and constructing irrigation ditches from Applegate Creek.

The Offenbacher brothers purchased the Long claim on contract from George Neuber for $3,000 (Vol. 33, p. 381, Deed Records, January 15, 1898. Two years later Henry sold his interest to John and Fred for $2,000. (Vol. 4, p. 307, Deed Records, August 9, 1900). Henry moved to Klamath Falls, where he lived for many years.

Home of Fred Offenbacher, early 1900s. This is at 10800 Highway 238 between Ruch and Applegate. Pictured: Beatrice O'Brien, Carrie Cameron Offenbacher (mother), Leon, Lance, Fred (father). (Author collection)

Offenbacher place, remodeled, in 1989. (Author photo)

Fred Offenbacher had a large two-story house built close to the road across from Long Gulch. A similar house was built for John on an acreage adjoining the O'Brien ranch. This house was eventually destroyed by fire and a modern house was built on the same site. Fred brought his bride, Carrie Cameron, to live on his ranch in 1901. Their children, Leon, Lance, and Catherine, grew up, married and established homes of their own. In 1989 the original Fred Offenbacher house is still standing in good condition.

Lance married Stella Layton on September 24, 1924. Their children were Walter, Wesley and Rosella. They farmed on the Upper Applegate, but eventually returned to make their home on part of the original ranch. Leon married Lola Huber, and their children were Elvis, and Leroy (Dutch).

CHARLES OFFENBACHER

Charles Offenbacher married Mamie (Mary, Minnie) Cameron on November 26, 1891, at Sterling, at the home of Joseph Saltmarsh. She was the daughter of Ella Pool Cameron of Eagle Point and was no relation to the Camerons of Uniontown. Charles and Mamie had one son, Harry Ray, born in September 1892. When Ray was still a baby, Charles was killed in an accident while breaking horses. His widow, Mamie, met William Horace Venable in Jacksonville. Being mutually agreeable, they were married on May 13, 1894, at the home of her mother at Sterling. They lived at Sterling about five years. In 1899 Horace acquired a restaurant and saloon in Jacksonville and moved his family to a home on South Third Street. The saloon was located in the brick building on the corner of California and Oregon streets adjoining the Orth Building. This did not last long as Horace decided to go into farming and raising horses. He found a 160-acre ranch on the Applegate River near Ruch owned by Samuel Dunnington, who was willing to trade it for Horace's town property straight across. The deal was made on June 18, 1901. (Vol. 42, p. 263-264). The Venable family moved to the ranch and Sam and Martha Dunnington became owners of the brick saloon building which later was Dunnington's butcher shop. Horace and Mamie had a Happy New Year baby when they moved to the ranch. Her name was Bessie, born January 1, 1901. They were to live on the ranch thirteen years. Bessie and Ray grew up and went to Ruch School and Jacksonville High School. Bessie married Ralph Smith and had two children, Naomi and Stan. They had a career in the restaurant business.

In 1915 a young teacher named Maybelle Daniels came to teach at Uniontown. She met Ray Offenbacher and they were married on September 1, 1916. She gave up teaching to become a full time wife and mother. They had two children, Charles and Lorraine. In later years they built a home on part of the Horace Venable property. Maybelle went back to teaching during World War II. She taught one year at Ruch, then went to Applegate School, where she taught until retirement in 1965. She and Ray spent their last years in Jacksonville.

HERMAN OFFENBACHER

Herman Offenbacher lived across the river south of the O'Brien ranch. He had over 200 acres of farm land with house, barns and other buildings near the river. Herman married Zelpha Coleman Terril who had a daughter, Dorland.

For three generations, the Offenbacher family operated some of the most prosperous and successful ranches in the area. Some of the original acreage has now been subdivided. The remaining fields are being farmed by Fred (Fritz) and his nephews. Several family members have retirement homes in the area.

THE MATNEY FAMILY

Between Fred Offenbacher's ranch and William Ray's place was the homestead settled by Carroll B. Matney. He came to Jackson County in 1850 with his brother, W. J. Matney. He filed on a Donation Land Claim in the Rogue River Valley, northeast of Medford on Dry Creek, and settled the claim November 10, 1853. He proved up and the patent was issued August 8, 1856. He sold this property and moved to the Applegate Valley.

Matney purchased the LeClaire Donation Land Claim (William Ray ranch) in 1859, and sold it to R. W. Benefield in 1863. Apparently "W. J." and his family left the area as there seems no further information about them.

Carroll B. Matney took up a homestead of 143 acres on the Applegate River. The patent was issued October 15, 1874. (Vol. 8, p. 103, Deed Records). He and Margaret Ann Maupin were married July 27, 1859. Over the next twenty-five years they became the parents of seventeen children but not all of them lived to adulthood. Several are buried in Logtown Cemetery. On the

1880 census there were thirteen children: Jefferson, Alvis, Carroll B. Jr., Nancy, Martha, Sarah, Mary, William, John, Thomas, Issac, George, and Amanda. Three more children were born in the 1880s: Icie B., Anna and Maggie. Out of this big family, two of the boys married and raised families on part of the home place. Jeff and his wife, Mary, had five children: Ina, Ospert, Nellie, George and Oliver. They attended Ruch School from 1893 to 1910, when Jeff moved to Klamath Falls.

LEWIS C. GAREY

The original settler on the ranch acquired by Horace Venable in 1901 was Lewis C. Garey (Geary). He had come to Jackson County about 1854 and fought in the Indian War in Company J under Captain Thomas Smith. Later he became a miner near Jacksonville. He married Maranda Johnson May 5, 1858, and their first child, Phoebe, was born in 1859. They moved to Siskiyou County where six more children were born: William Francis (1860), Laura Jane (1861), Samuel Edward (1865), Mary Aseneth (1865), Sarah Alice (1868) and James Irvin (1869).

In 1870 Lewis brought his family to the Applegate Valley and took up a homestead on the south side of the river adjoining Carroll B. Matney, to the north and the Buckleys to the east. He built a house and barn, cleared the best land to plant crops and built a ditch for irrigation. Tragedy struck the family in 1873 when 15-year-old Phoebe died with the fever on March 17. Maranda had just given birth to a daughter, Minnie. One month later, on April 19, the mother, Maranda, also died of the fever. Phoebe and Maranda were buried side by side in Logtown Cemetery. Maranda's mother, Susan Johnson, took baby Minnie to raise. Lewis made a home for the other children on the ranch for several years on which he received the patent December 13, 1876. (Vol. 9, p. 99, Deed Records). Records show he sold part of the place to Martin Ellison for $500 in 1880. (Vol. 9, p. 98). He sold the rest of it to N. S. Drew for $700 on August 2, 1882. (Vol. 9, p. 742, Deed Records). Lewis moved his family to Upper Rogue and Elk Creek area where he died on July 12, 1885.

John Matney married Fannie Swartsfager August 20, 1906. Their children were Marie and Lee. John and Fannie lived out their lives on his place. In 1989 their house is still standing on a hill overlooking the road and farm fields. Among the subsequent owners of the original Carroll B. Matney homestead were William H. and Emma Smith who purchased thirty acres with a small cabin on it in 1916. In later years they bought the rest of the ranch, which included the board and batten house built by Carroll B. Matney. Two generations of the Smith family grew up on this place, which remained in family ownership until 1957. In 1989 the old house is still standing, shaded by huge trees. This is on the south side of the road about one fourth mile west of the Hamilton Road intersection.

With the settlers Matney and Garey, the geographical loop covered in this documentary is closed. Across Hamilton Road is Buckley's and Ray's and about one mile east is Ruch. □

Chapter 9

SCHOOLS

Jackson County schools were established under the government of the Territory of Oregon when the county was formally organized in March 1853. At the first meeting, school districts were assigned by geographical features and area as the county had not yet been surveyed.

District No. 1. Jacksonville, the town and surrounding lands
2. Griffin Creek (Heber Grove)
3. Colonel Ross, northeast of Jacksonville toward Central Point
4. Phoenix
5. Ashland
6. Manzanita (now Central Point)
7-8. Valley View, included all of the Valley east of Bear Creek from Ashland to Eagle Point
9. Eagle Point

Additional districts were formed from these nine as other areas were established and the need arose for more schools.

The first Jackson County Superintendent of Common Schools was Thomas Fletcher Royal who served in 1854-55. He was a minister who came to Jacksonville with his family in 1853 on assignment to the Methodist ministry. His school work was largely centered in Jacksonville School District as the outlying districts were just then becoming established.

When Oregon became a state in 1859, the Constitution established the office of State School Superintendent of Public Instruction. The legislature passed laws governing the operation of the schools, requirements for qualified teachers and school board members. The Public School Support Fund was established to provide funding, based on school district enrollments.

A man who had great influence on the early Jackson County

schools was Moses Allan Williams. He was an ordained minister of the Presbytery of Georgia. He had studied at Washington College and Columbia University, and graduated from Princeton College (Seminary) in 1849. He came to Jacksonville from California in 1857 and organized the First Presbyterian church. He was elected to the office of County Superintendent of the Common Schools in 1861 and served four one-year terms to 1864. His work has been well documented, as he kept detailed diaries of his life and experiences. These diaries have been preserved and copies are available in libraries. He made a lasting impression on the schools of Jackson County. Some of his decisions still stand.

In the early years, the school was the social and cultural center of the community. Children received basic education and parents depended on the school for a meeting place, entertainment and worship. They were proud of their school in most districts.

Teachers were required to pass an examination for a certificate. There were three grades offered, first, second and third. In Jackson County, some of the first teachers were men who had some college training. They included John Jeffrey, Charles Prim, Lincoln Savage, Gus Newbury and John Gore.

Teaching school was one of the very few generally accepted occupations for women in the early days. A few brave young women took the examinations and went out to teach in the one-room schools. Many of them soon married and had families, but they had a strong influence on the school and community in later years.

Many individuals who received their basic education in the one-room schools of the Applegate Valley grew up to lead successful and productive lives. The schools served their purpose and deserve a place in the history of the region.

LOGTOWN-RUCH SCHOOLS

The first school district organized in the Upper Applegate Valley was recorded on April 23, 1863. This was Upper Applegate-Uniontown No. 24. The boundaries included most of Little Applegate and Upper Applegate Valleys down to the Jacksonville-Crescent City Road. Later that year, in December, another school district was formed, taking in Poormans Creek and Forest Creek. This became Logtown No. 27. In 1866 districts No. 24 and 27 were combined and called Union No. 27. By 1871, the population had grown and the boundaries were changed again.

Uniontown was a settlement of several families by this time. The district became Uniontown No. 27. The boundaries extended along the Little Applegate and Big Applegate Rivers about two miles each way. Logtown District was assigned No. 3, which was dropped by the Colonel Ross District when it was consolidated with Manzanita No. 6. In this reorganization, Logtown District No. 3 was officially recorded on May 31, 1871.

This school district took in the watersheds of Poormans Creek, Forest Creek (Jackass Creek) and included the confluence of Forest Creek with Applegate River. In May 1872, William Ray was clerk of the district. There was a total of 51 pupils on the census: 25 male, 26 female. Twenty-four legal voters lived in the district. Two terms of school were held and the district received $98.78 from the County Treasurer to pay the teacher.

Early teachers included J. D. Farley, Kate Herriott Hyde, Jennie Moore, Stella Stidham, Frances Donegan and John Jeffrey.

The building was probably made of rough lumber with hand made benches and tables. It was located on the northeast corner of James Buckley's homestead, on a knoll overlooking the Jacksonville-Crescent City Road. A new frame schoolhouse was built in 1876, largely due to the influence of Martin Drake, who was a neighbor and good friend of the James Buckley family. Martin Drake was active in school matters and it soon became known as Drake School. His children were Fred M., Belle, May and Ella. In the office of the County School Superintendent, the district was listed as Logtown No. 3 until 1897 when it was redesignated Ruch District No. 3.

By 1912, the old frame building had become very dilapidated. On the school board at that time were Miles Cantrall, Charles Hamilton and Horace Venable. The clerk was "Cap" Ruch. Plans were made for a large one-room school to be built of concrete blocks on the same site as the old building.

Early in 1913, the school district voters approved a bond issue to finance construction of a new building. The old frame building was taken down by Edward Smith, a neighbor, and the lumber re-used for his house and other farm buildings.

Work on the new building was soon under way. The contractor was Fred J. Fick of Jacksonville, a hardware store owner. The concrete blocks were made on the site by Mr. Jones, who was an experienced stone mason. The cement was mixed by hand and poured into special molds, which left one side of each block roughly textured. When the blocks were cured, they were laid up

Ruch School about 1910 when it was also called Drake school (top). Because of the dilapidated condition of the building, the patrons of the school district voted to construct a new building in 1914. The concrete blocks were poured on the site. On May 16, 1914, the teacher was Nellie Collins. "Cap" Ruch was Clerk of the Board and the three directors were Miles Cantrall, Charlie Hamilton and Horace Venable. The pupils and most of the community turned out to celebrate the opening of their new building. Note that windows had been set high, so students could not be distracted from their work by gazing out-of-doors. (Photos: top from Lewis Buckley; lower from Maude Pool Ziegler)

Ruch School with addition for High School classes (top) in 1916. (Center) In 1950-51, the building was completely remodeled. The windows were lowered and the bell tower, porch and steps were removed. The buidling's main entrance was changed to the other end of the building. (Lower) The Ruch School complex in 1987 includes the Uniontown building, which was moved, by the flagpole. (Photos: top from Ina Persel collection; center from Earl Swift collection; lower by author)

by the stone mason. A carpenter, William Peckham, did all the wood work and finishing work inside and out. The windows were placed at a height that made it impossible for the seated pupils to see out. This was supposed to keep their attention on their lessons.

By December 1913, the building was completed. Between Christmas and New Years, the teacher, Nellie Collins, and her pupils, moved into the new school. Average attendance was 30 pupils spread through all eight grades. The term was eight and a half months.

The school was formally dedicated at a community gathering in May 1914 with people coming from miles around to attend a program and picnic.

In the summer of 1916, there were plans underway to establish a two-year high school. At that time only "towns" had high schools, the nearest being Jacksonville. Those who wished to attend high school could go to any school they chose and the home district would pay tuition. The concern was in getting to the classes. Many highschoolers worked for room and board near the schools, or stayed with relatives. The students only got home on weekends.

The Ruch High School was ready for classes in the fall of 1916. At first there was good attendance but high school classes lasted only two years, partly because there were not enough pupils. When the United States entered the First World War, many young men left home to enlist in the army or navy. By 1918, there were only 62 pupils on the census—presumably including those of high school age. The average daily attendance was 30. Although the records do not state the teacher's name, the teacher was paid $75.00 each month for the eight and one-half months the school was in session.

Over the next twenty years, Ruch was a one-teacher school. Some of these teachers were: Edna Allen, Harlan Cantrall, Nettie Armpriest, Mary Beatty and Opal Mooter.

In 1938 the school at Sterling closed, but the district, wanting to show its best for its pupils, hired a driver and a vehicle and provided daily "bussing" to Ruch. The school district changed its name to Ruch-Sterling. Two teachers were Grace Brownlee and Ina Pursel. Ruch remained a two-teacher school through the 1940s. In the 1949-50 school year, four one-room schools consolidated with Ruch, and the school expanded to five teachers. A building and remodeling program included three class rooms, an office and health room. The Uniontown building was moved to the site and remodeled into a cafeteria. The bell tower and porch were removed and a new doorway installed. The hyphenated name was dropped in 1951. It became Ruch School District No. 3 once more. In 1955, a gymnasium and one class room were added.

More changes took place in 1959 when Ruch and Jacksonville consolidated with Medford District No. 49. The Medford District became 549C, which meant consolidation of five districts with Medford No. 49. More improvements were made during the 1960s and 1970s and in 1971 Ruch School observed its one hundredth anniversary. A rustic sign was erected by the entrance to the buildings by Earl Swift, who was principal in 1971.

RUCH SCHOOL BUILT IN 1914 AS A COOPERATIVE PROJECT BY MEMBERS OF THE COMMUNITY, WHO POURED EACH BLOCK WITH MATERIALS AND LABOR DONATED. THE BELL WAS INSTALLED IN THE TOWER OF THE OLD STONE BUILDING WHICH IS STILL IN USE.

FOREST CREEK SCHOOL DISTRICT NO. 43

In 1878, School District No. 43 was partitioned off Logtown No. 3. The creek was commonly called Jackass Creek in those years. From the beginning, the school was named Forest School. The name of the creek was changed to Forest Creek about 1910. The first schoolhouse was located at the confluence of the east and west forks of the creek on a mining claim owned by Frank Logg. Early-day families whose children attended the school were: Sturgis, Armpriest, Smith, Winningham, McIntyre, Atterbury, Coffman, Pearce and Spencer. In later years, some of the families were Davies, Black, Stone, Coffman and Salsman. In the 1930s there were Meeds, Hoxworth, Carter, Pearce and Black.

A new frame schoolhouse was built on the same site in 1908 by Fred Fick, contractor from Jacksonville. One of the early teachers was Gus Newbury. Others were Ella Parks, Pearl L. Gould, Ada Ditsworth, Almeda Orr, Flossie Baily, Ruby Downing and Nettie Armpriest. In 1945 the school was closed and the children transported to Jacksonville until 1950, when the district consolidated with Ruch. The building was sold about 1956. It is still standing and in 1989 is a private home.

Forest Creek School building was put up in 1908. After some districts consolidated, the building was sold in 1956 and in 1989 is a private residence. Photograph made in 1933 by then teacher, now author of this book, Marguerite Black.

UNIONTOWN DISTRICT NO. 27

The next school district south of Logtown was organized April 23, 1863. It included the valleys of the Little Applegate and Upper Applegate with their major tributaries. There was a school on Cameron property in 1864, according to an entry in the Superintendent's Book of Common Schools (p. 50). The district had 35 legal voters. There were 21 students on the census, 19 of them male. J. W. Starr was clerk. School was held one term only. In 1866 there were 37 pupils—18 male and 19 female—on the census. The average daily attendance was 10 for the one term of school. Theodoric Cameron was clerk.

By 1871 there were 59 school-aged children on the census and Uniontown District No. 27 was separated from Logtown No. 3. This left Uniontown with 31 students and 21 legal voters.

In January 1877, William Cameron wrote in his diary there was a meeting at which subscriptions were raised to build a new school. The drive was successful, for that August men hauled foundation stones to the site and worked through the fall and winter 1877-78.

In March, Cameron wrote that he put up a stove in the building, then moved in the desks. The location of this school was on Robert Cameron's property one-quarter mile from the intersection of the Upper Applegate Road. It was to remain in use for over 40 years.

Another new building was constructed in the early 1920s. In the Medford *Mail Tribune*, September 8, 1927, was this article:

OLD UNIONTOWN SCHOOL HOUSE TAKEN DOWN

Since the new schoolhouse was built a few years ago, the old building still stood beside it, detracting from the appearance of the grounds. The old building marks the passing of the work of pioneer days, the house having been built about 50 years ago. The little white schoolhouse has welcomed innumerable students through its doors during its half century of usefulness, although at one time, only two pupils were in attendance for several months. The lumber from the old structure will be preserved and put to future use.

Settlers who served on the school board in the early years included Jacob Parks, S. B. Hamilton, William Cameron and Robert Cameron. Two of the first teachers were John A. Jeffrey and Bernice Cameron. Children in the school were from these early families: Cameron, Cantrall, Hamilton, Jones, Parks, Wilson, Haskins, Buck, Kleinhammer and Pursel.

In 1989, the Uniontown building is still part of the Ruch School complex.

STERLING SCHOOL DISTRICT NO. 33

The gold rush settlement of Sterlingville was the home of several miners with families as early as 1865. A school district was organized on June 15, 1865. Joseph B. Saltmarsh donated a site on his homestead for the first schoolhouse. School board members in those early days were Joseph B. Saltmarsh, John Haskins and William Jennings. Henry Ankeny served several terms as clerk. The pupils were from the families of Saltmarsh, Ankeny, Crump, Margreiter, Yocom, Gilson, Jennings, Haskins and Venable. Two early-day teachers were Amy Cantrall and Helen Holtan. A note on the clerk's report for 1895 reads, ''We owe Miss Amy Cantrall $40.00. And the district owes at this report for school charts $30.00. So we are still in debt. The clerk makes no charge.''

By this time the school was located on a knoll overlooking the

Uniontown School District dates from 1863. (Top) Teacher Eva Couch and her students: (left to right) Jessie Garrett, Ora Goldsby, Miss Couch _____ Wolf, Lloyd Cameron, Cora Goldsby. (Back row) Gladys Wolf, Paul Jennings, Bert Goldsby. Identification by Paul Jennings in 1982. (Photo from Jack O'Brien collection). (Right) Miss Ailene Inlow, teacher during 1935-36 school year in the picture collection of Mary Hansen DeLong.

Sterling Creek School House was located on knoll near Sterling Cemetery, was destroyed by fire in fall 1918. A replacement building was constructed and is shown here in 1925 when Flora Saltmarsh was teacher. John Black, co-author of this book, remembers the building was painted white but over the years the paint peeled off. (Top picture from Helen Sherman. Lower from author collection)

intersection of Sterling Creek Road and Griffin Lane. Nearby, on the same knoll, was the cemetery. The population in the district changed in the twenty years after 1900. New families were: Nelson, Chase, Arnold, Atterbury, Wilsey, Turnbough, Ginet and others. L. A. Nelson came to Sterling in 1907 with his wife and children: Grace, Ernest, Edgar and Albert. They all attended Sterling School. Albert, who was the youngest, was in the eighth grade in 1918. That year he was school janitor. The building had only a stovepipe for a chimney, which was badly rusted and in need of replacement. Albert reported it to the school board but nothing was done about it. The inevitable happened. Early one morning in the fall of 1918, Albert built a fire in the stove and went to get a bucket of water. Returning up the hill, he saw flames licking at the dry shakes around the stovepipe. The teacher, Olive Hogan, was there and the Fields children were coming. At first they all tried to put out the fire, then concentrated on moving everything out of the burning building. They were able to save the desks and most of the books before the roof caved in. Arrangements were made to hold school in a Sterling Mine Company building the rest of the term. In 1919, the Fields family moved away and Albert was the only school age pupil in the district. Two other preschool children on the census were Francis and Olivette Ginet.

Their father, Joseph Ginet, lived about a mile from Buncom on the Sterling Creek Road. He was chairman of the school board. The other board member was L. A. Nelson. Joseph Ginet donated the site for a new schoolhouse on a corner of his ranch. A small, unpainted building was put up on the hill above the road under a big oak tree. There was no playground. This building served the children of the district until 1938 when the declining population led to closing the school. Afterward, the children were transported to Ruch. An elderly bachelor lived at the school for several years, but eventually the building was dismantled. Even the oak tree is gone in 1989. All that remains is a bare hillside.

ECHO SCHOOL DISTRICT NO. 77

In the 1890s, several families with school age children lived in the north end of Sterling School District. They decided to divide off Sterling and start a school closer to their homes. Echo School District No. 77 was organized in the fall of 1895. A simple board building was put up on property owned by C. F. Dunford about two and one-half miles north of the Sterling schoolhouse on

This is believed to be the only picture of Echo School and was made about 1914. (Author collection)

The teacher in Echo School saw to it that even the boys learned the table graces. This included setting the table for the school lunch program and washing the dishes. The year was 1914. (Author collection)

Poormans Creek. First classes were held there in spring term, 1896. The board of directors were A. J. Beck, R. F. Yocom and Mrs. Rebecca Crump. Ollie W. Pursel was clerk. They had 21 pupils on the census, and eleven attended school. They were from the families of Yocom, Crump, Pursel, Beck, Mitchell and Margreiter. Mary Dawson was the teacher in 1898 for the fall term October 3 to December 23. The school board members were A. J. Beck, B. H. Olsen and R. F. Yocom. The clerk was J. Margreiter. There were sixteen pupils in school and 28 on the census. The new families were H. B. Olsen and James M. Coffer. The next year there were 19 children on the census, seven of them in school. The teacher was Gertrude Beaver and her salary for the term, October to December, was $25.00 per month.

The enrollment gradually decreased in the next fifteen years as times changed and population shifted.

In 1914, a teacher, Alma Gould, started a hot lunch project at Echo School. She prepared hot soup and cocoa and the children brought sandwiches. The luncheon was served on a white tablecloth with dishes brought from her home. The children were taught manners and domestic science at the same time. The boys were required to take their turn at washing dishes. A newspaper article describes this novel plan, and a photograph was taken of three boys at the table. The boys were Chester Carter, Homer and Walter Blevins.

Henry Mankins and Harrison Fields were on the school board in 1918-19. The census was down to seven children, six of school age. The County School Superintendent advised the board members to close the school and annex the district to Jacksonville. This was accomplished in 1921. Echo School District No. 27 had been in existence 25 years.

LITTLE APPLEGATE
SCHOOL DISTRICT NO. 87

For four families who lived on Little Applegate above Buncom, it was a five-mile trip one way to Uniontown School in the 1890s. The Saltmarsh, Crump and Kleinhammer children rode horseback or drove a horse and buggy to attend school. In 1903 Frank Crump, Arthur Kleinhammer and Bird Saltmarsh organized a school district, which they partitioned out of the Uniontown District. On the official records, this became Little Applegate School District No. 87, but some people called it Crump School and others called it Buncom School.

The first schoolhouse was built on the Crump ranch, out of 12-inch plank flume lumber. It was about 12 by 16 feet. There was a nice spring right behind it. Ramona Bissel was the teacher. The first clerk's report was filed June 20, 1904, in which there were 18 children reported on the census, only six in school, for a five-week term. A note on the back of this report read, "Teacher's wages, $35.00 not paid, donation toward seats $10.50." Children were from the families of Crump, Miller, Cantrall, Saltmarsh, Stafford and Kleinhammer. In 1906, Frank and Cora Crump donated land and a new school building was constructed not far from Crump's house. (Vol. 55, p. 84, Deed Records). The lot was only 124 feet by 100 feet in size. There was a woodshed and the privies, but no room for a play ground. Over the years, children came from the families of West, Combest, Wolf and Pursel.

Classes stopped at the Little Applegate School in the 1940s. This picture was made by Vieva Saltmarsh in 1963. The building was on the property of Rolland and Clara Smith but was dismantled in 1972. John Henderson got the beams and joists. The Smiths used the rest of the lumber to build a shop. (Author collection)

In his report on schools in 1917, Rural School Supervisor E. R. Peterson lists District No. 87 as "Buncom. Building in good condition, modern in plan, fairly well equipped. Waterbury system (heater). Ground quite steep. Little or no play apparatus. Some local interest shown but room for more. Livestock, hay, potatoes, general farm crops and some mining. Quite good road, passable most of the year. Reached from Jacksonville via Ruch or Sterling, some fifteen or twenty miles."

Some of the teachers included: Ina Pursel, Ethel Houston, Katherine Denzer, Carl Ayers, Lulu Metsger and Flossie Myers.

Children who attended in the early ears were: Dean Saltmarsh; Ethel and Doris Kleinhammer; Harold, Jack and Vivian Crump; Paul and Lewis Jennings; Lucille and Raymond Garret; George and Esther Pursel.

Irene Crump was the last teacher at Little Applegate in 1941-42. There were only six children of school age. Faced with the loss of their district, the people voted to transport to Uniontown. The little school was never reopened but the district hired a driver to haul the kids to Uniontown through the 1949-50 school year. On May 4, 1950, consolidation with Ruch was approved by the voters. The district had been in existence 47 years. In 1973 the old building was taken down by Rolland Smith and the lumber used on his ranch.

WATKINS SCHOOL DISTRICT NO. 68

In accordance with a petition now on file in my office, I hereby create a new school district that is to be known as Squaw Lake District No. 68 with boundaries to wit: To be embraced by the territory not included in the Uniontown School District on the north, Steamboat School District on the west, and the [California] State Line on the south, so as to include Squaw Lake; being a scope of country about 12 square miles and containing at present 24 school children of lawful age. The district, as asked for, will take in all of Township 40 south, range three west. The two easterly tiers of sections in Township 40 south, range 4 west, about all of Township 41 south of range 4 west.

This document was signed by C. S. Price, Superintendent of Schools, on March 21, 1891. The petitioners were Freeman Collings, Mark Watkins, William Dorn and Sylvester Arrasmith. Between them they did have a total of 24 school age children. They built a hewed log school with such skill that it remained in use for

Watkins School pupils in 1921: Front row, David Winningham, Lois Swayne, Roy and Paul Winningham. Rear row, Ione "Bill" Knutzen, Francis Edwards, Mildred Swayne, Hester Knutzen, Lee Winningham. Not pictured, Teacher Maude York. (Top photo from Carlos Morris collection. Lower from Louise Harr Allen collection)

over thirty years. The site chosen was on the riverbank about one fourth mile above the mouth of Squaw Creek. There was a spring nearby for water. The playground was limited to a narrow strip of land between the river and the road because farmland was much too hard to obtain to be used for a school yard. Parents felt that children could easily get their daily exercise by walking to school and helping with work at home. They did play games on this limited space at recess. The most popular game was baseball, using a homemade bat and ball, which frequently was lost in the river.

The first teacher was John Jeffrey and the first school board members were Mark Watkins, Freeman Collings and Ed Langley. Three years later, when Mark Watkins established a post office, named for himself, the official name of the school district was changed to Watkins No. 68.

In 1893 there were 30 children on the census and they had one four-month term of school. The teacher was T. K. Roberts, and he had 17 pupils. They were from the families of Byrne, Arrasmith, Dorn, Collings and Watkins. Teacher Roberts reported to the Superintendent that the school did not have accommodation for all of the pupils in the district; that there was not suitable furniture; that the playground was a public highway; that there was not sufficient supplies; but there was a supply of good water and wood. There was no woodshed and no water closet. The ventilation was the finest in the land. (Teachers Annual Report, Watkins District No. 68, for the year ending August 10, 1894.)

By 1897 there were 67 children on the census. The next year, 1898, Beaver Creek School District No. 82 was partitioned off, and the families in the lower end of the district went to Beaver Creek School.

In 1900, Nora Sheean was the teacher. The census listed 38 pupils, but she had only seven in the two terms of school. In her teacher's report she says the accommodations are sufficient. There are books, furniture and other supplies. The ventilation was very good, by windows and doors.

Ina Stoker and her mother, Roseltha Birchard, came to Jackson County from Iowa in 1906. Mrs. Birchard taught at Watkins in 1907. Her pupils were from the families of Collings, Watkins, Byrne, Harr, Dorn and Thurman. Christine Beaver was the teacher in 1911. She had eight pupils. Among them were Mamie Watkins, Oscar Collings, Ida Rhoten; John and Kate Byrne; Hazel and Mildred Swayne.

After her marriage to Bert Harr, Christine lived most of her life in the Watkins School District.

Rural School Supervisor in 1917 was E. R. Peterson. He reported that Watkins had the only log schoolhouse remaining in Jackson County, that it was in fairly good repair, neat and attractive inside, but equipment was limited. The grounds were fairly good, unfenced and little or no play apparatus.

Maude York was teacher in 1921. Her pupils were David, Paul and Lee Winningham; Lois and Mildred Swayne; Hester Knutzen and Francis Edwards. Ina Pursel was the last teacher in the log building. She taught two years, 1922 to 1924. A new modern school was built in 1924 on a small piece of government land, which had been fenced in with Bert Harr's homestead. He reset his fence where it belonged, thus the school was on government land. In later years, when the School Board tried to buy it, the Forest Service would not sell it.

Ina Pursel returned to teach at Watkins from 1933 to 1937. Over the next five years the population changed. In 1942-43 there were only seven children in the district. Mary Esther Davis was the teacher and she was the last one until 1946. The few children were

Watkins District built a new school in 1924. This Sunday School class met there in 1929: Standing, Pearl Whitney, (unknown), _____ DeWolf, Guy and Polly Watkins, Mamie Winningham. Seated: Valera Winningham, (girl, unknown), Louise Harr, Violet and Ruth Whitney. (Dorothy Heckert collection)

transported to Uniontown from 1942 to 1946. But the school district was not to die yet. In 1946 school was reopened with Russel A. Mitchell as teacher. There were fifteen on the census and nine in school. The next teacher was Minnie Fox. She taught three years. In 1950 there were only five children again. A successful consolidation with Ruch took place on April 1, 1950. The Watkins building stood vacant until the 1970s when it was used as an office during preparation for the Applegate Dam construction project.

BEAVER CREEK SCHOOL DISTRICT NO. 82

Between Uniontown and Watkins schoolhouses in the 1890s, there was a distance of some six miles. About halfway between these schools was Charles C. Pursel's sawmill, with a small settlement surrounding it. In 1897, it was decided to organize a school district and build a school more centrally located for their children. The boundaries of Uniontown District were moved to include the families of Charles C. Pursel, William Lewis, Newton Lewis and Austin Sargent. From Watkins district were A. D. (Deb) McKee, James M. Dews and Oliver Dews. The organization was completed in early 1898. The first board of directors were Charles C. Pursel, W. H. Lewis and I. N. Lewis. James M. Dews was clerk. Lumber from Pursel's mill was used to build the school with Charles Pursel and Oliver Dews doing the work.

The site chosen for the school was about a mile down the river from Pursel's mill. The first teacher was Daisy Walker. She taught a three-month term in the spring of 1898. Her pupils were from the families of I. N. Lewis, A. N. Sargent, Charles C. Pursel, Manuel Silva, Charles Buck and William Bendick.

Teachers over the next ten years included Kate Buckley (1899), Dora Hurley (1903), Lucia Chapman (1904), Susie Boyd (1905), Maude Harr (1906 and 1909), Ina Stoker (1907), and Bertha Peachy (1911). Nine-month terms began in 1912. Mabel Thomas was the last teacher in the old schoolhouse that year.

In 1913 a new schoolhouse was built about a mile up the river on the east side. It was located on government ground between the road and the hillside. There was no playground, but they did have a commercially built slide. Almost every school had one of these devices. The first teacher in the new school was Lucille Barber. Her pupils were from the families of McKee, Phillips, Lewis, Stephenson and Culy. Teachers from the 1920s included Eva Beebe Collins, Mabel Thornton, Elizabeth Meir, Jeanette Gore,

Cheryl Smith and Lois Fretewell. Families were Culy, McKee, Pence, Port, Anderson, Byrne and Lewis. In the 1930s there were Offenbacher, Childers and Fletcher.

As times changed, the population decreased and by 1942 there were only the Offenbacher and Phillips families with children in the district. The school board closed the school and arranged for transportation to Uniontown, where Ina Pursel was teaching with an average of 10 pupils. (This was wartime and gasoline was rationed. Special dispensation was required of the wartime Office of Price Administration for special ration stamps that would authorize purchase of extra gallonage for transporting students to schools when there was no public transportation available.)

In 1944-45, three new families moved into the district with eight children of school age. They were Childers, Evans and Ford. The school was reopened for them. Flossie Myers was the teacher. She left in the middle of the year to join the army. Hilda Sutherland finished out the year with four pupils. There was very strong sentiment among the parents and the school board against closing the school. One more time they hired a teacher for the year 1945-46. Her name was Wanda Broyles. She, too, was unable to finish the year and Christine Harr substituted the last few weeks. That summer the school board held a consolidation election with Ruch on August 3, 1946, ending 52 years as a school district. Morris Byrne purchased the building and dismantled it to use the lumber on his ranch.

STEAMBOAT SCHOOL DISTRICT NO. 58

Among the miners and one or two ranchers in this area, there were a number of children who were miles from the nearest school in 1889. George Culy, with his neighbors, J. H. Shearer and A. W. Shearer, petitioned Jackson County Superintendent of Schools for a school district. The boundaries were to be from the California line at the southwest corner of Jackson County, running north to Thompson Creek, then east to Squaw Mountain, then south to the California line. The petition was granted on January 17, 1889, by H. H. Mitchell, County School Superintendent.

The board of directors were George Culy, J. H. Shearer and H. C. Shearer. A. W. Shearer was clerk. They built a hewed log building for a school house, which was located on the Culy ranch. The exact site is unknown.

The clerk's report for 1894 lists the teacher as Jessie Rose and

(Opposite) Beaver Creek School served for all community activities including use by this Sunday School class sometime after 1915 which was about the year this new building was constructed. (Center) "Trolley" crossed the Applegate River to Beaver Creek School. There were at least two "rope-and-pully" aerial tramways over the river. (Lower) Student body of the old Beaver Creek School, spring term 1912: Teacher Mabel Thomas. Back row: Fern Phillips, Orpha Lewis, Luella, Doris McKee, Merritt Dews (with glasses), Lydia Stephenson. Front row: Emmett Phillips, Omar Culy, Dorothy McKee, Helen Culy, Orie Phillips, Earl Stephenson. (Above, this page) This picture appears to be about 1906-07 when Beaver Creek School was also known as McKee School. Seated at desks, Fort McKee, Ernest Bostwick, Leatha Buck, Luella and Floyd McKee. By window, Henry Bostwick, teacher Maude Harr (later Ditsworth), Orpha Lewis, Clarence Buck—in very back. (Photos: top from Dorothy Hackert, center from Pearl Byrne collection, lower from Dorothy Hackert. Photo this page from Maude Ditsworth collection)

Steamboat School and pupils about 1904-05. Teacher (left) Nettie Lewis Thompson. Students standing. Of the three boys two are Ned Culy and Dan Shearer. Lucy Shearer in white dress. Lora Culy Owen. Seated: Branch Culy, Frank and Harold Loosly. (Author collection)

her seven pupils as: Albert, Cary, Lora and Neldrett Culy; Dan and Charley Shearer; and Rachel Mee. In 1896 there was a sudden influx of miners and the census jumped to 27 with nineteen in school. They were from the families of Lewis Copeland, Guy Blood, Thomas Henry, W. E. Finney, James Young and Prosper Gantry.

The people did not stay long and, by 1906, there were only ten children of school age. Maude Harr was the teacher in 1905, her first school. She admitted she was scared at first as there was a big girl, 21 years old, and Maude was only eighteen. The children were so anxious to please the teacher that she soon lost her fear. She taught there for the three-month term in 1906 and again in the summer of 1907.

Nettie Lewis Thompson taught about 1904. She and her pupils

were photographed in front of the schoolhouse. This photograph has been handed down in the Culy family. They have generously shared it with historians.

Steamboat School was annexed to Thompson Creek in 1916 after 27 years of providing basic education to the children of this remote community.

THOMPSON CREEK DISTRICT NO. 34

The original boundaries of Thompson Creek School District No. 34 were described as being all of the area from the Duncan ranch to the divide between Upper Applegate and Thompson Creek, also to include all the sections of Thompson Creek and its tributaries.

This district was taken by petition from Missouri Flat District No. 21 and was created November 20, 1974. The first building was made of logs and was located about three and one-half miles up the creek. An early teacher was Eudora Godfrey. A new frame schoolhouse was built in 1890, and Effie Green was the first teacher in the new building. Children were of the William Jordan, Kendall, John Knutzen, Marion and John Bingham families. Others were Hoffman, Darnielle and Mee families.

In 1893 the school board members were D. W. Winetrout, S. Louden and J. H. Knutzen. Children were from the Winetrout, Oldaker, Hoffman, Mee, Culp, Lathrop and Louden families. In 1918-19 there were 22 children in the school. The board members at this time were M. F. Bingham, Albert Borde and S. J. Johnson. George Hoffman was clerk.

A third Thompson Creek School was built in 1921. It was a modern frame building located about four miles up the creek across the road from the Thompson Creek Fire Guard Station of the U.S. Forest Service.

Teachers who taught at Thompson Creek School in the 1920s were Viola Hogan, Dorris Applegate, Esther Messenger and Olive Hogan. In the 1930s June Rudd taught four years. She lived in a teacherage provided by the district. Wanda Heinze taught in 1937-38. During the 1940s there were Ruth Foster, Ethel Ludwig and Ruth Hood. Ethel Maxwell was the teacher in 1943-44 and she was hired for the next year. In October 1944, she died of a heart attack at the wheel of her car on the way to school. Marguerite Black was hired to finish out the year. There were 12 children from the families of Decker, Turnbough, Cody, Best, Nielsen, Bross,

Chausse and Beard. The school was operated here for two more years when the people voted to consolidate with Applegate in the summer of 1947. Thompson Creek School closed after 74 years.

APPLEGATE SCHOOL DISTRICT NO. 40

The settlers around Applegate Crossing organized a school district on February 17, 1876. The boundaries of Missouri Flat and Thompson Creek districts were rearranged to form the new district. The first board of directors were Abraham Cougle, John O'Brien and Orlando Rose. John Bolt was clerk, a position he was to hold for twelve years. The district was named Bridge Point No. 40. School classes were held somewhere in the area in 1886-87 for a three-month term. The teacher was Charles Prim. Since there were not yet any county school funds available, parents were assessed a tuition fee of $2.00 for each of their scholars. Those who paid were John O'Brien, John Bolt, John Knauss, William Herriott, Joseph Shoemaker, John Knutzen and Thomas Dews. John Bolt and Rial Benedict were appointed to select a site for a schoolhouse. They reported that the best-suited place nearest the center of the district was on the west side of Humbug Creek and north of the county road on a piece of ground owned by Mr. Benedict. He agreed to donate it for school purposes.

In order to finance the building of a schoolhouse, buy furniture and supplies and pay a teacher, the school board held a series of balls in William Herriott's hall. The first was held on May 1, 1878. After the expenses were paid, $75.35 was turned over to the school clerk. Several more events were held in 1879 and 1880. As each event was successful, a small frame building was constructed on the site donated by Benedict. It was between the road and the hill, and had no playground. Teachers in those early years included Dora Godfrey and John Butterworth. By 1909 there were over 60 pupils on the census, and the little frame schoolhouse could not hold them all. The school board acquired land on the bench above the old building and made plans to build a large two-room brick schoolhouse. A professional brickmaker was hired to set up a temporary brick yard in a field across the road. The bricks were made from clay dug from the nearby hillside. The bricks were partly dried in the sun first, then laid up in a kiln built for the purpose and fired. The brick mason and carpenter had the new school ready for occupancy by December 1912. Teacher Nell Callahan and her pupils moved in during Christmas week.

Applegate School and gymnasium in 1985.

Athletics played a major role at Applegate School in the early days to a point of being criticized in an official 1917 inspection report. In 1989 the district has a "well-rounded curriculum." In the picture of the Girls Athletic Club Field Meet 1916: Front row: Dorothy Head, Stella Layton, Audrey Layton, Elizabeth (Bessie) Rowden, Bernice Grubb, Roberta and Blanch Clute, Thelma McDaniel, Eva Hanson. Second row: Josie Wright, Alice Bingham, Beatrice O'Brien, Violet Thompson, Gladys Miller, Edith Kubli, Ethel Topping, Lois Rice, Margaret Brown. (Edith Kubli Scott collection)

By 1919, records show that a two-year high school had been established under one teacher. Another teacher taught the first eight grades in the other room.

E. R. Peterson's report in 1917 stated that Applegate District No. 40 had a two-room building of modern construction but it was not well-built. Two-year high school. Fairly good equipment. Waterbury System (heaters). Grounds in fair condition. Much interest has been taken in annual field and track meet. Tendency, however, is too much toward professional athletics stressing the strong and neglecting the weak. The small schools are invited, but to participate are absolutely barred by conditions. There has been too much rivalry between Applegate and Ruch for the cup at the expense of the real benefit that should result from such events. Prosperous farming section, dairy products, livestock, alfalfa, beans, general farming. About twenty miles from Medford via Jacksonville and Ruch: about the same distance from Grants pass. (Journal of E. R. Peterson 1917, p. 16).

Two years later an addition of two rooms was built of brick on the rear of the original building. The high school used two rooms and the grade school occupied the other two. When Ruch High School was closed, students from Ruch went to Applegate and lived in two small cabins on the edge of the school grounds while they attended high school. Among them were Glenn and Everett Smith and the Rice boys. The high school closed in 1926, after which date the pupils were transported to Jacksonville. The first bus was a homemade body on a Model T Ford truck chassis. It took two hours to make the trip one way. It made a long day but most of the students stayed with it and graduated from Jacksonville High School. Teachers who taught during the 1920s include Velma Gearhart, Twila Rader, Dorothy Head and Thelma Jones. In the 1930s there were William and Ethel Ludwig, Mary Beatty, Kathryn Denzer, Thelma Stringer and Leora Pease. Some who were there in the 1940s were Bertha Haskins, Lucille Neiter, Ruth York Hood, Marguerite Black, Nettie Armpriest and Catherine Walker. During the summer of 1945, Missouri Flat voted to close their school and transport to Applegate. In 1947, when Thompson Creek consolidated with Applegate, it became a three-teacher school. Those teachers were Cleo Shannon, Catherine Walker and Maybelle Offenbacher. A gymnasium was built in 1952 after a successful bond election. It was a quonset hut-type building with a concrete floor. The school population remained stable during the 1950s and four teachers were able to carry the enrollment. By the 1960s enrollment increased. In 1962 Bruce Matheny became principal. He was to remain twelve years. He guided the growth from four teachers with 76 students to eight teachers and 152 students in 1978. Bruce resigned at the end of the school year 1978. The new principal was Ed Daniels. He soon received notice from the State Department of Education that the school was non-standard, thus a campaign was conducted for a bond issue to build four classrooms and remodel the basement of the brick building. On May 20, 1980, the bond issue was passed on the second try. The building project was completed and the school was declared standard. In 1983 Bruce Matheny was re-hired and remained until his retirement in 1987.

Applegate School is one of only two independent school districts in Jackson County. The school board members and people of the community have so far successfully defended their school from repeated attempts to get them to consolidate with Medford or Josephine County. A new Superintendent, Jeff Fagan, was hired and started work on July 1, 1989. Then he received news in September that the school was again non-standard. Regulations require that necessary adjustments and improvements to meet the standards be completed in one year. Superintendent Fagan said that the State's requirements were primarily in the "paperwork" and that no fault had been found with the curriculum.

The rural schools of Upper Applegate Valley have served their purpose in educating about five generations of pupils in the 187 years they were in existence. Consolidation has brought modern, well-equipped buildings, better-trained teachers, adequate transportation and equalization of taxes. Good quality education is available in the 1990s. □

Chapter 10

POST OFFICES

Many early-day post offices were in remote places with business conducted in the postmaster-farmer's home, in a barn or converted woodshed. Pictured is the Watkins, Oregon post office, in shed marked X in 1898. (Opposite) Maude Harr, Grace Lewis, postmaster, and "Katie" Byrne stand in the doorway to the post office which was near the mouth of Squaw Creek, a branch of the Applegate River, near the California line. Apparently the mail (in sacks on steps) has just been delivered by the contract carrier in buggy at left edge of photograph. (Author collection)

202

WATKINS, OREGON

Few things are more important to the life of a community than the delivery of its mail. For nearly forty years the two days each week when the stage brought the mail up Applegate were red-letter days at Buncom, Watkins and all along the river.

In 1892 the only post office on the Upper Applegate was Herling, later known as the Bauten place, four miles west of Jacksonville (on the Crescent City Road). At that time Anthony Watkins was 18 years old, and he carried the mail once a week free gratis for the people living up the river. On March 25, 1893, a post office was established at Watkins. Mark Watkins was postmaster and held that office for seven years. Ed Fawcett was next to assume the duties of postmaster and the office was moved to his home (February 27, 1901). After several years, another change was made back across the river to the Ed Langley ranch with Albert Collings as postmaster (February 9, 1904). His wife, Mary, actually took care of the mail). From there the office traveled up Squaw Creek to Byrnes' (January 5, 1920). Katie Byrne was postmaster. Next it went to Harr's (October 17, 1912) where Mrs. Louise Harr served as postmaster. Grace Harr was appointed January 23, 1914, and again in October 1914, after her name became Grace Lewis. During these years the mail carriers endured many hardships. The Little Applegate had to be forded. The Big Applegate was forded at what is now the Straube ranch and again at Rippey's, six miles above. Often high water made it impossible to cross with a team and hack or buggy. At such times, if the mail was to be delivered, the driver must proceed on horseback. Jim Louden was the first who took a mail contract up Applegate. While August Wolf had the contract, he died, and his wife, Elizabeth, undertook to fulfill the arduous task. Their son, Harry, used to go with her and wield the whip while she handled the reins. One of the horses she drove was white and the other one black. The white horse made a practice of balking in midstream while crossing the fords.

When Henry Wendt died during his term as mail carrier, his sons, George and Chester, took over the route and made the change from horse-drawn hack to a gas burning Model T Ford. Eugene Thompson held the next contract, and through his effort an additional delivery each week was assured. Other mail carriers in later years were E. S. (Slats) Wilson, John Norris, Oscar (Duke) Lewis, Cliff and Ellen Childers. In the 1970s-80s, Katherine Dennis was the carrier.

Three times a week for twenty years the hum of a motor announced the arrival of the mail, a service of such value it could scarcely be estimated in cold cash.

Watkins continued until November 20, 1920, when it was closed.

STEAMBOAT, OREGON

A post office to serve the residents of this remote community was established January 10, 1888, and operated 27 years. Closure came on August 15, 1915. The first postmaster was Wilfred E. Finney. He served until 1893, when H. Shearer was appointed on November 20, 1893. The post office was closed on August 15, 1915, when servicing the area was transferred to Applegate.

The Steamboat, Oregon post office was conducted in the old Culy house in the 1890s. Inset: The Culy family: George ''and wife'' and boys Branch, Ned, Cary and daughter Nellie. (Author collection)

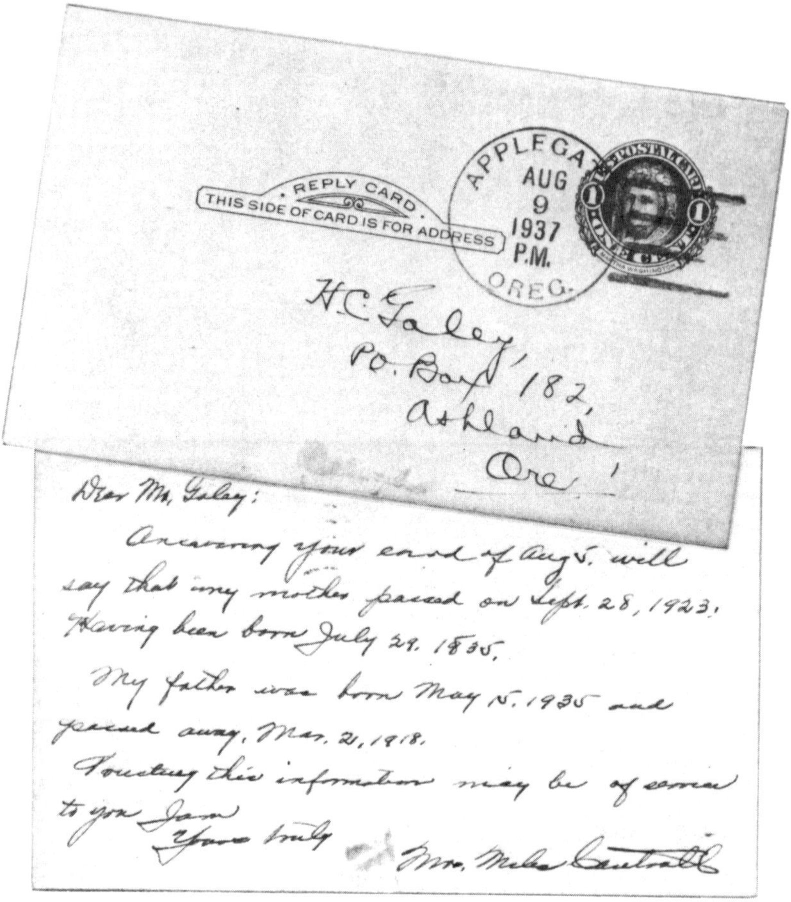

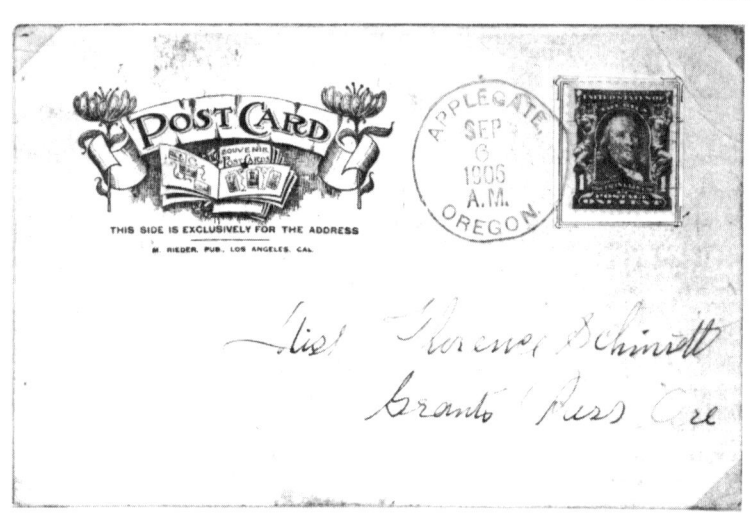

REPLY CARD
THIS SIDE OF CARD IS FOR ADDRESS

APPLEGATE
AUG
9
1937
P.M.
ORE.

U.S. POSTAL CARD
ONE CENT

H. C. Galey
P.O. Box 182,
Ashland
Ore.

Dear Mr. Galey:

Answering your card of Aug 5. will say that my mother passed on Sept. 28, 1923. Having been born July 29, 1835.

My father was born May 15, 1935 and passed away, Mar. 21, 1918.

Trusting this information may be of service to you I am

Yours truly

Mrs. Miles Cantrall

POST CARD
SOUVENIR POST CARD
THIS SIDE IS EXCLUSIVELY FOR THE ADDRESS
M. RIEDER, PUB. LOS ANGELES, CAL.

APPLEGATE
SEP
6
1906
A.M.
OREGON

UNITED STATES

Miss Florence Schmidt
Grants Pass Ore

APPLEGATE, OREGON

Applegate Post Office was established on August 30, 1858, while Oregon was still a territory, and the road was yet a pack trail. The first postmaster appointed was John O'Brien. Apparently he did not serve at all. Records show that John W. McKay was appointed on September 4, 1858. Less than a year later George W. Keeler was appointed June 19, 1860. Following him was William W. Fowler on September 24, 1861. Keeler and Fowler had the post office at their trading post. This lasted until September 3, 1863, when James A. Wilson became postmaster. Kasper Kubli was appointed August 26, 1868, and the post office was located at his ranch. The next was Rial Benedict effective May 31, 1871. He had the post office at his home and stopping place. John H. Luman took over on August 7, 1874, followed by John E. Pearson on March 26, 1875. John Bolt was appointed on August 9, 1875, and the post office was in the Kubli and Bolt Store on the Kubli ranch. Henry D. Kubli took over on November 23, 1887, and served fourteen years. Orlando Rose was appointed on September 13, 1895. He had it at his ranch and stopping place on the south side of the river until John Pernoll built his store in 1900. John was appointed postmaster and served until his death in 1938. His wife, Laura, took over the store and was appointed postmaster. She continued until her retirement in 1953. Applegate post office was converted to a rural station of Jacksonville Post Office on May 1, 1959. It is still operating in the Applegate Shopping Center in 1989. For over 130 years there has been an Applegate Post Office.

HERLING, OREGON

Henry A. Bauten operated a stopping place about four miles southwest of Jacksonville in the 1880s. With the nearest post office at Uniontown, Bauten recognized the need for a post office to serve the area of Forest Creek, Logtown and Bishop Creek. He applied for a post office and was appointed postmaster July 28, 1888. The name chosen was Herling, for Louis Herling the original settler on his homestead. The post office was in service until July 9, 1895. Henry Bauten was the only postmaster and served seven years. Following closure, the mail for this area was handled from Jacksonville.

RUCH, OREGON

Soon after Casper (Cap) Ruch established his blacksmith shop at the intersection of Uniontown and Jacksonville-Crescent City Road in 1896, he applied for a post office, naming it for himself.

The post office was established on May 4, 1897. A store building was constructed, where the post office was located for the next 42 years. After Cap Ruch died in 1930, his wife, Anna, was appointed to fill his place. She continued to operate the store and post office until mid-1939, when she received notice from the Post Office Department in Washington, D.C., that her office was to discontinue business on Saturday, July 15. She was advised that the mail would be carried on a rural route the next Monday to all who mounted mail boxes along the way and listed them with the Jacksonville Postmaster.

Over 70 neighbors, patrons of the Ruch Post Office, signed a petition to the Post Office Department requesting that Ruch post office be kept open and operated at the Sunnyside Service Station. Rural boxes had been sprouting up along the road for a month, thus all procedures were set for the transition. Records do not indicate if the petition was received and if so what action was taken about it. Rural Free Delivery (RFD) service had started elsewhere about 1901. It took nearly four decades to reach Oregon's Applegate Valley.

UNIONTOWN, OREGON

Uniontown was a well-established settlement when the post office was opened on April 21, 1879. Theodoric (Tod) Cameron was appointed postmaster. The post office was in his store, which

was operated by his brother, William Cameron. Tod was postmaster the entire 12 years the post office was in existence. It served the Little Applegate area and about six miles up Big Applegate until September 14, 1891. The mail came through Herling till 1895 when it went to Jacksonville.

STERLINGVILLE, OREGON

While the Sterling Mine was in its heyday, a post office was established on April 12, 1879. George Yaudes was postmaster. The post office was only in existence four years, closing on July 11, 1883, and the mail went to Jacksonville, but miners and settlers could call for their mail at Uniontown or Jacksonville for several years.

BUNCOM, OREGON

Settlers on Little Applegate were a long way from a post office after Uniontown closed in 1891. A petition for a post office at Buncom, located near the mouth of Sterling Creek, was presented to the Post Office Department in 1896 when an application for a "Special Post Office" was filed on May 20 by Jacob Parks and Henry E. Ankeny. The application stated that the site for the desired post office was three miles from the existing mail route,

Map showing Proposed New Route
from Jacksonville, to Buncom and
Watkins. Jackson County. Oregon

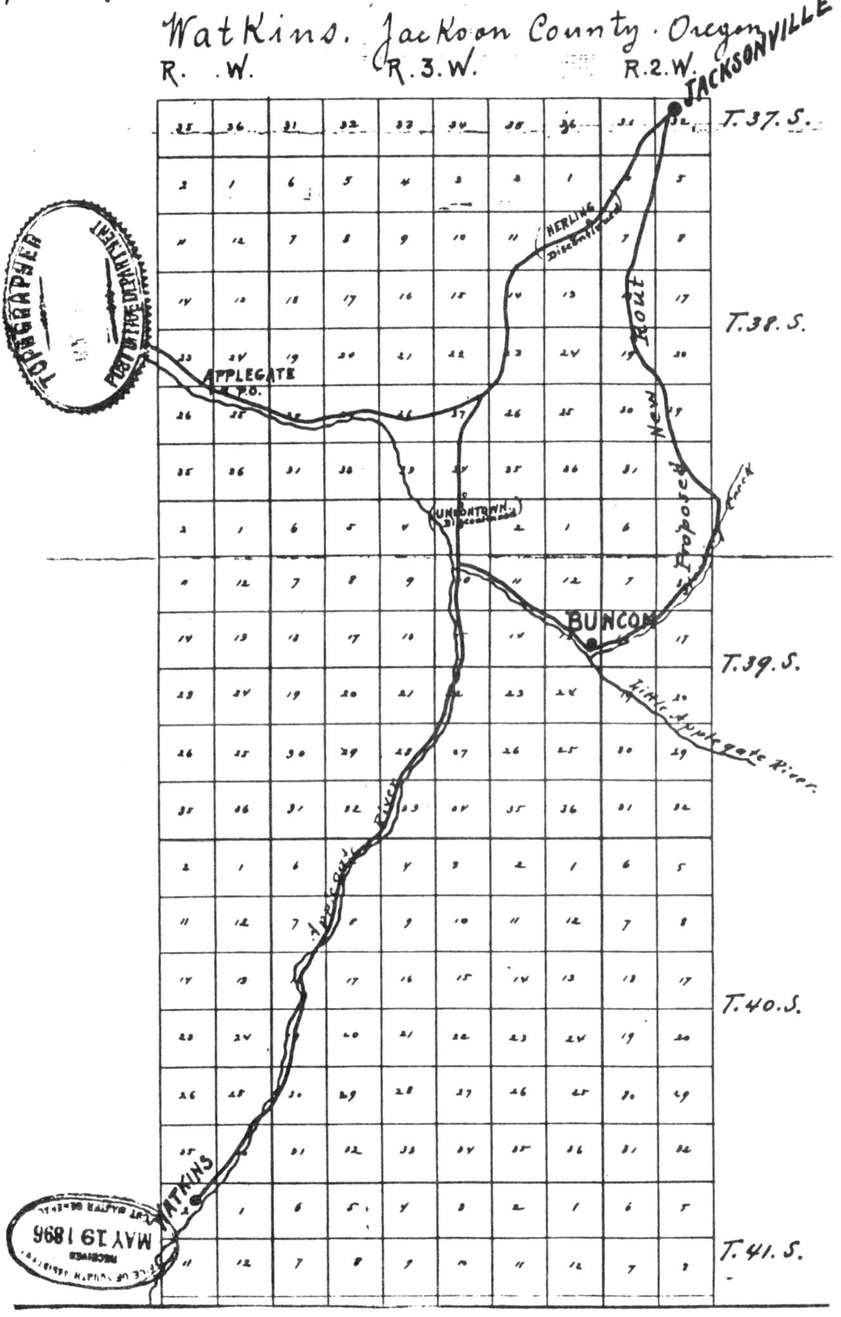

R. _. W.   R. 3. W.   R. 2. W.   JACKSONVILLE

T. 37. S.
T. 38. S.
T. 39. S.
T. 40. S.
T. 41. S.

APPLEGATE P.O.

HERLING Discontinued

UNIONTOWN Discontinued

BUNCOM

Little Applegate River

Applegate River

Proposed New Route

WATKINS

TOPOGRAPHER POST OFFICE DEPARTMENT

MAY 19 1896

twelve miles from an existing post office on one side (Jacksonville) and twenty miles from an existing post office on the other side (Watkins). The population to be served was listed as 175 people scattered in a country area. A map accompanied the application showing that the proposed route was from Jacksonville on the old road to Sterling Creek, following said creek to its confluence with Little Applegate where the new post office was to be located. The mail route then went to Little Applegate Crossing and up Big Applegate to Watkins. The return trip would be over the same route. The post office was approved and opened on December 5, 1896. It served the people until December 15, 1917.

PURSEL, OREGON

The Pursel Post Office was on the James Dews ranch about halfway between Little Applegate Crossing and the Watkins Post Office. It was established on February 11, 1898. It was in existence six years. Charles C. Pursel was its only postmaster. When he moved his sawmill to Yale Creek the post office was discontinued on January 30, 1904.

WRIGHT, OREGON

Nicholas B. Wright was postmaster at his ranch and stopping place on Upper Applegate near Mule Hill for nine years. He was appointed on April 25, 1879, and served the neighborhood until the office was discontinued December 22, 1888. Henceforth, the mail was handled from Uniontown.

COPPER, OREGON AND ITS STORE

A post office named Copper was established on Elliot Creek over the line in Siskiyou County, California, on June 5, 1914. Charles E. Huff was the first postmaster. The post office served the miners and workers in the Blue Ledge Mine until 1924, when it was moved to Jackson County, Oregon, on November 15.

Jim Winningham had taken up a homestead adjoining the Watkins property in the early 1920s. The patent was issued October 26, 1926 (Vol. 180, p. 199, Deed Records). Jim and his wife Mamie made their home in a cabin on the road to Elliot Creek and Steamboat. It was an ideal place for a post office.

When Copper Post Office was re-established in Jackson County, Mamie Winningham was appointed postmaster. She served eight years. Jim worked for the Forest Service and was transferred to various stations in the district. They sold the homestead to Raymond R. Rooney. He was appointed postmaster on November 9, 1931. The deed was signed April 28, 1932. (Vol. 191, p. 201, Deed Records). Rooney only lasted eight months for when he was involved in a disagreement with a Postal Inspector who showed up without notice (a normal practice), it is reported that Rooney handed over the keys and resigned on the spot. This resulted in the closure of the post office on May 31, 1932. From that time until the area was covered by the waters behind the Applegate Dam, area patrons received their mail on a rural route from Jacksonville.

The property changed hands several times in the next two years. Raymond Rooney sold to Carrie A. Wiggins, a widow, on March 13, 1933. (Vol. 194, p. 52, Deed Records). On July 14, 1934, she sold to Henry and Adelaide Petri. (Vol. 201, p. 257, Deed Records). During this time, it went to the County for taxes. The next owner was R. C. Crow. He purchased it from Henry Petri, November 3, 1934. (Vol. 201, p. 458, Deed Records). He also obtained a Quit Claim Deed from Jackson County by paying the back taxes.

R. C. Crow and his wife Gladys soon had a house and store building under construction with all the latest equipment available. The neighbors predicted that the store would be a failure but neighbors can be wrong as the little store prospered. The Crows stocked basic groceries and picnic supplies and the gasoline pumps were a great convenience for travelers and residents alike. The store became a gathering place for the neighbors, who stopped in to visit and exchange stories. In 1938 Mr. Crow deeded the property over to his wife, Gladys, and left the area. (Vol. 218, p. 417, Deed Records, May 23, 1938). Gladys operated the store with the help of a neighbor, Guy Watkins, for many years. When she died, Guy inherited the estate and continued to operate the store until the late 1970s. Along with all the other landowners in the proposed Applegate Dam and Lake area, Guy sold to the U.S. Government about 1978. He retired to a comfortable new home on a bluff overlooking the river near Mule Hill. He died October 15, 1989—the last of his generation.

Rural post offices served a real purpose during the years of settlement and development of the Upper Applegate Valley. Preserving their history and postmarks of each one is an ongoing project. □

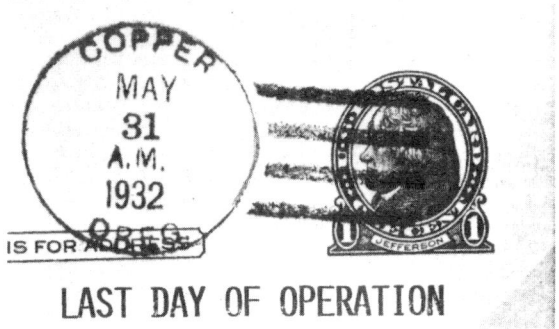

LAST DAY OF OPERATION

(Opposite) John Black, co-author of this book, standing at fender of Model A Ford truck with a load of shakes hauled for Mark Winningham at Copper in fall 1936. (Author collection) Folks drop by Copper store (center) for rest and chat in early 1970. (Above, this page) The Copper ARCO gas station with its glass-top gravity-flow pumps, and nearby store were all dismantled to make way for the lake that would form behind Applegate Dam. Entire area is now under water. Photo made in February 1970 by Bert Webber.

Ch. 5   Settlers: Ruch to Uniontown

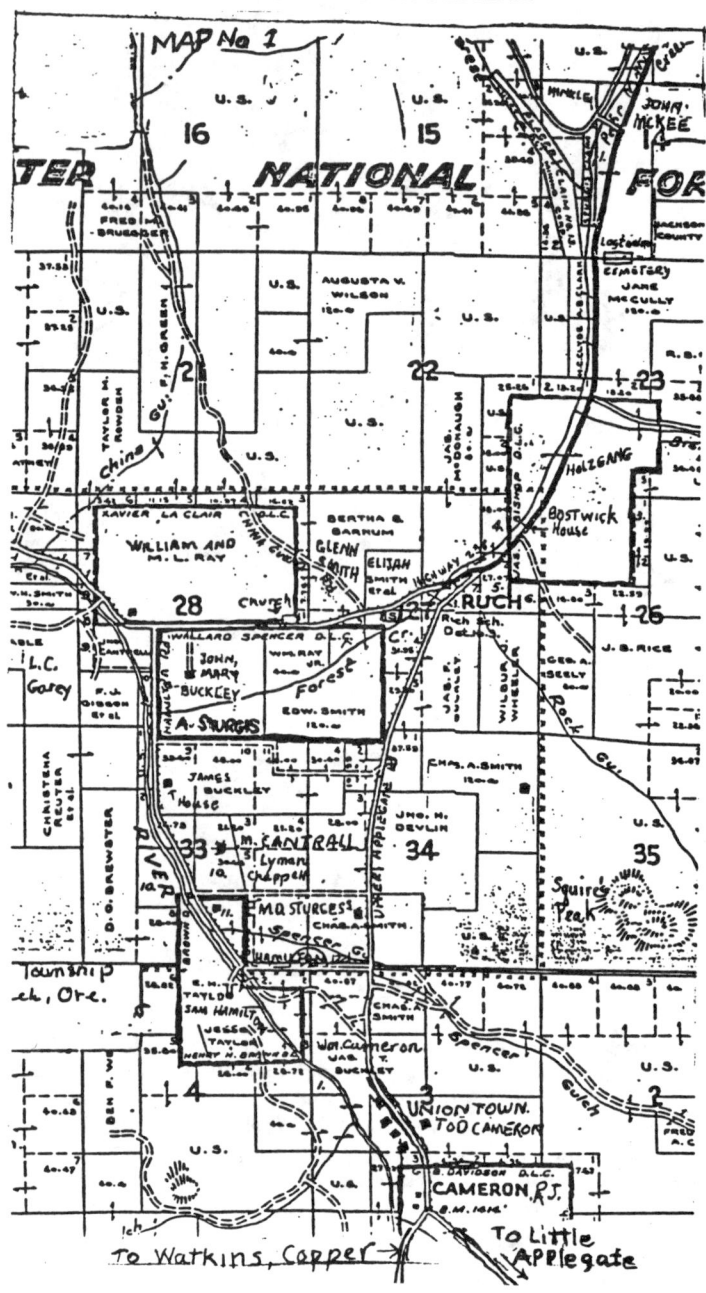

Ch. 6 Buncom: Sterling, Little Applegate

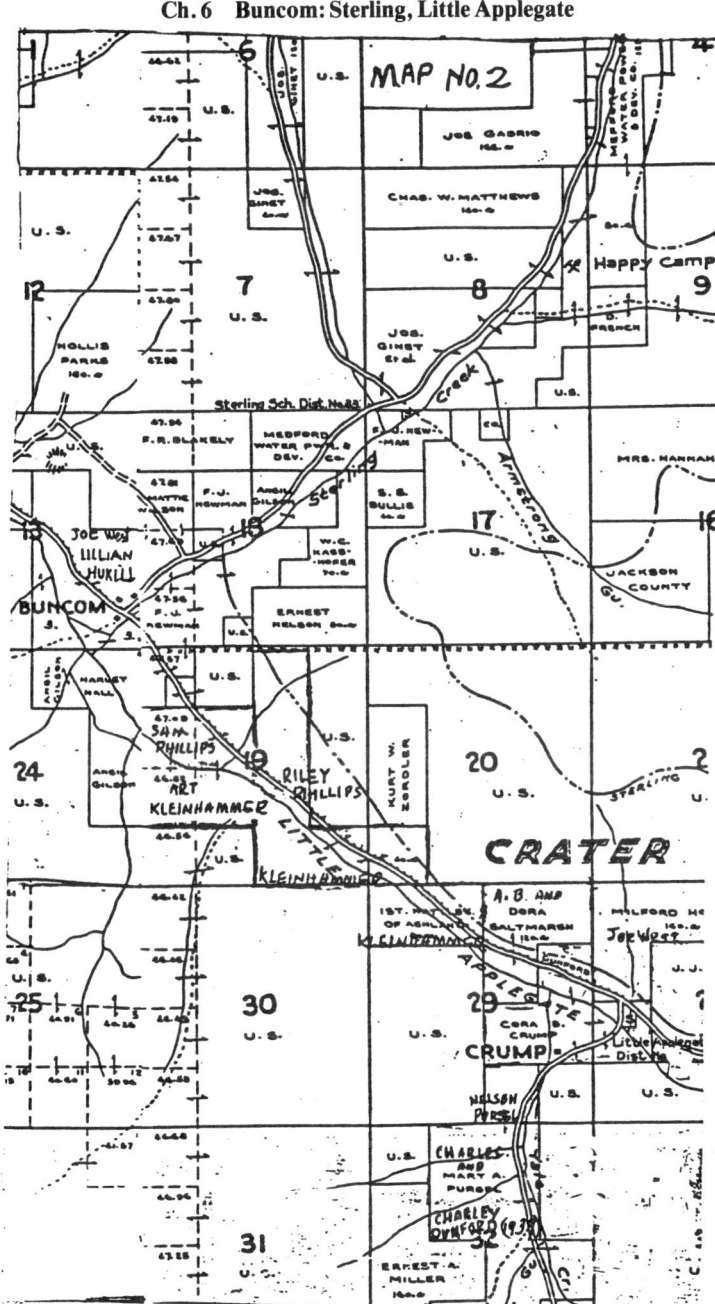

Ch. 7   Little Applegate Crossing to Steamboat

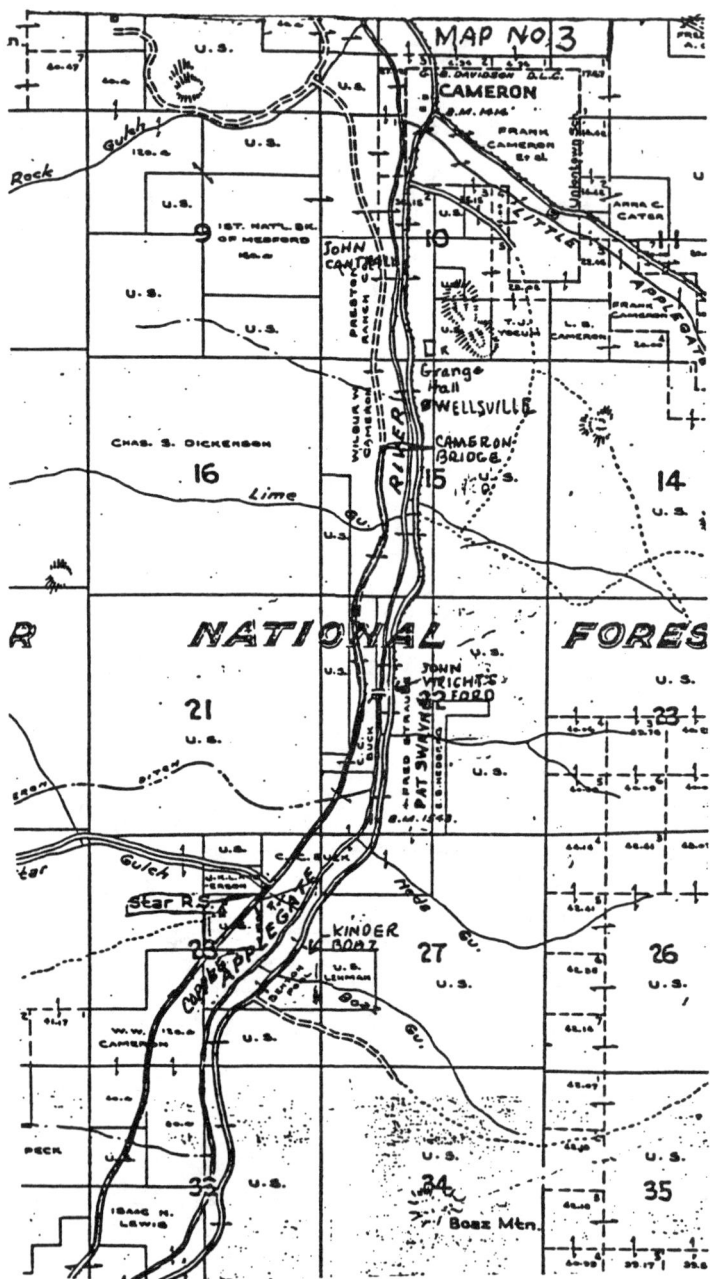

Ch. 7 McKee Bridge to French Gulch

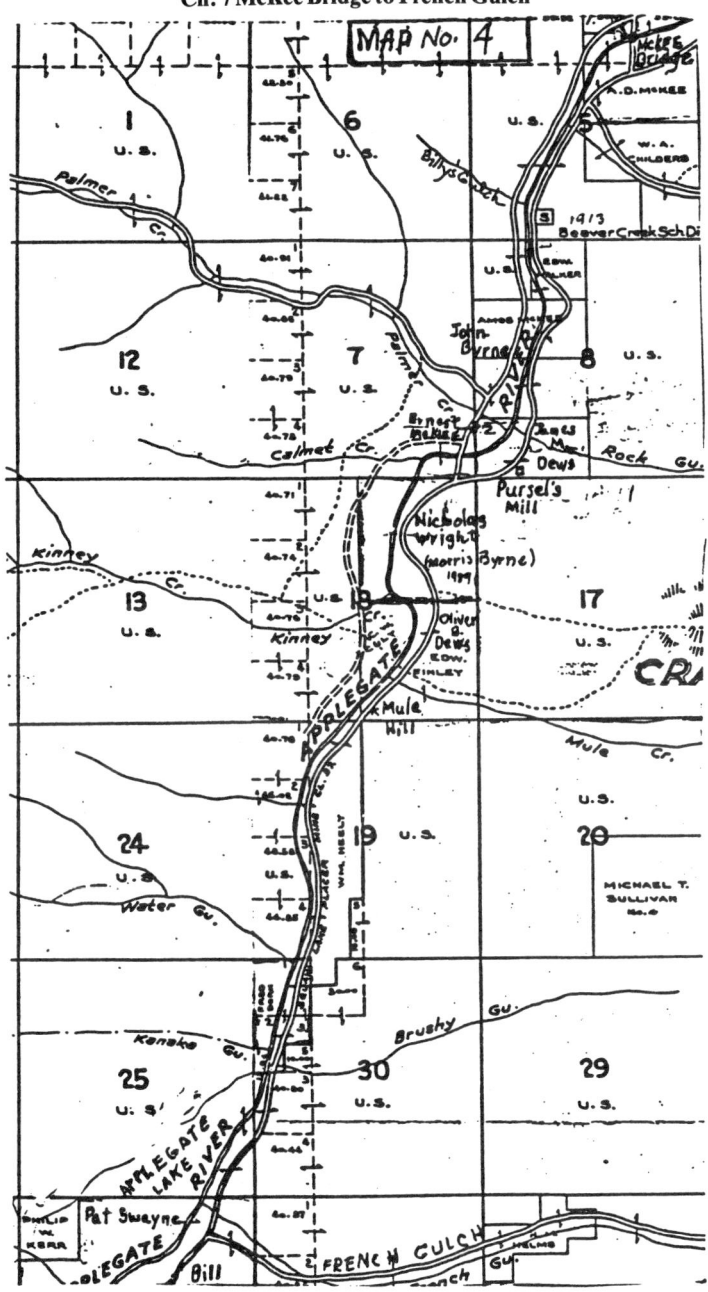

Ch. 7   Squaw Creek, Copper, Watkins

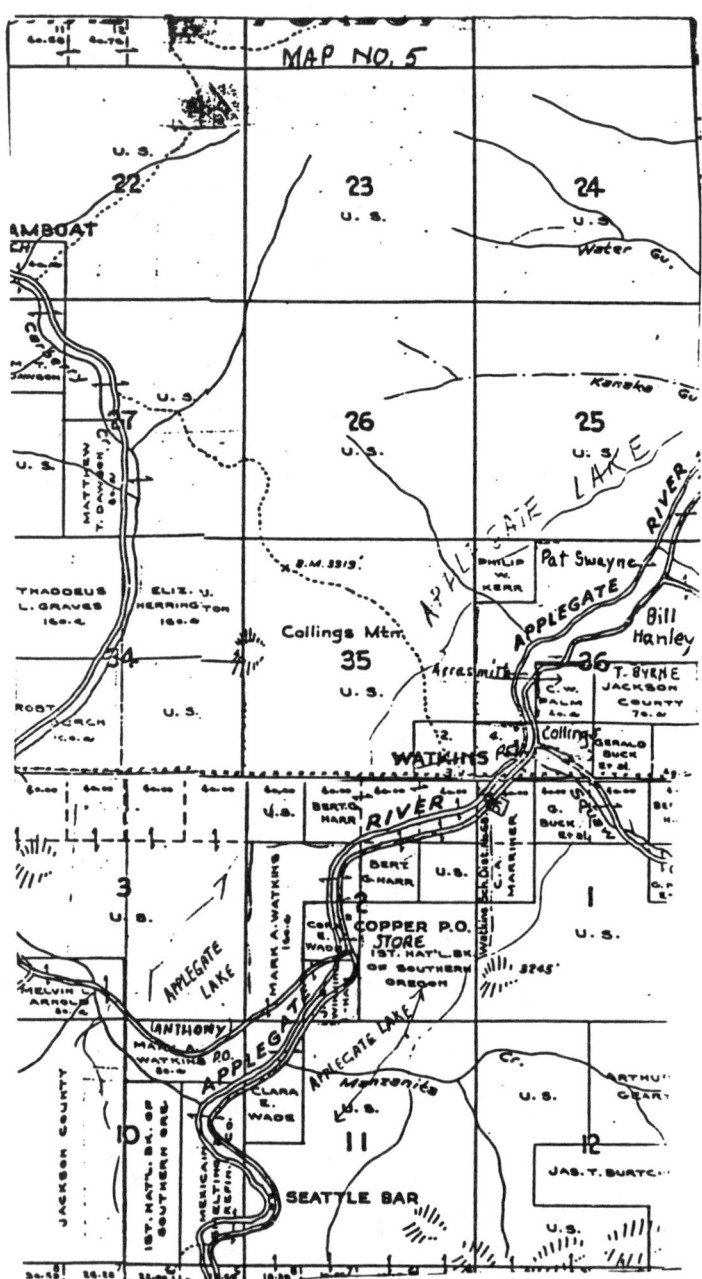

Ch. 7   Steamboat

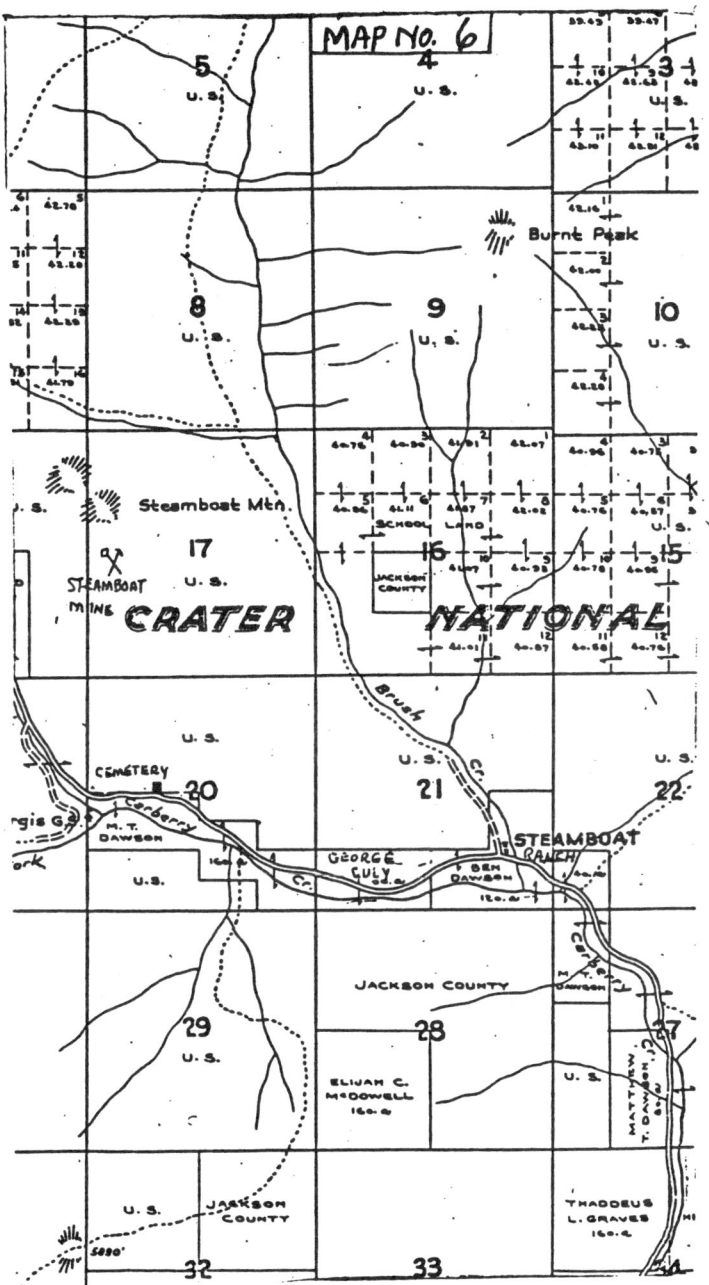

Ch. 8   Lower Applegate, Kubli, O'Brien, etc.

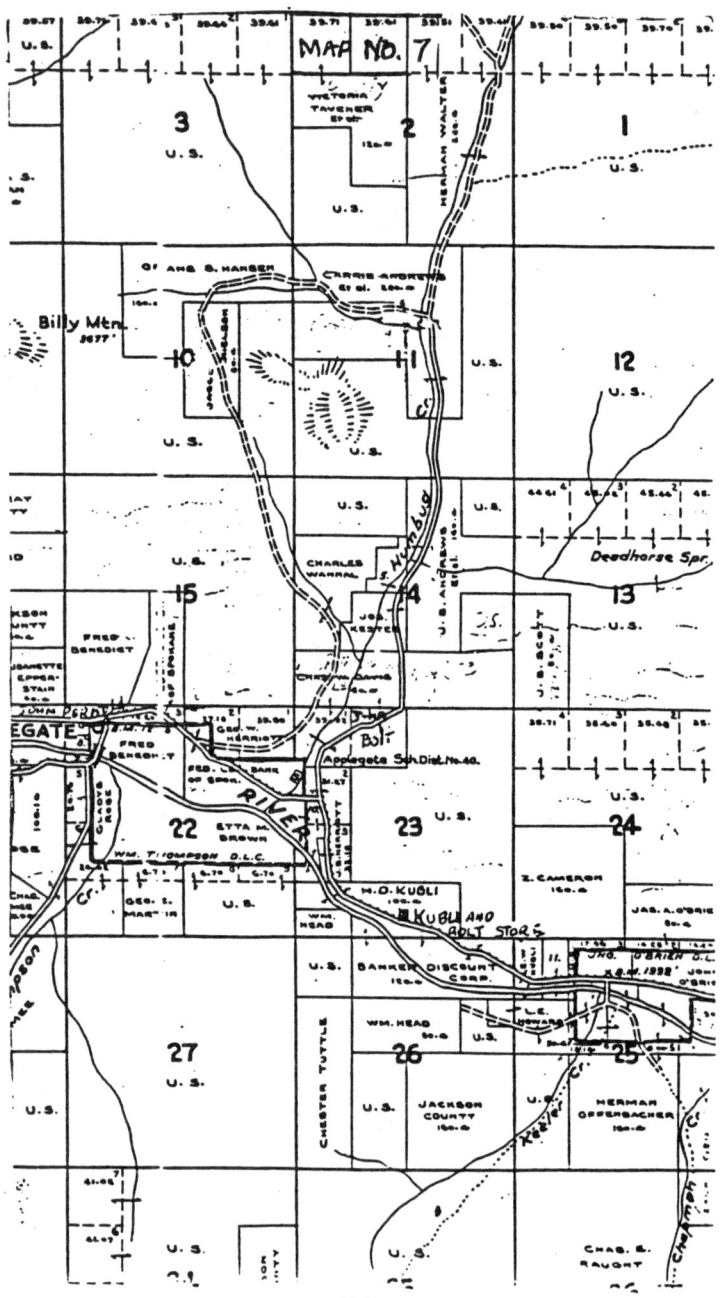

Ch. 8   Lower Applegate, Offenbacher, Matney

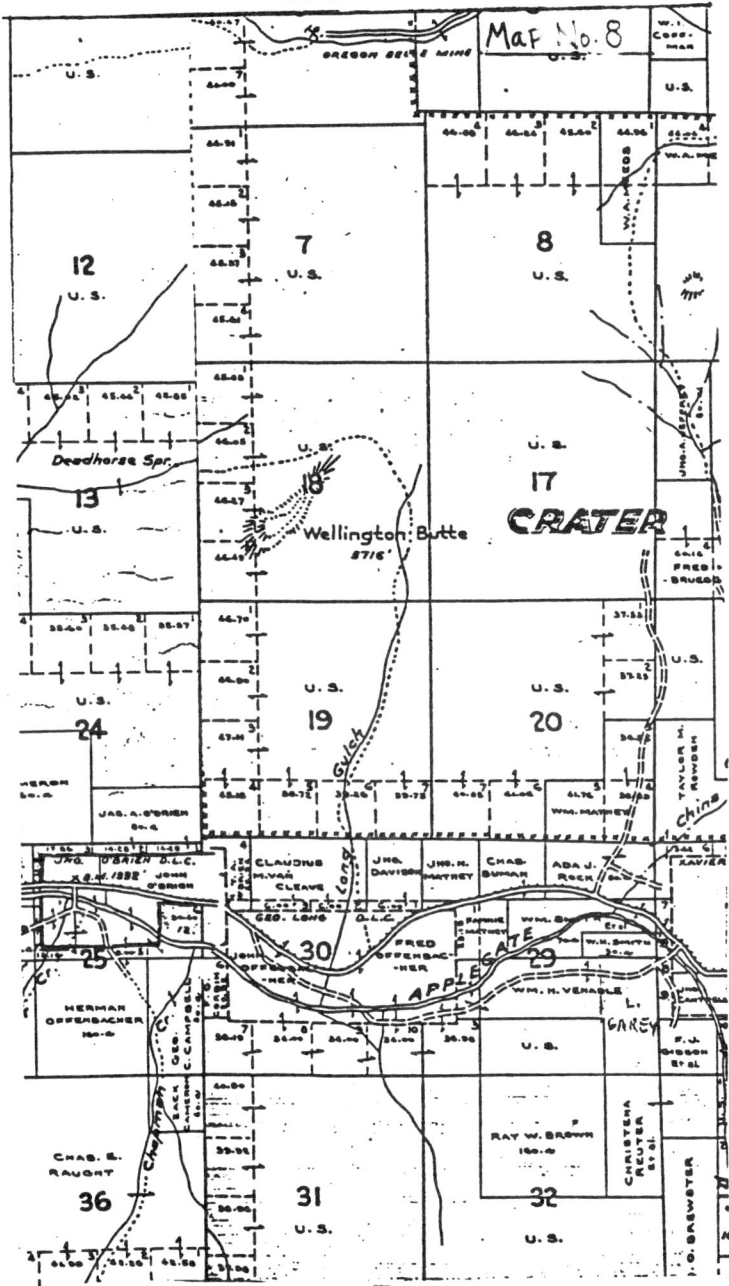

Bibliography

BOOKS

Atwood, Kay. *Jackson County Conversations.* Educ. Service District, Medford. (1975)

Black, Marguerite. *The History of Beaver Creek School, Jackson County, Oregon District No. 82.* Privately Pub. (1987)

Brown, Carroll E. *History of the Rogue River National Forest.* vol. 1. 1893-1932. (n.d.)

Chase, Don M. and Marjorie Neill Helms. *Pack Saddles and Rolling Wheels.* Privately Pub. (1959)

Gaston, Joseph. *Centennial History of Oregon.* Clark. (1912)

Genealogical Material in Oregon Donation Land Claims. Genealogical Forum of Portland, Ore. Vol. III (1962)

Haines, Francis D. Jr. and Marjorie O'Harra. *Applegate Trail: Southern Emigrant Route, 1846.* American Revolution Bicentennial Committee. (1976)

Haines, Francis D. Jr. and Verne S. Smith. *Gold on Sterling Creek.* Privately Pub. (1964)

Heckert, Elizabeth. *The People and the River.* Privately Pub. (1977)

Hegne, Barbara. *Unforgettable Pioneers.* Privately Pub. (1985)

Helbock, Richard W. *Oregon Post Offices 1847-1982.* La Posta (1982)

Johnson, Olga Wedemeyer. *They Settled in Applegate Country.* Privately Pub. (1978)

Kresek, Ray. *Fire Lookouts of the Northwest.* Ye Galleon. (1984)

La Lande, Jeff. *First Over the Siskiyous.* Oregon Historical Society Press. (1987)

_____. *Pre-History and History of the Rogue River National Forest.* U.S. Forest Service. (1980)

McArthur, Lewis A. *Oregon Geographic Names.* Fourth Edition: Oregon Historical Society. (1974)

Nesheim, Margaret. *One Hundred Twenty-Three Years' Search for Community.* Privately Pub. (1977)

Bibliography

Portrait and Biographical Record of Oregon. Chapman. (1904)

Sampson, Mary, Myrtle Krouse and Marguerite Black. *Applegate School 75th Anniversary Memory Book*. Applegate School District No. 40. (1985)

Scott, Edwin. *California to Oregon by Trail, Steamboat, Stage Coach and Train, 1850-1887*. Pasadena City College. (1976)

Siskiyou Sites and Sagas. Yearbook of the Siskiyou Pioneer Sites Foundation, Vol. 2 No. 1. (1967)

Sutton, Jack, *110 Years with Josephine*. Josephine County Historical Society. (1966)

Thompson's Dry Diggings, Shasta Butte City, Wyreka, Yreka. Siskiyou Pioneer and Year Book. Siskiyou County Historical Society, Yreka. (1976)

Walling, A. G. *History of Jackson, Josephine, Douglas, Coos and Curry Counties*. (1884)

Webber, Bert. *Indians Along the Oregon Trail; the Tribes of Nebraska, Wyoming, Idaho, Oregon and Washington Identified*. Webb Research Group. (1989)

Webber, Bert, and Margie Webber. *Jacksonville, Oregon; The Making of A National Historic Landmark*. YeGalleon. (1983)

Williams, Evelyn Byrne. *Maryum's Yellow Rose*. Privately Printed. (1984)

Winther, Oscar Osburn. *The Old Oregon Country*. University of Nebraska. (1950)

NEWSPAPERS

"Valley Pride Creamery Picnic" in Medford *Mail Tribune*, May 14, 1915.

"Applegate Span Dedication Will Honor Pioneers" in Medford *Mail Tribune*, June 21, 1934.

Vroman, Bob. "Log House in Applegate Being Torn Down" in Medford *Mail Tribune*, September 1958.

Williams, Evelyn Byrne. *Newspaper Clippings, Upper Applegate Grange Scrap Book, 1935 to 1985*.

Ziegler, Maude Pool. *Newspaper Clipping Scrap Book from Medford Mail Tribune and Medford Daily News, 1927-1940*.

PERIODICALS

Table Rock Sentinel (Newsletter of the Southern Oregon Historical Society), June, 1984; February, 1986; December, 1986.

Helbock, Richard W. "A Relative Scarcity Index for 19th Century

Oregon Town [Post]marks" in *The Postal Historian* Vol. 2. No. 4, April 1968

PUBLIC RECORDS

Black, John. *Logtown Cemetery Records, 1862-1989.*

Clay, L. Scott and Marjorie Edens. *Jackson County Historical Sites Survey, 1979.* Oregon State Historic Preservation Office, Salem, Oregon. (n.d.)

Jackson County. *Index of Liquor and Ferry Licenses, 1866-1905.*

Jackson County Deed Records, 1853-1930.

Jackson County, Oregon, Directories, School Officers and Teachers, 1918-1960. Office of Jackson County School Superintendent.

Jackson County Road Records, 1853-1930.

Jackson County Oregon School Census, 1893. Rogue Valley Genealogical Society. (1984)

Jackson County Oregon Schools. *Superintendent's Book of Common Schools, 1853-1880.* Carlos Morris Collection. (1974)

Jackson County Title Company, Vance Anderson Mining Company, Abstract of Title. (1914)

Jacksonville Cemetery Records, 1860-1980. Southern Oregon Historical Society Library.

Lacy, Ruby. *Jackson County Oregon Marriages, 1853-1877* Vol. I, 1974.

_____. *Jackson County Oregon Marriages, 1877-1888* Vol. II, (1974)

_____. *Jackson County Oregon Marriages, 1889-1896* Vol. III, (1976)

_____. *Jackson County Oregon Marriages, 1896-1907* Vol. IV. (1986)

Lacy, Ruby, and Lida Childers. *Jackson County Oregon Marriages 1908-1915* Vol. 5. (1986)

_____. *Jackson County Oregon Marriages, 1916-1924* Vol. 6. (1986)

_____. *Jackson County Oregon 1900 Census.* (1988)

Peterson, E. R. *The Journal of E. R. Peterson. Rural School Supervisor, Jackson County Schools, 1917.* Jackson County Education Service District. (1983)

Strom, Ora. *Index of Twenty Nine Rural Jackson County Cemeteries.* Rogue Valley Genealogical Society. (1979)

Bibliography

United States Census of Jackson County, Oregon, 1860 1870 1880. Genealogical Forum of Portland, Oregon. (1964)

UNPUBLISHED PAPERS

Applegate 8th Grade Class of Applegate Elementary School. The Applegate Valley. Applegate School District No. 40. (1974)

Black, Marguerite and John Black. *Early Jackson County Roads and River Crossings.* (1979)

Cameron, William. *Personal Diaries, 1865-1878.*

Harr, Christine. *Watkins Post Office.* (1942)

Morris, Carlos. *Interviews with Dean Saltmarsh, Maude Harr Ditsworth, Jim Winningham, Bert and Christine Harr, Ray and Maybelle Offenbacher.* (1974)

Smith, Emma Jean. *Development of Ruch Grade School.* Archives of the Southern Oregon Historical Society, Jacksonville. (1960)

Port, Lee. *Notes on Historical Events, Applegate Ranger District, 1945.* Archives of the Southern Oregon Historical Society, Jacksonville, Oregon.

MAPS

Jackson County, Oregon General Highway Map. Cedar Pub. Co., Cedar Rapids, Iowa. n.d. (ca 1982)

Metsker's Atlas of Jackson County, State of Oregon. 1932, 1955, 1970. Charles E. Metsker, C. E., Tacoma, Washington.

Official Map of Jackson County, Oregon. Jackson County Abstract Company. (1910)

ABOUT THE AUTHORS

Marguerite Watson Black has been a resident of the Jacksonville area since 1925. She attended Jacksonville and Medford High Schools then she graduated from Southern Oregon Normal School in 1932 with a teacher's certificate. Her first teaching experience was at Forest Creek School in the Applegate Valley. While there she met and married John M. Black. She spent the next ten years as wife and mother with John and his father, Lee, on the Black Ranch.

During World War II, Marguerite renewed her teacher's certificate and taught in four of the rural schools in the Applegate Valley. She attended evening and summer sessions at Southern Oregon College of Education and graduated with a B. S. Degree in Education in 1955. She taught in the Gold Hill and Central Point Schools a total of 22 years, retiring in 1968.

John Black was born and grew up on his parent's ranch on Forest Creek. After his father's death, he operated the 500-acre cattle and timber ranch while working as a seasonal fire warden for the State Department of Forestry for 20 years. In 1989, he is still operating the ranch.

Retirement gave Marguerite and John time to pursue local history. They served as volunteer guides on bus tours of the Southern Oregon Historical Society and worked with the Trails Committee.

Together they did the research and Marguerite prepared a paper, *Early Jackson County Roads and River Crossings* which is not yet published.

Marguerite wrote the text for the *Applegate School 75th Anniversary Memory Book* (1985). She also wrote and published *The History of Beaver Creek School, Jackson County, Oregon, District No. 82* (1987). Other writing includes the Introduction and Afterword for *The Oregon and Overland Trail Diary of Mary Louisa Black in 1865* (1989) published by Webb Research Group.

Although Marguerite does the writing in the present book, this is possible because of the couple's uncanny perseverance in rooting out details from official records. But cold, austere records are enlightened here by John's life-long adventure of participating in and making notes of activities of the people in the heart of the area covered in this volume.

The couple make their home on the family ranch on Forest Creek. They have three children, nine grandchildren and four great-grandchildren. □

Index

230